SKY SPORTS
A YEAR IN SPORT

£12.95

SSA02

Published by

Pedigree

Books Ltd

Under license from
BRITISH SKY BROADCASTING LTD

Pedigree Books Ltd
The Old Rectory
Matford Lane
Exeter
Devon
EX2 4PS
books@pedigreegroup.co.uk

All editorial, design and repro by
Final Score Ltd
finalscore@compuserve.com

EDITOR: Steve Pearce
CONTRIBUTORS: Tim Barnett; Bill Day;
Tony Grimsey; Nick Leaves; Alexander
Pearce; Ruth Pearce; Ian Piercy; Jessie
O'Shea; Gavin Willacy; Nick Wright.
PICTURES:
Action Images; Pete Norton (Billy Mims,
page 128); Allsport (Tony Rickardsson
136, Lee Radford 165); Horse and Hound
magazine (Vere Phillipps, page 179);

Check out the latest sports news on
www.skysports.com

The views expressed in this book are not
necessarily those of Sky Sports.

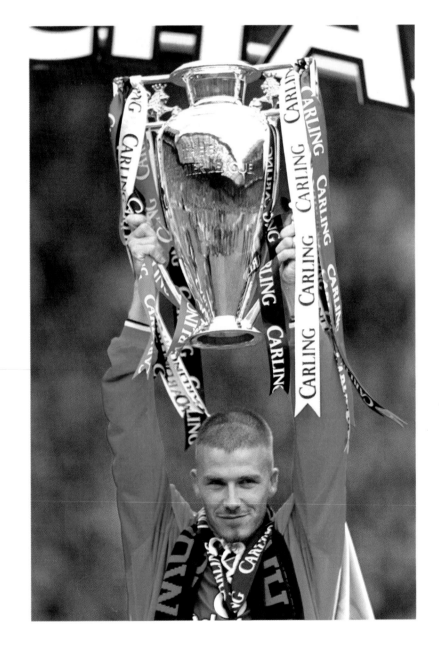

CONTENTS

FOOTBALL   14
The Premiership   16
Sir Alex Ferguson profile   38
Cup football   42
Nationwide League   46
Scottish season   52
Europe   56
International football   62

CRICKET   74
The Ashes   78
England's other Tests   80
County scene   86
Michael Atherton profile   88
The best team ever?   92

GOLF   96
The Majors   98
Tiger Woods profile   100

SNOOKER   106
The big tournaments   108
Rocket Ronnie O'Sullivan   110

RUGBY UNION   112
Lions Tour   114
League and Cups   116
Martin Johnson profile   118

BASKETBALL   124
The BBL season   126
Star of 2001   128

MOTOR SPORTS   130
Formula One   132
Michael Schumacher   134
Speedway/Superbikes   136

BOXING   138
Brits in the ring   140
Lennox Lewis profile   142
Ricky Hatton   147

TENNIS   148
Grand Slam events   150
Wimbledon wizard Goran   152
Andy Roddick   153

RUGBY LEAGUE   154
Saints clean up   156
Super League   158
Paul Sculthorpe profile   160

ATHLETICS   166
World Championships   168
Track and Field events   170
Jonathan Edwards   172

HORSE POWER   174
Equine elite   176
Wonder horse Galileo   178

OTHER SPORTS   180

A YEAR IN SPORT
A YEAR IN SPORT
A YEAR IN SPORT
A YEAR IN SPORT
A YEAR IN SPORT
A YEAR IN SPORT

A YEAR IN SPORT
A YEAR IN SPORT
A YEAR IN SPORT

THINK SPORT THINK SKY

SKY SPORTS passed the 10 year milestone in 2001 and there is no doubt the broadcaster has taken the presentation of sports events on to a different planet.

In that time Sky has been at the forefront of sports broadcasting and now features five channels and a 24 hours a day news service that is often the first to break the major stories as they develop.

Sky Sports has brought the drama of the Ryder Cup, World Cup cricket, international rugby, Premiership football and so much more. The cameras have been at the centre of the action, ready to bring the moments that matter, the glory, the despair, the winners and the losers. Every angle explored, every story covered.

It's that blanket coverage, combined with technological expertise, that Sky have introduced that has not only shaken up the presentation of sport, it has stirred the sports themselves.

Take football, Sky's technological developments have not only added something a little bit different to the Monday Night Football Show, but have been copied right round the world.

Even the players, management and coaches in the world of football, who may have been sceptical of the graphs, stats, speed measurements and match analysis at first, watch and take on board the information that is presented on screen.

"I got into the technology simply because we wanted to change the way to view the game at home and give people more options," says Andy Gray, who - as a wizard of the gadgets - has become a cult figure among millions of football fans.

"And when it was decided to go ahead with it there was no hanging about. We were using it the next week. There was no 10 week course. It was a case of let's get on with it now.

"We have done so much and pushed the barriers back so far that it is amazing. We have gone from being the outsider to being the forerunner that everyone judges themselves against."

The technology that Sky has used in their coverage of cricket has also prompted the game to look at ways of helping the umpires with the decision-making process.

The introduction of the 'third eye' to help decide on stumpings and run-outs is now seen as a major step forward in the cricket world and with cameras now covering every angle around the wicket, perhaps umpires will one day have further technical backup in making crucial decisions.

But while Sky's expertise and vision may stimulate improvements in the way the sports are run, the number one priority has always remained the same - to provide the very best in sports broadcasting.

"We all believed in the early days that a good, dedicated sports channel could prosper, but that belief was not based on any research," says Sky Sports' Managing Director, Vic Wakeling.

"It was gut instinct, some of it based on when I used to sit on the tube and watch guys going to work and reading their newspapers from the back page in.

"There is a real passion for sport out there and that is true of everyone who works at Sky Sports.

"The talent of our presenters, commentators, reporters and our entire production team has paid rich dividends.

"We have encouraged them to take risks in event coverage, and in their programming.

"The staff of Sky Sports have been true pioneers and the most important thing now is to keep pushing the barriers, always looking for innovation.

"It's that passion which provides a unique and genuine bond between Sky Sports and the subscribers.

"They are real sports fans who know their sport and who want to hear and learn more about it. Our job is to get them even closer to the action, and to keep them informed.

"Our audience want a choice of quality live events from around the world - and they want different ways of watching it.

"The days of the Big Fat TV Controller offered the occasional choice of one live sports event, with late at night highlights on others are a distant memory. The pace of change and growth has been amazing and will continue - with Sky Sports staying out in front of all the competitors."

It has been Sky Sports' vision and ability to look at different ways of presenting sports events that has taken them on to a different level over the last few years.

'We have encouraged them to take risks in sports event coverage'

"If anyone had told me when we started 10 years ago that we would have developed five dedicated channels and be fully interactive, I would never have believed it," adds Wakeling.

"Just look at what is on offer on Sky digital today - a choice of camera angles, highlights, commentary - all at just a single touch of a button.

"On our US Open tennis coverage, and on domestic snooker, we offer menus and a choice of three different live matches, again all at a touch of a button.

"It all means that on some days we can offer five different live events on five channels - plus a choice of three more live matches from one of those events. That's eight different choices all at the same time.

"That is what our audience wants - a choice of top quality live sports action. That is what we deliver."

Wakeling is also keen to stress the fact that Sky Sports has put something back in to the sports as well.

"We have played our part in helping sport. The evidence is clearly there," he says.

"The Premier League continues to be very popular, a new and younger audience are watching cricket, there is a revived interest in speedway and bigger gates than ever before at club rugby. And they are just some of the success stories - there are many more.

"Some people may say that is down to Sky money, but I think the exciting images our producers and directors have created have played a major part.

"Sport is exciting, real-life drama - and fun. We want the same to be said of Sky Sports."

The freedom to choose what sport you watch and how you watch it and the continued search for new ways to improve coverage of events is

Frank Bruno - Heavyweight champion of the world in 1995

Sky Sports provided over 150,000 hours of sport in their first 10 years of broadcasting. Here are some of the highlights since the launch in 1991.

1992: The Cricket World Cup was shown exclusively live on Sky Sports. It was the first overseas World Cup to be shown live from first ball to last in the UK.

1992: Teddy Sheringham scored the winner for Nottingham Forest against Liverpool in the first live Premiership match.

1993: Manchester United lifted the first Premiership title, their first League Championship triumph in 26 years. Sky Sports' cameras were there to see it.

1994: Brian Lara scored a Test world record 375 for West Indies against England in Sky's ball-by-ball coverage.

1995: Europe's golfers beat the Americans on foreign soil in the first Ryder Cup to be shown live from start to finish.

1995: Frank Bruno won the World Heavyweight title at Wembley.

1996: Rugby League began a new era with the launch of Super League.

one of the factors that Sky Sports' top football presenter, Andy Gray, believes has kept them at the top of sports broadcasting.

"The brilliant thing about Sky Sports' coverage is that the fans have a choice," says the former Scotland international striker, who has played a leading part in the development of Sky's football presentation.

"If they don't want to listen to my opinions on the game, they can go to the FanZone, which gives them the atmosphere of sitting in the crowd, with all the noise that goes with that. Or they can choose the camera angles to track one player, like you would at a game.

"The choice is at their fingertips. It's as simple as that.

'I love the excitement that using a new piece of technology brings'

"And the advances we have made since I covered my first game some 10 years ago still amaze me.

"Every time a new season comes around I think, there is little else we can do and each year we come up with something new, something special.

"I must admit I love the excitement that using a new piece of technology brings. That chance to do something in the studio that has never been seen before.

"That is one of the reasons why I still get a buzz driving to a game, even though I must have covered hundreds of matches over the past 10 years.

"In those early days the coverage was very much in its infancy, now it's so good that it's

almost as though the fans are sitting in the dug-out.

"And that's not just in football, it's right across Sky Sports' coverage. We put the fans right at the heart of the action."

Right at the heart of the action is where Sky Sports have been for over 10 years and that is where they intend to stay.

Teddy Sheringham and David Beckham celebrate England's qualification for the 2002 World Cup finals

1997: The British Lions won the Test series in South Africa. Sky Sports showed every one of the 10-game tour live for the first time in the UK.

1997: Europe, led by Seve Ballesteros, retained the Ryder Cup at Valderrama.

1997: England qualified for the World Cup finals with a goalless draw in Italy.

1999: Australia beat Pakistan in the Final to win the Cricket World Cup.

1999: England and Scotland clashed in the Euro 2000 Play-Offs. Both legs were shown live on Sky Sports.

2000: England manager Kevin Keegan resigned live on air after his side lost a World Cup qualifier to Germany in the final game played at Wembley Stadium.

2001: Nasser Hussain's England clinched a Test series victory in Pakistan in a game that finished in the dark.

2001: Manchester United clinched their third successive Premiership Championship.

2001: David Beckham scored a last minute equaliser in the 2-2 draw with Greece to give England a place in the 2002 World Cup.

Australia win the 1999 Cricket World Cup - the third successive time Sky had covered the competition

Andy Gray and Richard Keys on the set of Monday Night Football

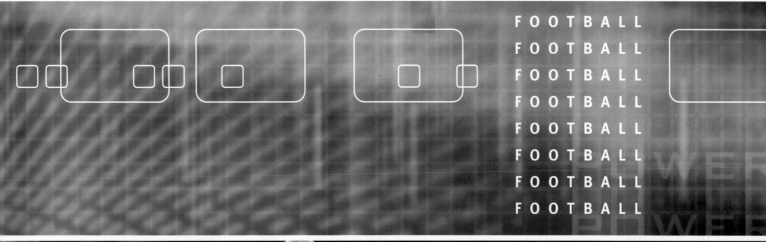

FOOTBALL
FOOTBALL
FOOTBALL
FOOTBALL
FOOTBALL
FOOTBALL
FOOTBALL
FOOTBALL

FOOTBALL
FOOTBALL
FOOTBALL

PREMIERSHIP

SEVEN UP FOR UNITED

CARLING CHAMPIONS 2001

MANCHESTER UNITED picked up their seventh Premiership title in nine years as their domination of English football showed no sigh of abating.

The Old Trafford club, who also finished runners-up to Blackburn in 1995 and Arsenal in 1998, ended 10 points clear of the Gunners and the margin of victory could easily have been greater but for United's run of three defeats in their last three games.

By then the silverware was well and truly locked up in the trophy cabinet, with victory ensured in mid-April, the earliest the Premiership title has been decided.

According to manager Alex Ferguson, the Championship race was as good as over by the turn of the New Year, with the rampant Reds going 11 points clear of the chasing pack.

"After we beat West Ham on New Year's Day, I thought it was all over then really," said the United boss.

"To win the title so early is a remarkable achievement by the players and is testament to the ability we have in the squad."

It was United's third successive Championship,

following in the footsteps of Huddersfield (1923-26), Arsenal (1932-35) and Liverpool (1981-84), with Ferguson the only manager to remain in charge for all three successes. Now he wants another place in English history.

"No team has ever won four Championships on the trot so that is the challenge for us now," said the Scot, who will stand down from the manager's seat at United at the end of the 2001-02 season.

'The title was won by the New Year'

While Ferguson eyes a fourth crown as he brings to a conclusion the most successful spell of management in United's history, the challenge to the chasing pack is to close the gap on the Reds.

Arsenal, Liverpool, Leeds and Chelsea were heavily criticised for their failure to prolong the title race beyond Easter 2001 especially after the Old Trafford club had finished a staggering 18 points clear a year earlier.

Chelsea upset their fans by sacking Gianluca Vialli early in the campaign and replacing him with another Italian, Claudio Ranieri, who had as much trouble learning the language as he did getting his team to chalk up an away win.

A sixth place finish and UEFA Cup participation was a grain of comfort from what was a disappointing season.

Liverpool rallied late on with a blistering run of form that saw them win six of their last seven League games to clinch third spot.

Their triumph in the Worthington Cup, FA Cup and UEFA Cup completed a remarkable treble. A magnificent season, no doubt, but to finish 11 points adrift of their bitter rivals was not good enough for players, manager or fans at Anfield.

Leeds were hindered by a string of injuries and a court case involving Jonathan Woodgate and Lee Bowyer, but boosted by the £18 million arrival of Rio Ferdinand, and just missed out on a second successive Champions' League place.

But David O'Leary has assembled a good young squad at Elland Road and their run to the Semi-Finals of the Champions' League has

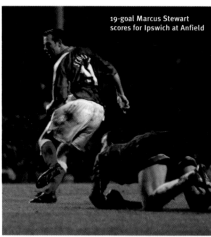
19-goal Marcus Stewart scores for Ipswich at Anfield

won them respect on the continent now as well as at home.

So what about Arsenal, runners-up for the third successive year?

An ageing defence, the lack of a clinical goalscorer and a hole in their midfield following the sale of Emmanuel Petit were all major contributors towards another season of disappointment. Arsene Wenger knows the Gunners' fans are growing impatient.

While Highbury may have shed more tears than cheers in 2001, Ipswich Town emerged as the success story of the season.

Favourites to be relegated after their Play-Off Final win over Barnsley, they stunned

Ipswich: the surprise team of the year

the critics and their opponents by challenging for a Champions' League place right up to the final day of the campaign.

A fifth place finish and a spot in the UEFA Cup was the eventual reward for George Burley's side, who won many friends as well as games with their stylish football. The Scot's Manager of the Year trophy, the first won by a non-title winning boss since Ron Saunders with Aston Villa in 1975, was well merited.

Like Ipswich, newly-promoted Charlton adapted to the step up to the Premiership well, just missing out on a place in Europe, along with Sunderland, who finished seventh for the second successive season.

Southampton marked their last year at The Dell with a 10th place finish, much of that due to Glenn Hoddle's astute management before his return to Tottenham in April.

Aston Villa, Newcastle and Tottenham would have all been hoping for better things when the campaign kicked off in August, but Villa boss John Gregory seemed to be at loggerheads with either his chairman, Doug Ellis, or some of his players for much of the term. Meanwhile, Bobby Robson had more injury victims than a whole series of ER at St James' Park and Spurs only hit the headlines when George Graham was dismissed.

Leicester topped the table for the first time in nearly 40 years in October but finished the

campaign with eight successive defeats, equalling the Premiership record, and pressure mounting on manager Peter Taylor.

Middlesbrough were rescued by Terry Venables, who steered them to safety, just. West Ham and Everton endured miserable times. Calls for Walter Smith's head at Goodison passed by, but Harry Redknapp was not so lucky at Upton Park, getting the chop in the last week of the term.

Derby, who did not record a League win until they beat Bradford in mid-November, eventually secured their place in the Premiership for another season thanks to a 1-0 win at a coasting Manchester United with former skipper Colin Todd, brought in from Swindon as Jim Smith's assistant, credited with shoring up a defence that was leaking more than two goals a game before his arrival.

And so to the bottom three: Coventry, Manchester City and Bradford. The Bantams sacked Chris Hutchings early on but Jim Jefferies could not turn around a season that started with the arrival of Benito Carbone, included a cameo role from Stan Collymore and ended in a punch-up between skipper Stuart McCall and team-mate Andy Myers as they trailed 5-1 at Leeds before half-time.

Manchester City returned from whence they came, minus Joe Royle, sacked two days after the end of the campaign in a meeting that apparently lasted one minute with his chairman. Kevin Keegan replaced him as the manager at Maine Road.

And Coventry ended their 34-year stay in the top flight with John Hartson's rescue act coming too late to keep the great escapologists afloat. Pity, manager Gordon Strachan's wit will be missed in the Premiership.

Leeds' £18m man Rio Ferdinand and Thierry Henry, of Arsenal, do battle

HOW THEY FINISHED

Club	P	W	D	L	Pts
Man Utd	38	24	8	6	80
Arsenal	38	20	10	8	70
Liverpool	38	20	9	9	69
Leeds	38	20	8	10	68
Ipswich	38	20	6	12	66
Chelsea	38	17	10	11	61
Sunderl'd	38	15	12	11	57
A Villa	38	13	15	10	54
Charlton	38	14	10	14	52
So'ton	38	14	10	14	52
Newcastle	38	14	9	15	51
Tottenham	38	13	10	15	49
Leicester	38	14	6	18	48
M'boro	38	9	15	14	42
West Ham	38	10	12	16	42
Everton	38	11	9	18	42
Derby	38	10	12	16	42
Man City	38	8	10	20	34
Coventry	38	8	10	20	34
Bradford	38	5	11	22	26

TOP LEAGUE SCORERS

Jimmy Hasselbaink	Chelsea	23
Marcus Stewart	Ipswich	19
Thierry Henry	Arsenal	17
Mark Viduka	Leeds	17
Michael Owen	Liverpool	16
Teddy Sheringham	Man Utd	15
Emile Heskey	Liverpool	14

FAIR PLAY TABLE

CLUB	BOOKED	SENT-OFF	PTS
Ipswich	33	2	111
Man Utd	44	3	150
So'ton	49	1	153
Charlton	45	3	153
Arsenal	46	3	156
Tottenham	48	3	162
Bradford	57	1	177
Liverpool	49	5	177
Newcastle	49	5	177
Leicester	57	2	183
Aston Villa	63	3	207
West Ham	69	2	219
Man City	69	3	225
Leeds	70	3	228
Chelsea	75	2	237
Coventry	76	4	252
Everton	77	4	255
M'boro	74	6	258
Derby	81	3	261
Sund'land	76	6	264

(6pts for a red card, 3pts for a booking)

WHAT THEY WON

THE PREMIERSHIP PRIZE MONEY:
Man United £6.73m; Arsenal £6.39m; Liverpool £6.06m; Leeds £5.72m; Ipswich £5.38m; Chelsea £5.05m; Sunderland £4.71m; Aston Villa £4.37m; Charlton £4.04m; Southampton £3.70m; Newcastle £3.36m; Tottenham £3.03m; Leicester £2.69m; Middlesbrough £2.35m; West Ham £2.02m; Everton £1.68m; Derby £1.35m; Man City £1.01m; Coventry £672,844; Bradford £336,422. (Does not include Sky TV revenue)

PREMIERSHIP DIARY

AUGUST

High-profile players continued to move around the Premiership as the new season approached at pace...

WEAH IS CITY'S MAINE MAN

AUGUST 2 Former World Footballer of the Year George Weah turned down moves to Roma in Italy, as well as clubs in France and Greece to join newly-promoted Manchester City on a free transfer.

The Liberian international became a free agent when his contract at AC Milan expired during the summer of 2000 and after a successful loan spell at Chelsea the previous season - in which time he picked up an FA Cup winners' medal - he decided to return to the Carling Premiership.

The 33-year-old Weah, who moved to Maine Road in a deal reported to be worth £3 million over two years, said: "I had lots of options but Manchester were truly willing to sign me. They really wanted me at their club and that is very important to me.

"Now my message to the fans is let us work together to win a place in Europe this season."

BANTAMS GO BARMY FOR BENNI

AUGUST 9 Hundreds of excited Bradford fans turned out to mob new signing Benito Carbone as he was unveiled at a press conference at Valley Parade.

The Italian striker, who joined as a free agent, signed a four year contract said to be worth a staggering £6 million, the biggest deal the club have ever been involved in.

Chairman Geoffrey Richmond announced Carbone's arrival as "the most exciting transfer in the club's history" and breathed a huge sigh of relief after Coventry had made a last ditch bid to sign the former Aston Villa player and had gone as far as agreeing wages with him.

But Carbone insisted: "Money is not as important to me as the club. I have signed a contract for four years and want to respect that.

"Bradford have a mission to grow and that is why I came here."

FRANKLY SPEAKING

AUGUST 15 The war of words that had broken out between Frank Leboeuf and Chelsea manager Gianluca Vialli during the month escalated when the defender accused his boss of trying to force him out of the club.

"I do not want to leave Chelsea but the manager told me that I could not expect to play so often because he was going to bring in another defender," said Leboeuf.

"It is clear that he does not have much faith in me and that makes it very difficult for me to stay.

"He has not forgiven me for getting sent-off against Leeds last season. I apologised for that and hoped he would support me but he didn't, he just criticised me in public."

Chelsea managing director Colin Hutchinson responded by calling Leboeuf "totally unprofessional and out of order".

UNITED HINT AT VAN NISTELROOY DEAL

AUGUST 19 Manchester United manager Sir Alex Ferguson revealed that Dutch forward Ruud Van Nistelrooy would be invited to Old Trafford to assess his fitness with a view to joining the club.

The highly-rated PSV Eindhoven striker was on the verge of a club record £18 million move to United in 1999/2000 before suffering cruciate knee ligament damage which kept him out of action for several months.

"The reports are that Ruud is well ahead of schedule and we have invited him to train with us in October to see how he is getting on," said Ferguson.

"If all goes well then, and he comes through alright, the deal will be right back on as far as we are concerned."

Van Nistelrooy had already indicated that he still had ambitions of playing at Old Trafford when he was fit.

VIEIRA SEES RED AGAIN

AUGUST 22 Patrick Vieira was sent-off for the second successive game in Arsenal's 2-0 win over Liverpool.

The French international followed up his red card at Sunderland on the opening day of the season with another at Highbury in a game that also saw Liverpool pair Gary McAllister and Dietmar Hamann dismissed.

In addition, referee Graham Poll showed nine yellow cards in a pulsating game that was littered with hefty challenges.

McAllister went for a late and high tackle on Vieira that left the Gunners' midfielder needing treatment for more than five minutes.

Vieira himself went after picking up two yellow cards in three minutes and was almost immediately followed by Hamann, with Poll later accepting that he had made a mistake in dismissing the German international for a second yellow.

Vieira's red card put him alongside Martin Keown, Francis Benali, Jason Wilcox, John Hartson and Frank Sinclair on five sendings-off in the Premiership and one behind the worst offender, former Wimbledon, Chelsea and Leeds midfielder Vinnie Jones.

The Frenchman's dismissal took the tally of red cards at Highbury, since Arsene Wenger took over in October 1996, to 31.

SOCCER SHORTS

The FA charged Arsenal boss Arsene Wenger with misconduct and bringing the game into disrepute after he allegedly pushed fourth official Paul Taylor in the tunnel after the Gunners' opening day defeat at Sunderland.

Craig Bellamy joined Coventry from Norwich in a club record £6.5 million deal.

Harry Kewell signed a new four year contract with Leeds as Dominic Matteo arrived at Elland Road from Liverpool in a £4.75 million transfer, even though he was injured.

Arsenal splashed out a club record £13 million to sign striker Sylvain Wiltord from Bordeaux.

Southampton pair John Beresford and David Hughes announced their retirements from the game through long term knee injuries.

Croatian international Alen Boksic marked his debut in the Premiership with two goals for Middlesbrough in their 3-1 win at Coventry.

Duncan Ferguson returned to Everton in a £3.75 million move from Newcastle while Ipswich smashed their transfer record to sign Hermann Hreidarsson from Wimbledon for £4 million.

PREMIERSHIP DIARY
SEPTEMBER

There were dark mutterings at Derby and a shattering blow at Portman Road, while Stan Collymore was on the move - again...

ROBSON ACCUSES DERBY OF CHEATING

SEPTEMBER 6 Middlesbrough boss Bryan Robson claimed Derby cheated to earn a point in a 3-3 draw at Pride Park.

Boro were 3-1 up with eight minutes left when Paul Ince played the ball in to touch to allow team-mate Phil Stamp to receive treatment. But instead of returning the ball, Dean Sturridge took a quick throw which brought Derby a corner, Branko Strupar headed in the cross and a few minutes later the Rams levelled the scores.

"Derby cheated, it's as simple as that," said an angry Robson after the game. "Everyone knows when someone is injured you return the ball. That is what my players were expecting and they were caught out when it didn't happen."

OWEN HAT-TRICK EASES INJURY WORRIES

SEPTEMBER 6 Michael Owen shot down Aston Villa with a first-half hat-trick that revived memories of his World Cup 98 performances.

Question marks were raised about the Liverpool striker's ability to recapture the form that made him a world star at that tournament, especially given the hamstring problems that had dogged him throughout last season. But Owen was back to his best, leaving the Villa defence in shreds as the Anfield side cantered to a 3-1 victory.

"I am feeling much sharper now. I can't say the injuries are never going to happen again but at least when I go on the field now, I am not thinking about them," he said.

NILIS NIGHTMARE

SEPTEMBER 9 Aston Villa's 2-1 win at Ipswich was overshadowed by a serious leg injury to Luc Nilis that cast a huge doubt over his career.

The Belgian international broke his right leg in an accidental clash with Ipswich goalkeeper Richard Wright and players from both sides were clearly upset by the incident.

Nilis was rushed to Ipswich Hospital for immediate surgery and at 33, serious question marks were raised about his ability to recover from such a bad injury.

"Luc had his eye on the ball and so did the goalkeeper," explained Villa's assistant boss, Steve Harrison.

"It was just one of those things that happen. No-one was to blame but it does look to be a very serious situation for him."

VIALLI SACKED

SEPTEMBER 12 Gianluca Vialli was dismissed as Chelsea boss only five games into the season – and after a two-and-a-half year stay at the club that had seen him become the most successful manager in the club's history.

The Italian led the Blues to victories in the Coca-Cola Cup, European Cup-Winners' Cup, FA Cup and Super Cup plus the Charity Shield triumph over Man United in August 2000.

His full record as Blues boss read: Played 143; Won 76; Drawn 38; Lost 29. But a poor start to the campaign resulted in his shock departure.

Commenting on the decision to axe his manager, chairman Ken Bates said: "I have much admiration for Luca's work but in a wider context, it is in the best interests of the club to seek a change of direction now."

COLLYMORE CAN GO, SAYS TAYLOR

SEPTEMBER 24 Controversial striker Stan Collymore was put on the transfer list at Leicester.

After lengthy discussions between the former Liverpool front man, his advisors and Foxes' boss Peter Taylor, the player was told his future was away from the Midlands side. The decision followed a lacklustre performance by Collymore in Leicester's draw with Everton at the weekend but the friction between him and his manager had been brewing since the start of the season when the player's advisors asked for a new contract for their client.

"They came to me with demands for a new contract. The timing was poor and the money they wanted was unacceptable," revealed Taylor.

"It is a shame because we have bent over backwards to keep Stan here but it's in the best interests of everyone concerned if he moves on."

At one stage Collymore indicated that he was going to walk out on the club, but he decided against that and was made available on a free transfer instead.

SOCCER SHORTS

Paul Gascoigne made a successful return to Middlesbrough, inspiring Everton to a 2-1 win at the Riverside.

Claudio Ranieri was named as Chelsea's new manager.

Emerson Thome became Sunderland's record buy, moving from Chelsea for £4.5 million.

Leeds' Harry Kewell was ruled out of action for three months after an achilles operation.

Newcastle's Daniel Cordone was instructed by the FA to have two permanent earrings surgically removed.

Steve Walsh ended his 14-year career at Leicester to join Norwich City on a free transfer.

Sunderland skipper Steve Bould announced his retirement from the game after being told that if he played on with a toe injury, he could suffer permanent damage.

Manchester United revealed a new sponsorship deal with Nike worth £300 million to the club over 15 years. Kicking off at the start of the 2002-03 season, it is three times higher than the deal the American sportswear company have with the Brazil national team.

PREMIERSHIP DIARY

OCTOBER

Goalscorers were in the headlines thanks to a wonder strike from Thierry Henry and a return to form for Shearer and Collymore...

KING HENRY

OCTOBER 1 A spectacular strike by Thierry Henry gave Arsenal a memorable victory over Manchester United at Highbury.

The live-wire French striker - who finished the campaign with 17 goals to his credit - stunned his international team-mate Fabien Barthez in the Reds' goal with a 20 yard volley into the top right hand corner, after flicking the ball in the air with his back to goal and spinning past defender Ronny Johnsen.

"It was one of the best goals I have ever scored, not only because of the way it went in but also because it was against Manchester United and Fabien," said Henry after the game, which lifted the Gunners into second place in the Premiership.

Even United boss Sir Alex Ferguson admitted it was a special strike and added: "It was brilliant. I'm sure he won't score one like that again in a hurry."

SHEARER FEAR

OCTOBER 1 Newcastle manager Bobby Robson revealed he had a long chat with Alan Shearer about the striker's goal drought.

The former England skipper ended a run without a goal in open play, which went all the way back to Euro 2000 and the winner against Germany in Charleroi, with a header in the 1-0 victory at Manchester City.

Shearer had clearly not been happy with his form and Robson explained: "Alan came to see me recently and told me of his concerns over his poor scoring run. He was clearly worried about the way things were going for him in front of goal.

"I told him what I first said to him 18 months ago when I took the manager's job at Newcastle. He was static in games; he was only working in the parameters of the 18-yard box.

"I told him he had to get behind defenders instead of playing with his back to goal all the time."

WENGER HANDED 12 MATCH BAN

OCTOBER 10 Arsene Wenger was banned from the touchline for 12 matches and fined four weeks' wages following an alleged confrontation with fourth official Paul Taylor at Sunderland on the opening day of the season.

The Arsenal boss was found guilty of 'threatening behaviour' and 'physical intimidation' following allegations that he waded into Taylor in the tunnel after the Gunners' 1-0 defeat in an incident that was also said to involve Thierry Henry and the Black Cats' Darren Williams.

Patrick Vieira was sent-off during the game after apparently elbowing Williams. Arsenal indicated they would appeal against the ban.

TV DEAL FALLS THROUGH

OCTOBER 18 The £328 million pay-per-view deal between cable giants ntl and the Premier League broke down.

The package, which involved ntl showing 40 Premiership games per season in a three year deal, had been discussed since the summer but the parties couldn't agree on the terms of the contract.

Premier League chief executive, Richard Scudamore said: "We all worked long and hard and there is disappointment that an agreement could not be reached but we have to respect ntl's decision."

The deal would have worked alongside Sky's £1.2 billion agreement with the Premier League, which allows the broadcaster to show 66 live games a season.

DEBUT DELIGHT FOR COLLYMORE

OCTOBER 29 Stan Collymore marked his home debut for Bradford with a spectacular goal in the 1-1 draw with Leeds.

The striker only arrived at the club in midweek, after joining from Leicester on a free transfer, but made an immediate impact with a brilliant overhead kick. Collymore was brought in by Bradford on a £13,000 a week deal with instructions to score the goals to take the club away from the Premiership basement.

"Bradford have a lot of quality players but they are looking for more firepower and that's what I can provide," said the former Liverpool and Aston Villa frontman.

"I could have gone abroad but I wanted to stay in the Premiership and scoring on my debut was a great start to my career at Bradford."

SOCCER SHORTS

Yugoslav international Slavisa Jokanovic became Claudio Ranieri's first signing as Chelsea boss when he joined the club from Deportivo La Coruna for £1.7 million.

Arsenal boss Arsene Wenger ruled himself out of contention for the England manager's job following Kevin Keegan's resignation.

George Weah walked out on Man City and signed a two year contract with Marseille.

Ugo Ehiogu's debut for Middlesbrough after his £8 million transfer from Aston Villa lasted four minutes at Charlton before a calf strain forced him off.

Jimmy Floyd Hasselbaink became the first Chelsea player to score four goals in a League game since Gianluca Vialli against Barnsley in 1997 in the 6-1 win over Coventry.

Derby's 4-1 defeat at Aston Villa left them as the only club without a League win in the 2000-01 campaign.

Leicester headed the top flight for the first time in 37 years after their 0-0 draw at Sunderland.

Everton's new signing, Alessandro Pistone, was ruled out for six months after suffering cruciate knee ligament damage in training.

PREMIERSHIP DIARY

NOVEMBER

Mark Viduka was the man in form, while Roy Keane blasted Old Trafford's 'prawn sandwich brigade' and Arsene Wenger got paranoid about United...

VIDUKA STUNS LIVERPOOL

NOVEMBER 4 In an amazing victory over Liverpool, Mark Viduka became the first Leeds player to score four times in a game since Allan Clarke against Burnley in 1971.

The Australian international grabbed all four goals in his club's 4-3 win over the Reds at Elland Road, with Leeds coming from 2-0 and 3-2 down to pick up the three points.

"I scored a couple of hat-tricks for Celtic but had never scored four in a game before," said the striker.

"This was just one of those games when everything went well for me."

Viduka's haul took his impressive goal tally to 10 in nine games since returning from the Sydney Olympics.

Sami Hyypia, Christian Ziege and Vladimir Smicer scored the Liverpool goals.

KEANE HITS OUT AT UNITED'S SILENT FANS

NOVEMBER 9 Manchester United skipper Roy Keane attacked a section of the club's supporters for their lack of noise at Old Trafford – and their understanding of the game.

The Republic of Ireland midfielder's comments followed a Champions' League victory over Dynamo Kiev, a game in which he felt the team did not get the backing they needed from some Reds' fans.

"Some people come to Old Trafford and I don't think they can even spell football, never mind understand it," he said.

"Away from home, our fans are great. They are what I call hard-core supporters. But at Old Trafford, some of them have a few drinks and their prawn sandwiches and do not realise what is going on out on the pitch.

"It's as if they expect us to cruise to victory every week.

"We had to win the game against Kiev and we did but a few passes went astray and some fans started to get on the players' backs. It's out of order."

RECORD BREAKER RIO

NOVEMBER 25 Rio Ferdinand became the most expensive defender in the world when he completed his £18 million move from West Ham to Leeds United.

The England international was unveiled to the Elland Road supporters before Leeds' 1-0 win over Arsenal after a week of negotiations that resulted in Ferdinand accepting a reduced £300,000 loyalty bonus from the Hammers, instead of the £1.3 million that he was entitled to as he had never asked for a transfer.

Leeds had been chasing the central defender since the summer of 2000 and had a bid of £15 million turned down before agreeing to up their offer to a record level.

"I never wanted to leave West Ham but as soon as they said they had accepted Leeds' offer, I knew it was time to go," revealed the highly-rated Ferdinand, who had been at Upton Park since his schooldays.

"The Leeds chairman Peter Ridsdale impressed me all the way through our discussions regarding the move and made it clear how ambitious Leeds are to win honours at home and in Europe."

INCE GOAL SAVES ROBSON

NOVEMBER 25 Paul Ince believed Bryan Robson was 45 minutes away from quitting as Middlesbrough manager.

The Boro skipper claimed the Riverside boss would have walked away if they had lost to Bradford and at two goals down at half-time, that looked very likely.

But Ugo Ehiogu reduced the arrears early in the second-half and Ince equalised a few minutes from time to salvage a point.

"Because of all the speculation about the gaffer, I thought he might walk if we lost to Bradford and at 2-0 down, it looked all over," said the former Manchester United team-mate of Robson's.

"At half-time I said my bit because it's not just about the manager's job. It's about ours as well. A new boss might come in and want to change things around. Half the squad could be out on the dole.

"As skipper I felt it was my responsibility to say something and the reaction from the lads was great."

CHELSEA AXE WILKINS AND RIX

NOVEMBER 28 Ray Wilkins and Graham Rix were sacked from their backroom staff jobs at Chelsea.

Rix, assistant to Gianluca Vialli in his time as manager at Stamford Bridge, and coach Wilkins, had been gently eased out of their prominent roles by Ranieri, who preferred to bring in his own Italian backroom team.

Both were offered compensation, along with fitness coach Antonio Pintus and goalkeeping coach, Eddie Niedzwiecki, who had their roles changed to more junior positions, leaving them with little option but to leave the club.

SOCCER SHORTS

Arsenal mourned the loss of George Armstrong. The former Gunners' winger spent 16 years at the club and was working as reserve team boss when he died suddenly from a brain haemorrhage.

James Beattie scored one of the goals of the season with a 40 yard strike for Southampton in their 2-2 draw at Sunderland.

Sir Alex Ferguson missed United win the first Manchester derby in five years because he was in South Africa to attend his son Mark's wedding. David Beckham scored the only goal at Maine Road.

Jim Jefferies became the new manager of Bradford. The former Hearts boss replaced Chris Hutchings, who was sacked after just 12 games in charge.

Arsenal boss Arsene Wenger accused the rest of the Premiership of not trying hard enough to beat Man United. "They have gained so much respect in England that clubs do not really have a go at them," he said.

Bradford striker Stan Collymore was given a three match ban after being found guilty of elbowing Paul Gascoigne in his last appearance for Leicester, against Everton in September.

PREMIERSHIP DIARY

DECEMBER

Terry Venables got back into full-time football and Spurs' Ledley was the speed king of the Premiership. Meanwhile, Di Canio made some new friends...

VENABLES JOINS MIDDLESBROUGH

DECEMBER 4 Terry Venables returned to football, agreeing to join struggling Middlesbrough until the end of the season.

The former England national team coach was brought to the club by chairman Steve Gibson to work alongside manager Bryan Robson - who was Venables' assistant during Euro 96 - in a bid to lift the club away from the relegation zone.

Venables joined with Boro second from bottom in the Premiership after suffering seven defeats in eight games.

The ex-Tottenham and Barcelona boss was put in charge of selecting the team while former Man United midfielder Robson remained in control of transfer matters at the Riverside Stadium.

"Terry gets respect from players and they respond to him. That is what this club needs," said Robson.

"We need him to come up with a few new ideas. That will give the players, the staff, the fans and the whole club a lift and maybe help us to compete a bit better."

Venables agreed to put aside his TV commitments for six months to take up the Boro offer.

LEDLEY'S THE GOAL KING

DECEMBER 9 Ledley King wrote his name in the record books with the fastest goal in Premiership history in Tottenham's 3-3 draw at Bradford.

The Spurs midfielder (pic right) gave his side a dream start after only 10 seconds when his 25 yard shot deflected off Jamie Lawrence and cannoned into the net past the despairing dive of Matt Clarke.

King's strike beat the previous record of 13 seconds held jointly by Dwight Yorke and Chris Sutton.

SOCCER SHORTS

FAIR PLAY, PAOLO

DECEMBER 16 Paolo Di Canio showed a remarkable act of sportsmanship by catching the ball instead of firing it into the unguarded net as Everton 'keeper Paul Gerrard lay injured.

West Ham were drawing 1-1 at Goodison Park when Gerrard damaged his knee making a last minute save from Frederic Kanoute. The ball rebounded to Trevor Sinclair who crossed for Di Canio but the Italian striker caught the ball and then immediately made his way in the direction of the prostrate Everton No.1.

The home fans gave the Hammer a standing ovation and Upton Park boss Harry Redknapp said: "It was sportsmanship of the highest merit and it is nice to know that kind of thing still exists in the modern game.

"Paolo thought their 'keeper was badly injured, maybe even had a broken leg and refused to put the ball in the empty net."

MURPHY ENDS UNITED RUN

DECEMBER 17 Gerard Houllier celebrated his 100th game as Liverpool boss by watching his side end Manchester United's unbeaten Premiership run at home that had stretched two days short of two years.

Middlesbrough were the last visiting team to leave Old Trafford with all three points, with a 3-2 win on December 19, 1998, in a sequence that extended to 36 games.

Danny Murphy's free-kick winner also gave the Anfield club their first victory at United in 10 years and their first over them in any match for five years to the day. Murphy curled his kick around the wall and past Fabien Barthez in the 43rd minute and Liverpool always looked the more likely winners after that with the home side reduced to 10 men in the last few minutes after Luke Chadwick was dismissed for a professional foul.

Murphy's goal was the first an English player had scored against the Champions since Chris Armstrong notched for Spurs at Old Trafford in May 2000. It was also Houllier's 50th victory as Liverpool boss – and his sweetest.

ROBBIE'S KEANE ON LEEDS

DECEMBER 20 Leeds won the battle to sign forward Robbie Keane from Inter Milan on loan until the end of the season.

The highly-rated Republic of Ireland striker was wanted by a host of Premiership clubs including Aston Villa, Chelsea, Charlton and West Ham, but opted for Elland Road thanks to the lure of Champions' League football.

Keane joined Inter from Coventry in a £13 million move in the 2000 close season but after a successful start at the San Siro, lost his place in the first-team and the Italian club agreed that a loan move would be in the best interest of all parties.

The deal included an option for Leeds to make the move permanent at the end of the season, with a figure of £12 million placed on the 20-year-old's head should David O'Leary be tempted to open the chequebook.

The FIFA world player rankings were published with Manchester City's Paulo Wanchope appearing in 22nd place: ahead of Roy Keane, Dennis Bergkamp and Andy Cole among others. An oversight by FIFA in allowing Costa Rica coach Gilson Nunes Siqueira to vote for his striker was the reason behind Wanchope's shock rating.

Rio Ferdinand made an unhappy Leeds debut as his club conceded three goals in the first 30 minutes at Leicester to lose 3-1.

Neil Lennon joined his boyhood heroes Celtic from Leicester for £6 million.

Reports from Germany claimed Bayer Leverkusen had turned down a £24.5 million offer from Arsenal for defender Jens Nowotny.

Sir Alex Ferguson announced that he would stay on at Manchester United in some capacity after he steps down as manager at the end of the 2001-2002 season.

South African striker Shaun Bartlett struck twice on his home debut for Charlton Athletic in their 3-3 draw with Manchester United.

Arsenal finally signed Brazilian Edu from Corinthians for £6 million, five months after his original move was scuppered because he arrived in Britain with a fake Portuguese passport.

ENIC agreed a deal with Tottenham chairman Alan Sugar to take a 27 per cent controlling stake in the club.

PREMIERSHIP DIARY
JANUARY

The Gunners were spiked by Charlton and Dennis changed his mind about leaving home. Meanwhile, an Angel landed in the West Midlands...

Dennis Wise - staying at Chelsea

NEW YEAR CHEER FOR CHARLTON

JAN 1 Charlton kicked off the New Year in style with a 1-0 win over Arsenal at the Valley.

Jonatan Johansson scored his 13th goal of the season to give the Addicks the points against a below-par Gunners, who should have equalised 15 minutes from time but saw Nelson Vivas' penalty saved by Dean Kiely.

Charlton boss Alan Curbishley was delighted with the victory and said: "In the end the penalty save got us the points but we fully deserved them."

MUM'S THE WORD FOR DENNIS

JAN 8 Dennis Wise pledged his future to Chelsea only two days after announcing that he wanted to leave the club.

The Blues skipper was angered after being relegated to the bench for the 1-0 win over Aston Villa on New Year's Day and was set to quit Stamford Bridge, with the Londoners agreeing a £2 million fee with Blackburn for the England international.

But only a day after travelling to Ewood Park to discuss the move, Wise changed his mind and declared he was staying at the club he one day hopes to manage.

"Ken Bates, Colin Hutchinson, Gianfranco Zola, the tea ladies, they all had a go at me and said that I had to stay here," said the midfielder.

"Even my mum was upset at the thought of me leaving the club and told me to stay. I am Chelsea through and through and the blood is obviously thicker than I thought."

Zola claimed that Chelsea would not be the same club without the tigerish former Wimbledon player in their ranks.

"Dennis Wise has a big part to play for Chelsea Football Club," said the Italian.

"He is an excellent player, his team-mates love him, the fans love him. It would not be the same without Dennis being here."

WALSH WOE

JAN 13 Bradford goalkeeper Gary Walsh produced one of the most bizarre moments of the season when he gifted Manchester United their opening goal in a 3-0 win at Valley Parade.

The Bantams were holding the Champions to a goalless draw with only 20 minutes left when Walsh, who spent 10 years at Old Trafford, completely missed a backpass and let in a startled Teddy Sheringham to fire into an empty net.

"It was a real howler and probably cost us the chance of getting something out of the game," said Bradford boss Jim Jefferies.

"He just sat in the dressing-room after the game with a towel over his head and couldn't face the lads."

ANGEL DELIGHT AT LAST FOR GREGORY

JAN 15 John Gregory finally landed the £9.5 million signing of Colombian international Juan Pablo Angel after weeks of on-going arguments with his chairman about the deal.

The striker (pic right), who joined from Argentine club River Plate, became Villa's record buy only a week after chairman, Doug Ellis, had said the deal was off because of all the problems that were involved in the move.

Reports of Angel's agent pocketing a large chunk of the fee amid claims that he part-owned the player threatened the deal and prompted Villa to bid for Robbie Fowler instead.

Gregory said: "In buying Angel the chairman has established his intentions. He has provided the money and you can't say fairer than that. Now we want to move forward together."

NUT CRACKERS

JAN 31 Andy Cole and Alex Rae saw red after they literally went head to head in the top of the table showdown between Sunderland and Manchester United.

United's Cole, who scored the only goal of the match at the Stadium of Light, and the Black Cats midfielder squared up to each other early in the second-half and left referee Graham Poll with

little option but to dismiss both. Sunderland's Michael Gray had already been sent-off for dissent after chasing Poll to the halfway line to argue about Cole's goal, claiming the striker had handled the ball in the build-up.

"Andy claimed he was head-butted but we were disappointed with his reaction. You can't go around retaliating like he did," said United boss Sir Alex Ferguson.

United's 1-0 win took them 15 points clear at the top of the Premiership with bookies already paying out on them winning the title.

Cole and Rae are sent-off

SOCCER SHORTS

Newcastle goalkeeper Shay Given handed in a transfer request only four months after signing a new four year contract.

David Beckham confirmed he wanted to sign a new contract at Old Trafford as speculation mounted that he would become Britain's first £100,000 a week player.

Leeds chairman Peter Ridsdale flew to Australia in a bid to establish a 'partnership' with one of the leading sides Down Under and build on his club's growing appeal in the country.

Goalkeeper Mark Bosnich joined Chelsea on a free transfer from Man United.

Sven Goran Eriksson watched his first Premiership game as England boss, Sunderland's 2-0 win at West Ham.

Carling withdrew their £13 million a year offer to continue their eight year sponsorship of the Premiership for another three years after running out of patience over a decision on whether their bid had been accepted.

Marcus Stewart went to the top of the Premiership goalcharts with his 14th League goal of the season in Ipswich's 2-0 win over Leicester, prompting calls for his selection for England.

PREMIERSHIP DIARY
FEBRUARY

Wenger got off the hook, while United added a few million more to their already bulging bank account and Derby's latest signing went missing...

WENGER REPRIEVE

FEBRUARY 2 Arsene Wenger won his battle to overturn a 12 match touchline ban for his confrontation with fourth official Paul Taylor at Sunderland in August.

The Gunners boss, who had the original charge of violent and threatening behaviour reduced to misconduct, was given a reprimand and fined £10,000.

The decision, after a two-day hearing at the FA, left Wenger satisfied with the outcome - but nothing more.

"I have had 18 years in football management and not had one disciplinary problem before," he said.

"It was important for me that the charge of threatening behaviour was dropped, but I still have a blemish on my record and that upsets me."

Wenger stepped in to break up a scuffle between Thierry Henry and Darren Williams in the tunnel after the Gunners' 1-0 defeat at the Stadium of Light on the opening day of the season.

UNITED'S STARS AND STRIPES

FEBRUARY 7 Manchester United and American baseball giants the New York Yankees announced they were teaming up to form the biggest joint-marketing deal in sports history.

The deal allows Yankees' merchandise to be sold throughout the United Megastores around the world, with the name of Manchester United being pushed into the foreground in the potentially lucrative untapped soccer market of North America in return.

"North America is a significant marketplace for us," confirmed United chief executive, Peter Kenyon.

"And when you look at the strength of the Yankees in North America and Manchester United in soccer, you know this deal makes the utmost sense."

The partnership is expected to add between £15 million and £30 million a year to United's already sizeable income.

HODDLE CALL FOR PRO REFS

FEBRUARY 10 Glenn Hoddle received backing from the League Managers' Association (LMA) in his campaign for the introduction of professional referees to the English game.

The Southampton boss spearheaded the call for officials to become full-time and his club chairman, Rupert Lowe, revealed that the LMA had already lent their support to the idea.

"You are never going to eliminate mistakes completely but Glenn believes that if some referees were made full-time, it would help reduce the number of errors that can occur," explained Lowe.

"We have supported him in this and now the Managers' Association have backed the idea as well and will present it to the Premier League."

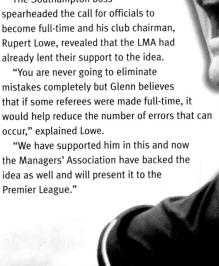

Nolberto Solano

DWIGHT'S TREBLE STRIKE

FEBRUARY 25 Dwight Yorke struck three times in the first 22 minutes as Manchester United hit nearest challengers Arsenal for five in an amazing opening half of this top of the table clash.

The Old Trafford striker, who had struggled to capture his best form during the opening half of the season, began the scoring with just 120 seconds on the clock as Arsenal 'keeper David Seaman conceded his first Premiership goal in 391 minutes.

The Gunners soon equalised through Thierry Henry but two minutes later United were back in front through Yorke and never looked back.

Roy Keane and Ole Gunnar Solskjaer added to the Trinidad international's treble before Teddy Sheringham completed the scoring in the last minute.

After the game, which saw United move 16 points clear of Arsenal in the race for the Premiership title, Old Trafford boss Sir Alex Ferguson said: "We finished superbly and that is the League Championship over for Arsenal now."

PASSPORT PROBE

FEBRUARY 12 The Football Association sent out clear instructions to clubs to check the legality of their overseas players after fears that some Premiership stars were playing under 'false passports'.

Newcastle's Nolberto Solano, from Peru, and Arsenal's Lithuanian striker Tomas Danilevicius were just two of around 50 players in the top flight playing under an EU passport, even though they originated from outside the EU.

FA chief executive Adam Crozier said: "We are not suggesting that players are actually here on false passports but it is clear that all clubs need to verify the authenticity of paperwork around all players who come to the UK on an EU passport when they hail from a non-EU country."

The passport issue not only affected English football but the whole of the European scene.

Dwight Yorke celebrates his hat-trick against Arsenal

SOCCER SHORTS

Stan Collymore joined Spanish club Real Oviedo on a free transfer from Bradford with 2,000 fans turning up to greet him on his arrival.

Derby's four day search for their defender Taribo West ended when he turned up at Pride Park saying he had stayed in Nigeria with his sick mother after playing for his country in a World Cup qualifier against Sudan.

Man United beat Everton 1-0 without having a shot on target in the game. Andy Cole's drive was going wide before being deflected in off Steve Watson.

Chelsea chairman Ken Bates quit as vice-chairman of the troubled Wembley Stadium project.

John Hartson joined Coventry from Wimbledon in a unique 'pay as you play' deal. Injury fears had seen the Welshman miss out on proposed moves to Spurs and Rangers.

Newcastle boss Bobby Robson set a 7pm curfew on his players while they were on a break in Spain following their defeat at Charlton a few days earlier.

Eric Cantona was voted Manchester United's best ever player in a poll conducted in the club's official magazine.

PREMIERSHIP DIARY

MARCH

Sitting room only in the Premiership as the game's governing bodies finally resolved the great transfer debate and George Graham moved on...

GAZZA PUTS 23RD OPERATION ON HOLD

MARCH 3 Everton's freefall down the table persuaded Paul Gascoigne to delay the 23rd operation of his career so that he could play his part in keeping the club in the Premiership.

The England international had already missed four months of the season with groin and thigh problems and was due to go under the surgeon's knife to have a metal plate taken out of his arm after breaking it in a challenge on Aston Villa's George Boateng in February 2000.

"I've had 22 operations in my career and have to have the metal bit taken out of my arm. It should have been done by now but I have already missed enough football," said Gazza, before he returned to the Everton side for their 1-1 draw against one of his former clubs, Newcastle United.

"And with the club struggling, I want to get back and help us climb up the table."

STILL NO STANDING AT PREMIER GROUNDS

MARCH 5 Sports Minister Kate Hoey's campaign to bring back standing areas at Premiership grounds was shelved following a report by her own department criticising the idea.

The Football Licensing Authority were asked to provide a report on the possibility of returning to 'standing' at grounds and studied the system used at Hamburg where a small section of the German club's stadium had seats removed to allow fans to stand.

Hoey had campaigned for space at Premiership grounds to allow around 2000 supporters to stand, but the report stated that it was not practical to convert such small areas and would also provide the possibility of a breeding ground for hooliganism.

Premiership grounds became seating-only following the Taylor Report, commissioned after the Hillsborough Disaster in 1989.

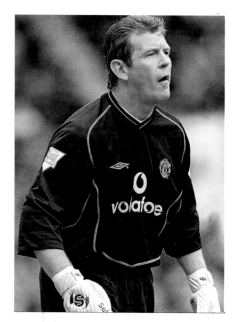

NEW TRANSFER SYSTEM AGREED

MARCH 5 UEFA, FIFA and the European Union agreed new rules governing the transfer system after more than nine months of discussions.

The regulations include ensuring that no player can sign a contract that lasts longer than five years; the introduction of two transfer windows - during the summer and a mid-season period - when movement of players can take place; and sanctions set up that include banning players from playing for clubs for a fixed time if they decide to break their contract and join a new club.

The sanctions decrease as the player moves further into his contract.

GRAHAM SACKED AT SPURS

MARCH 16 Comic Relief Day, but there was no fun and games at White Hart Lane where George Graham was told his stay as manager was over after 29 months.

The Scot (pic right) was dismissed by Spurs' executive vice-chairman, David Buchler, who made the decision after Graham is said to have revealed to the press details of a meeting he had with the new owners of the club, ENIC.

"I asked George for an explanation but no answer was forthcoming. He had a defiant attitude," said Buchler.

"I am building from top to bottom a cohesive team and I am not prepared to have someone who is not a team player. We agreed that we could not work together so he has gone."

VETERAN GORAM JOINS UNITED

MARCH 22 Manchester United ended their search for a new goalkeeper when they snapped up 36-year-old former Scottish international Andy Goram from Motherwell (pic left).

Old Trafford boss Sir Alex Ferguson brought in the ex-Rangers star as cover for Fabien Barthez and Rai Van der Gouw, who were both sidelined with injury.

Goram, who signed on a three month loan deal, admitted he was stunned at the move.

"I was born and brought up in Bury, just down the road from United," he said. "I always wondered what it would be like to play for them but it's ridiculous me joining them at this stage of my career," he said.

"You never know what is going to happen in this game, but nothing is ever sensible with me anyway. To be joining the biggest club in the world is like a dream though."

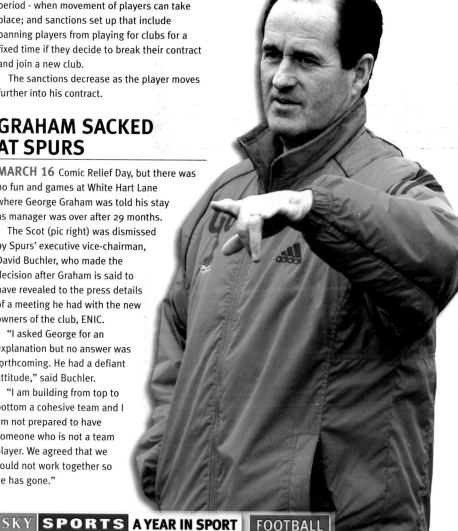

SOCCER SHORTS

Southampton were prevented from selling 9000 red plastic seats from the Dell because they were dangerous to eat. European Commission rules stopped the sale because the seats' paint contained small amounts of cadmium, which experts say can cause cancer if swallowed in large quantities. Saints' marketing director Paul Blanchard said: "It's crazy. If it happened on April 1, everyone would think it was a joke."

Newcastle's Kieron Dyer was told he would be out for the rest of the season after his shin splint operation.

Everton striker Francis Jeffers turned down the biggest contract offer in the club's history, a five year deal worth £8m.

The England team's official supporters' club was disbanded because too many members were 'thugs'. A report showed that eight out of 10 fans arrested at Euro 2000 belonged to the club.

Arsenal and Tottenham fans stood silent for one minute before the North London derby at Highbury in tribute to former Gunner, David Rocastle, who died of cancer.

Liverpool completed their first League double over Man United in 22 years with a 2-0 victory at Anfield.

Stan Collymore announced his retirement from football.

PREMIERSHIP DIARY

APRIL

The League campaign came to a premature end as Arsenal imploded at home, and a retrial was ordered for Bowyer and Woodgate.

Marcus Stewart enjoys his hat-trick at Southampton

STEWART IS TALK OF THE TOWN

APRIL 1 Marcus Stewart grabbed his first Premiership hat-trick to give Ipswich the points at Southampton and take the club within sight of a Champions' League spot.

The Town striker took his tally to 20 goals for the campaign, the first player to achieve that feat for the Suffolk club since John Wark in 1984, by scoring all three goals in the 3-0 win at the Dell.

The victory carried Ipswich, favourites for relegation at the start of the season, into third place and dreaming of Europe.

"It made me very proud to follow in the footsteps of John Wark because he is a legend at Ipswich," said Stewart.

"We have all heard the stories about the Ipswich team that won the UEFA Cup 20 years ago, now it's this team's target to qualify for European football next season, that would be a fantastic achievement."

HODDLE GOES HOME

APRIL 1 After a week of wrangling between Southampton and Tottenham, Glenn Hoddle became the new boss at White Hart Lane.

The former England manager spent most of his playing career at Spurs and was always favourite for the job following George Graham's departure from White Hart Lane at the end of March, but Saints chairman Rupert Lowe was left fuming about the move.

Arguments over compensation, the movement of backroom staff from Saints to Tottenham and confidentiality clauses raged with Lowe saying: "The way Spurs have handled the matter has not been in the essence of good business practice."

But Hoddle, who signed a five year contract, was only concerned with the future and said: "I had a great time here as a player and am looking forward to the challenge of being a manager here now.

"There was a lot of red tape involved in the deal but I just let the clubs get on with it and now I want to get on with bringing the good times back to Tottenham."

RETRIAL ORDERED FOR LEEDS DUO

APRIL 10 Jonathan Woodgate and Lee Bowyer were told they faced a retrial after their court case over an alleged assault on a student was stopped when the judge dismissed the jury as they were considering their verdict.

Mr Justice Poole brought the trial, estimated to have cost in the region of £8 million, to a halt after the Sunday Mirror newspaper published an article with student Sarfraz Najeib's father while the jury were contemplating their decision.

The Leeds pair, who had been in court for close on two months, were informed that they would have to return to Hull Crown Court in October to face the charges again in a fresh trial.

It was also revealed by the Football Association that neither player would be considered for England action until the legal process was completed.

GUNNERS GAFFS HAND UNITED TITLE HAT-TRICK

APRIL 14 Own goals from South American duo Edu and Silvinho gift-wrapped the Premiership title for Manchester United with a month of the season still remaining as Arsenal crashed 3-0 to Middlesbrough.

The Gunners needed to pick up at least a point against relegation threatened Boro at Highbury to take the title race (or should that be procession?) into another week but the Brazilian pair combined to put the ball past their own 'keeper David Seaman twice inside four crazy minutes in the first-half.

And when another South American - Colombia's Hamilton Ricard - added a third for the visitors early in the second period, it was all over bar the shouting.

The Premiership trophy was on its way to Old Trafford for the seventh time in nine years, equalling the record set by Liverpool between 1976 and 1984.

REDS FINALLY LAND £19M RUUD

APRIL 23 Manchester United completed the signing of Ruud van Nistelrooy from PSV Eindhoven for a new British record of £19 million.

The deal was finalised almost a year after the original transfer fell through because the Dutch international (pic above) suffered cruciate knee ligament damage.

Van Nistelrooy signed a five-year contract with the Old Trafford club and said: "It has always been a dream of mine to play for United so this has been a very easy choice for me to make."

SOCCER SHORTS

Man City conceded four goals in the first 36 minutes of their 4-0 home defeat by Arsenal.

Roy Keane was sent-off for a dreadful tackle on Alfie Haaland in the Manchester derby, which ended 1-1. On the same day, Leeds' David Batty was dismissed for appearing to elbow Joe Cole at West Ham and Seth Johnson's two footed lunge at Bradford's Stuart McCall resulted in a red card for the Derby star.

Ryan Giggs signed a new five year contract at Old Trafford worth a reported £15 million.

Michael Duberry was told his future was at Leeds after being cleared of conspiring to pervert the course of justice at Hull Crown Court in the case also involving team-mates Lee Bowyer and Jonathan Woodgate.

Industry analysts Deloitte and Touche warned that wages would overtake club income within six years if players' pay continued to increase at the same rate as it had done over the last few seasons. They also revealed the average wage in the Premiership was £400,000 a year.

Leicester set a new club record with their eighth successive League defeat, losing 1-0 in injury-time at Newcastle United.

PREMIERSHIP DIARY

MAY

Sponsors Carling parted company with the Premiership, as did Coventry, Bradford, Manchester City, Harry Redknapp and the Dell...

BARCLAYCARD REVEALED AS NEW SPONSORS

MAY 1 Barclaycard emerged as the new sponsors of the Premiership in a £48m three year contract.

The British Tourist Authority were also involved in the agreement, adding another £4m to the deal and enabling them to use Premiership stars in their campaigns to attract visitors to Britain.

Barclaycard replaced Carling as the official sponsors of the Premiership and FA Premier League chief executive, Richard Scudamore, welcomed them aboard.

"This is an exceptionally good deal for both parties and we are looking forward to an exciting partnership," he said.

SKY BLUES DOWN

MAY 5 Coventry's 34-year stay in the top flight of English football finally came to an end at the home of their biggest rivals and Midlands neighbours Aston Villa.

The Sky Blues made a name for themselves as the Houdini of football after providing numerous escape acts from the relegation trap door over those 34 years but their time finally ran out at Villa Park.

Coventry let slip a two goal first-half lead against Aston Villa to lose 3-2, sending them into the First Division.

Having parted company with a number of top class players over the previous few months - including Robbie Keane, Gary McAllister, Dion Dublin, George Boateng, Noel Whelan and Darren Huckerby - it was perhaps no surprise that the Sky Blues struggled to make enough of an impact in attack to save themselves.

Despite the setback, and the consequent loss of earnings, Highfield Road chairman Bryan Richardson confirmed that manager Gordon Strachan would stay in charge for the new season.

HAMMERS AXE HARRY

MAY 9 West Ham parted company with Harry Redknapp only a few days after the club secured their Premiership safety with a 3-0 win over Southampton.

The decision ended Redknapp's seven year stay as boss at Upton Park and stunned Hammers fans – and Harry (pic below).

He entered a meeting with chairman Terry Brown eager to outline his plan to strengthen his squad with some of the money generated by the £18m sale of Rio Ferdinand to Leeds.

"I had a meeting planned with the chairman and leaving the club was the last thing on my mind when I went into it," said the former West Ham player.

"I never dreamed what would happen but after talking to the chairman, I found myself out of work."

Redknapp's assistant, Frank Lampard senior, also left the club by mutual consent.

SHERI AT THE DOUBLE

MAY 10 Teddy Sheringham completed his own 'double' by adding the Football Writers' Footballer of the Year award to the PFA trophy he collected in April.

The England international followed in the footsteps of his Manchester United skipper Roy Keane, who scooped both honours in 2000.

"When I look down the list of players who have won this award, it gives me great pride to see my name alongside them," said Sheringham.

PERFECT MATT FINISH

MAY 19 Matt Le Tissier (pic below) fittingly marked the last League game at The Dell with a trademark spectacular goal.

The Southampton legend bagged his first Premiership strike of the season in the last minute to give his side a 3-2 win over Arsenal, turning brilliantly to fire into the top corner.

Le Tissier, who has spent his whole career with the South Coast club, was mobbed by fans at the final whistle, many wearing replica shirts with 'God' on the back in tribute to his talents.

"It was great to score the last goal at the Dell. That would have been the way I would have planned it. Now hopefully I can score the first one at our new stadium," said the England midfielder.

The Dell was Saints' home for 103 years before their summer move to a 32,000 capacity stadium at St Mary's.

SOCCER SHORTS

Alan Shearer netted a £1 million bonus from Newcastle after completing five years at the club.

Manchester United unveiled their new away kit which has a reversible shirt, giving two kits for the price of one. On one side the shirt is white and black and on the other, gold.

Southampton ended their goal drought that had lasted nine hours and 23 minutes when Marian Pahars scored in the 1-1 draw at Newcastle.

Gianfranco Zola signed a new two year contract with Chelsea which gives him an option of staying on as a coach at the club after that period.

Derby became only the second Premiership club to win at Old Trafford during the season, a 1-0 win ensuring they avoided relegation.

Man City were relegated after just a year back in the top flight following a 2-1 defeat at Ipswich.

Bradford pair Andy Myers and Stuart McCall were involved in a bust-up on the pitch during the club's 6-1 defeat at Leeds.

Ipswich's George Burley picked up the Manager of the Year award after guiding his club to fifth place in the table.

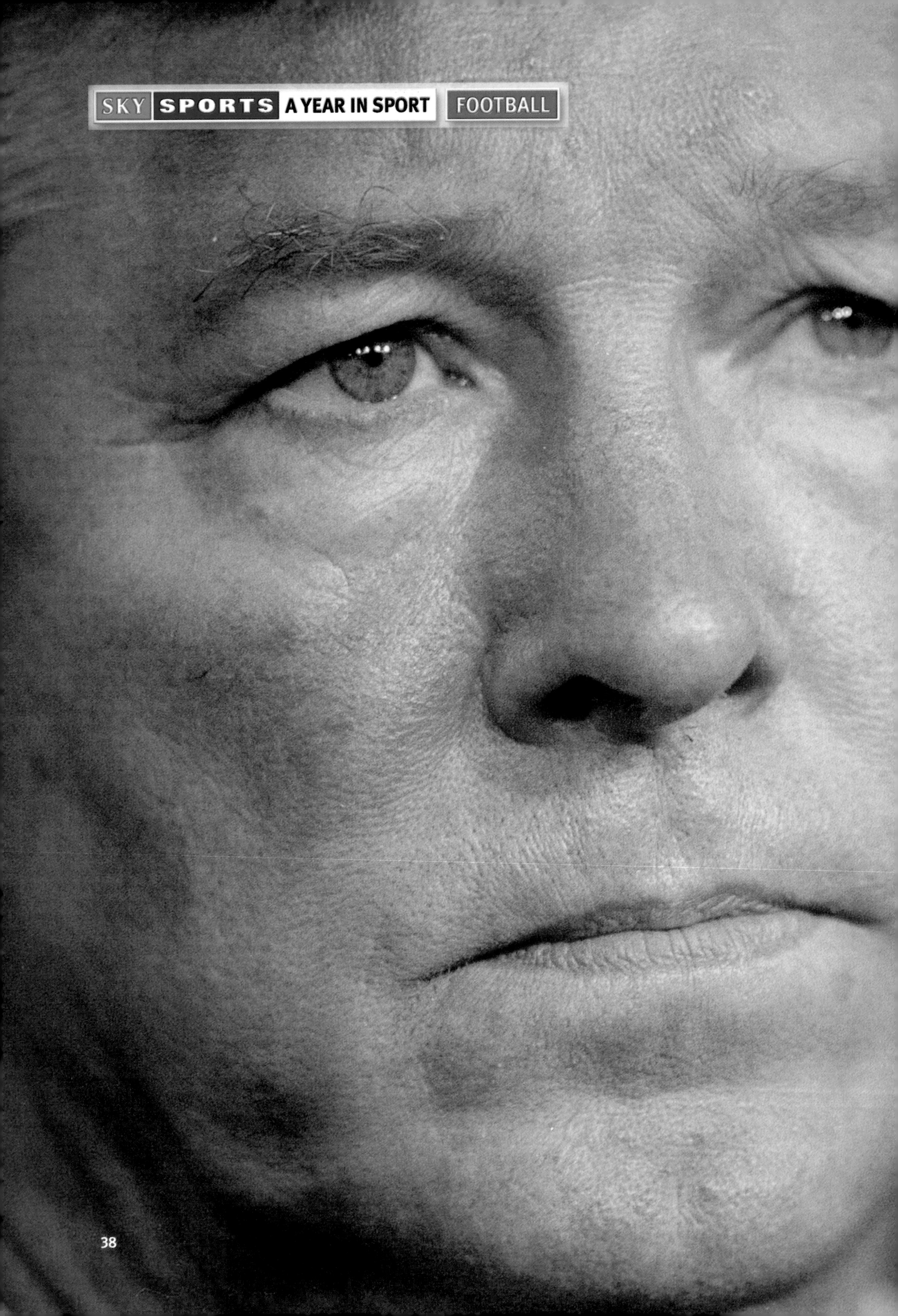

THE KING OF OLD TRAFFORD

In 1986 Alex Ferguson arrived at Manchester United to take on the hardest job in football – resurrecting the famous club to its former glories. Little did anybody realise what an amazing impact the tough Scotsman was to make on the game.

Alex Ferguson was already an accomplished manager when he burst through the front door at Old Trafford for the first time.

After serving his apprenticeship at East Stirling and St Mirren, where he first showed that famous temper and penchant for hurling tea cups around the dressing-room at half-time, he moved on to Aberdeen.

It was at Pittodrie that Ferguson first came to the attention of the English clubs. Celtic and Rangers were the dominant forces north of the border until he nurtured his young side to the Scottish Premiership title in 1979-80.

Further League glory followed in 1983-84 and 1984-85 along with Scottish Cup success in 1982, 1983, 1984 and 1986 and a League Cup triumph in 1985-86.

He was also in charge in Aberdeen's finest hour at a rain-soaked Gothenburg in 1983 when the little club from the granite city beat mighty Real Madrid 2-1 after extra-time in a

thrilling European Cup-Winners' Cup Final. That victory more than any other brought him to the attention of Manchester United.

Ron Atkinson had promised much as Old Trafford boss in his five year spell between 1981 and 1986 with two FA Cup Final wins in his time at United but like Frank O'Farrell, Tommy Docherty and Dave Sexton before him, he paid the price for not bringing the trophy the club most wanted back to Manchester – the League Championship.

Ferguson spent the summer of 1986 as caretaker boss of Scotland in the World Cup finals but the heat in South America was nothing compared to his first few seasons at Old Trafford after he arrived to take over from Atkinson in November that year.

Living in the shadow of the great Sir Matt Busby, who built not one but two brilliant sides at Old Trafford, one destroyed by the Munich Air Disaster in 1958, the other winning

DID YOU KNOW?

Ferguson's roll of honour at United in total reads: Premiership Champions 1993; 1994; 1996; 1997; 1999; 2000; 2001. FA Cup winners 1990; 1994; 1996; 1999. League Cup winners 1992. European Cup-Winners' Cup winners 1991. European Cup winners 1999.Charity Shield winners 1990 shared; 1993; 1994; 1996; 1997. Super Cup winners 1991. World Club Championship winners 1999.

Before turning to a career in football he worked in the Govan shipyards where he became a renowned union leader.

By August 2001 he had won the Manager of the Month award 12 times and Manager of the Year on six occasions.

He was a centre-forward in his playing days and turned out for Queen's Park, St Johnstone, Dunfermline, Falkirk, Ayr and Rangers.

Ferguson is the only manager to win League Championships in Scotland and England.

In 1993 he became the first manager to win Manager of the Year awards both north and south of the border.

He is learning to play the piano.

He was voted the Best Coach in Europe in 1999.

In 1991 he joined Johan Cruyff as the only managers to win the European Cup-Winners' Cup with teams from different countries. Ironically, Cruyff was manager of the Barcelona team that United beat in the Final that year.

Alex Ferguson's place in football folklore had been assured. For the first and probably only time, an English club had won the League, FA Cup and European Cup treble.

the European Cup at Wembley 10 years later, was proving to be tougher task than he imagined, even for someone as determined as Ferguson.

United finished 11th in his first season in charge, acceptable considering he inherited a team in the bottom four.

A runners-up position behind fierce rivals Liverpool in 1988 showed promise but with the likes of Millwall, QPR, Coventry and Norwich above United in the table the following year and another mid-table spot the end result, the calls for Ferguson to go were growing louder amongst the hordes of Reds' fans. The tea cups were certainly flying around the dressing-room at that stage!

By the time United travelled to Nottingham Forest for an FA Cup Third Round tie in January 1990, they were lying in the mid-table

wilderness again and speculation was rife that defeat would see the end of the fiery Scot's stay at Old Trafford.

"That period leading up to the Forest game was without doubt the lowest, most desperate point in all my years of management," recalled Ferguson.

Who knows what would have happened if Mark Robins had not stooped to head the only goal of the game at the City Ground, but he did and it kick-started a transformation in fortunes for the club and their manager.

Just like at Aberdeen, Ferguson had made the club's youth system a priority at United and one of his youngsters, Lee Martin, gave him his first trophy at Old Trafford, the FA Cup, four months after Robins' rescue mission.

The replay victory over Crystal Palace illustrated Ferguson's single-minded approach to what was best for his team. He had brought goalkeeper Jim Leighton down from Aberdeen, where they had been together for years, to be his number one at United but the Scottish international had been struggling with his form that season and looked vulnerable in the 3-3 draw at Wembley. Ferguson simply dropped him for the replay, replacing him with the extrovert Les Sealey. United won 1-0, their first trophy for five years, and the wounded Leighton's days were numbered from that moment on.

A year later, two Mark Hughes goals gave United victory over Barcelona at Rotterdam in the European Cup-Winners' Cup Final and the Ferguson bandwagon was gathering pace.

But it was the League Championship that the club craved more than any other trophy. The following season, 1991-92, they looked assured of taking top spot until fixture congestion and pure panic set in with the finishing line in their sights. Leeds nicked the title with Liverpool taking great delight in putting the final nail in United's Championship coffin at Anfield.

It was then that Ferguson made arguably

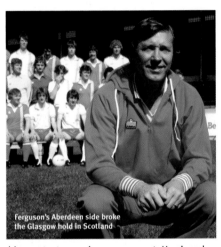

Ferguson's Aberdeen side broke the Glasgow hold in Scotland

his greatest move in management. He signed Eric Cantona from Leeds.

The controversial Frenchman had undoubted talent, but a temperament to match, with a reputation for being difficult to handle. He was also hardly the prolific goalscorer that United so desperately needed.

'The first Championship triumph breached the barrier that had defied so many talented people, world renowned players as well as managers'

But his signing proved a masterstroke, arguably the club's greatest ever buy at a mere £1 million.

Cantona proved the catalyst for United's first League Championship in 26 years, and the start of the club's domination of the English game.

"The Championship triumph, apart from ending 26 years of collective cursing and frustration, was unquestionably the breaching of the barrier that had defied so many talented people, world renowned players as well as managers," said Ferguson.

Inspired by Cantona and with the club's youth

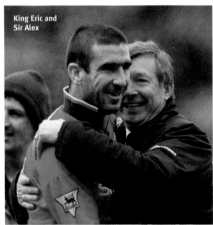
King Eric and Sir Alex

system providing a stream of stars from Lee Sharpe and Ryan Giggs to the new breed, Paul Scholes, Nicky Butt, the Neville brothers and David Beckham, United won their first League and FA Cup double in 1994, with only a Worthington Cup Final defeat by Aston Villa halting a domestic treble.

Cantona's infamous lunge at a Crystal Palace fan marred the following season and they ended up runners-up in both the Championship, to Blackburn, and the FA Cup, to Everton.

King Eric, as he became known to the United fans, made up for his aberration at Selhurst Park a year earlier by scoring the late winner against Liverpool in the 1996 FA Cup Final to put the club in the record books as the first to achieve the League and Cup double twice.

With Cantona retiring at the end of the 1996-97 season after another Championship triumph, critics predicted the bubble would burst, especially after Arsenal ensured there was no silverware at Old Trafford in 1998.

But Ferguson has never been one to stand still, always looking to the future.

He paid out a club record £12.6 million to Aston Villa for Dwight Yorke in August 1998. Another gamble perhaps, but the Scotsman, a respected racehorse owner, had signed another thoroughbred.

Yorke combined with Andy Cole with devastating effect, the pair sharing 35 goals in the League as United pipped the Gunners to the title on the last day of the season.

Victory over Newcastle in the FA Cup Final followed a week later before the drama of an amazing European Cup Final, with injury time goals from Teddy Sheringham and Ole Gunnar Solskjaer giving United a 2-1 win against Bayern Munich.

Alex Ferguson's place in football folklore had been assured. The first time, and quite likely to be the only time, an English club had won the Championship, FA Cup and European Cup treble. He became the first working manager to be knighted that year, truly following in the footsteps of Sir Matt Busby.

Now he is in his final year of management before taking an 'ambassador's role' at the club. And with 21 trophies at United before the start of the 2001-02 season, Ferguson has a strong claim to be called the greatest manager in British football history.

One thing is certain, when he steps down there will be a giant shadow hanging over his successor - probably carrying a teacup!

The Manchester United players and their boss celebrate European Cup glory

THE MEN TO FILL FERGIE'S BOOTS

MARTIN O'NEILL

Highly-rated young manager who has been successful wherever he has gone. Steered Wycombe in to the Football League, guided Leicester in to Europe and to two Worthington Cup Final successes and in his first year as Celtic boss, won the treble and not surprisingly the Manager of the Year award. Northern Ireland international in his playing days.

ARSENE WENGER

Has already proved he can be successful in the British game with Arsenal. Has a wealth of experience after managing in France with Monaco and also Japan. Wanted by the Japanese as their national team coach and also been linked with the French manager's role.

OTTMAR HITZFELD

Won the Champions' League with Borussia Dortmund in 1997 and then joined Bayern Munich the following year, leading them to three successive League Championships. Was boss when they lost to Manchester United in the 1999 Champions' League Final but got his hands on the trophy again in 2001. Has also worked in Switzerland and has nearly 30 years experience as a manager. Played for Germany in 1972 Olympics.

WORTHINGTON CUP

LIVERPOOL LIFT THE CUP FOR A RECORD SIXTH TIME

WORTHINGTON CUP FINAL
FEBRUARY 25 MILLENNIUM STADIUM
LIVERPOOL 1 BIRMINGHAM 1
(LIVERPOOL WON 5-4 ON PENS)

REDS HOLD
THEIR NERVE

LIVERPOOL picked up their first trophy under Gerard Houllier after beating Birmingham in a penalty shoot-out at the Worthington Cup Final.

Robbie Fowler's spectacular volley from 25 yards gave the Merseysiders a first-half lead and it looked good enough for victory until brave Brum won a penalty in the last seconds, which was calmly put away by Darren Purse.

Liverpool shaded the chances in the 90 minutes with Vladimir Smicer, Emile Heskey and Fowler all going close to adding a second before Birmingham's last gasp equaliser.

But Trevor Francis' side were the stronger in extra-time and should have had another penalty when Andrew Johnson was

brought down by a reckless challenge from Stephane Henchoz.

Dietmar Hamann smacked a long range strike against the post and Bryan Hughes brought the best out of Reds 'keeper Sander Westerveld but the extra 30 minutes could not provide a winner.

First blood went to Liverpool in the shoot-out with Gary McAllister scoring and Martin Grainger's effort kept out by Westerveld. But Ian Bennett saved from Dietmar Hamann, allowing Stan Lazaridis to level things up at 3-3.

Fowler, Hughes and Jamie Carragher all scored, leaving

teenager Andrew Johnson the responsibility of keeping Birmingham in the game. It proved too much and his shot was saved by Westerveld.

Johnson, who played a major part in Birmingham's resurgence after coming on as a half-time substitute for Dele Adebola, buried his head in manager Trevor Francis' arms and both shed tears of disappointment.

Meanwhile, Robbie Fowler lifted the trophy for Liverpool, a record sixth time the Anfield club had won the League Cup.

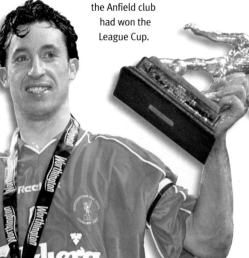

Robbie Fowler gives
Liverpool the lead

FOWLER LOOKS TO THE FUTURE

ROBBIE Fowler celebrated his man of the match display against Birmingham with a prediction that Worthington Cup success was just the start for the men from Anfield.

The Liverpool frontman, whose strike in the Final was his sixth goal in the season's competition, was part of the Reds side that won the trophy back in 1995 but said: "We should have kicked on from there but never did.

"It will be different this time. We now have a side that is capable of striding on to even bigger and better things.

"There is a mentality about the squad now that sees everyone playing for each other and we look well equipped to challenge for the major honours.

"Lifting the trophy was a special moment for me and I'm confident that it is just the start of some good times for this club after a barren run."

BRUM DEAL

BIRMINGHAM CITY left the Millennium Stadium complaining that it should have been their trophy and not Liverpool's.

When Andrew Johnson was sent crashing to the ground under a challenge from Stephane Henchoz, the blue half of the ground screamed for a penalty.

Referee David Elleray waved away Birmingham's appeals and manager Trevor Francis hopped, skipped and jumped down the touchline in frustration as the Midlanders' hopes of landing their first major trophy

UNITED AND ARSENAL LEAD CUP SNUB

WHILE the Worthington Cup carries the prize of a place in the UEFA Cup as reward for the winners, it continues to be low on the list of priorities for England's two biggest clubs, Manchester United and Arsenal.

The Gunners were missing a whole team of regular first-team players when they lost 2-1 to Ipswich in the Third Round while United combined the likes of Dwight Yorke and Ole Gunnar Solskjaer with a string of youngsters in their defeat at Sunderland.

"We play a high number of games in this country and it is not possible to field your best players in every match," argued Arsene Wenger.

"We have a strong squad of players at Highbury and the Worthington Cup has provided us with a chance to give some of the younger ones a chance."

since the 1963 League Cup disappeared.

"I couldn't believe the referee did not give a penalty, it was so clear cut," said Francis.

HOW THEY LINED-UP

LIVERPOOL: Westerveld, Babbel, Henchoz, Hyypia, Carragher, Gerrard, (McAllister), Hamann, Smicer, (Barmby), Biscan (Ziege), Fowler, Heskey.

BIRMINGHAM: Bennett, Eaden, Purse, M.Johnson, Grainger, McCarthy, O'Connor, Sonner (Hughes 71), Lazaridis, Horsfield (Marcelo 80), Adebola (A.Johnson 46).

Sander Westerveld makes the matchwinning save

RESULTS

THIRD ROUND ONWARDS

Aston Villa 0 Man City 1
Wimbledon 1 Boro 0
Arsenal 1 Ipswich 2
Soton 0 Coventry 1
Tottenham 1 Birmingh'm 3
Newcastle 4 Bradford 3
West Ham 2 Blackburn 0
Sheff Wed 2 Sheff Utd 1
Leicester 0 C.Palace 3
Tranmere 3 Leeds 2
Bristol Rvrs 1 Sunderl'd 2
Watford 0 Man Utd 3
Stoke 3 Barnsley 2
Liverpool 2 Chelsea 1
Fulham 3 Wolves 2
Derby 3 Norwich 0

FOURTH ROUND

Man City 2 Wimbledon 1
Ipswich 2 Coventry 1
Birmingh'm 2 Newcastle 1
West Ham 1 Sheff Wed 2
C.Palace 0 Tranmere 0
(Palace won on penalties)
Sunderland 2 Man Utd 1
Stoke 0 Liverpool 8
Fulham 3 Derby 2

QUARTER-FINALS

Man City 1 Ipswich 2
Birmingh'm 2 Sheff Wed 0
C.Palace 2 Sunderland 1
Liverpool 3 Fulham 0

SEMI-FINALS

C.Palace 2 Liverpool 1
Liverpool 5 C.Palace 0
Ipswich 1 Birmingham 0
Birmingham 4 Ipswich 1

FA CUP

FA CUP FINAL
MAY 12
MILLENNIUM STADIUM
LIVERPOOL 2 ARSENAL 1

OUT ON HIS OWEN

MICHAEL Owen snatched the FA Cup from Arsenal's grasp with two goals in the last seven minutes.

The Liverpool striker hardly had a kick in the first 83 minutes as the Gunners dominated the play and should have led by more than Freddie Ljungberg's 72nd minute goal.

But Owen reacted quickest when Gary McAllister's free-kick was headed back into the danger zone by Marcus Babbel and he twisted acrobatically to fire past David Seaman.

And a few minutes later the England international won the Cup for the Merseysiders when he latched on to a long pass from Patrik Berger, left Lee Dixon and Gunners' skipper Tony Adams in his wake and fired left-footed into the corner of the net.

Liverpool could have added a third when Robbie Fowler failed to release the unmarked Owen in injury time but it hardly mattered, referee Steve Dunn blowing his whistle seconds later to signal the start of a Scouse party at the Millennium Stadium.

But while Gerard Houllier's men danced around the pitch parading the club's first FA Cup trophy in nine years, man of the match Owen was putting the victory into perspective.

"It's great to win another trophy to go with the Worthington Cup but it's the Premiership we want really," he said. "The League table doesn't lie and we have been disappointed that we have not got closer to Manchester United.

"If you win over 40-odd games than that proves you are the best in England and if you are the best in England, you are going to be one of the best in Europe.

"We have to show we are more than a Cup team. We want to be the best side in the country and to do that you have to finish top of the Premiership."

HOW THEY LINED-UP

LIVERPOOL: Westerveld, Babbel, Henchoz, Hyypia, Carragher, Gerrard, Murphy (Berger), Hamann (McAllister), Smicer (Fowler), Owen, Heskey.

ARSENAL: Seaman, Dixon (Bergkamp), Keown, Adams, Cole, Pires, Ljungberg (Kanu), Vieira, Grimandi, Wiltord (Parlour), Henry.

GUTTED GUNNERS

DEFEAT by Liverpool left Arsenal with another trophyless season, their third in succession after winning the League and FA Cup double in 1998.

They were the better side in Cardiff but referee Dunn's failure to spot Stephane Henchoz handle Thierry Henry's shot on the line in the first-half and poor finishing in the second combined to leave the door open for Owen to shut in their faces in those closing seven minutes.

Arsenal boss Arsene Wenger felt the result was indicative of their year.

Owen grabs the winner for Liverpool

Henry shoots, Henchoz handles

"We had enough chances to have won the game comfortably but we didn't take them and then we lost our concentration right at the end," he said.

"I have said that many times during the season. We look like we should win but then lose it late on.

"We need to bring in new players now because we have lost two big games, against Valencia and Liverpool, in the last 15 minutes and that is no coincidence."

MILLENNIUM STADIUM PUTS WEMBLEY IN THE SHADE

THE controversial choice of the Millennium Stadium to host the FA Cup Final proved to be the right one.

While politicians and the FA were involved in discussions over the proposed new national stadium, Cardiff became the home of the first FA Cup Final outside Wembley since 1923.

And a fitting venue it was, with the pitch immaculate, every seat in the 72,500 capacity ground offering a perfect view and the transport chaos of the Worthington Cup Final eased considerably. Even the toilets were clean!

"We had some problems with the pitch but it was relaid a few weeks before the Final and was perfect," said FA chief executive Adam Crozier.

"The fans created a great atmosphere and from what we have seen and heard, the Millennium Stadium is a great venue for the Cup Final."

WYCOMBE CLAIM GIANTKILLERS CROWN

WYCOMBE were the giantkillers of the FA Cup 2001, grabbing the headlines with a Quarter-Final win at Leicester after victories over Wolves, Wimbledon and Grimsby in the earlier rounds.

Roy Essandoh (pic below) was the hero of their 2-1 win at Filbert Street, heading in an injury-time winner only a few days after making his debut.

He had seen that injury-hit Wycombe were looking for strikers on Teletext and his agent contacted the Second Division club to arrange a trial.

After impressing in a reserve game and then as sub against Reading, the 25-year-old, who had been playing in Finland for VPS Vaasa, won a place on the bench against Leicester and then wrote his name in FA Cup history.

Wycombe boss Lawrie Sanchez knows all about Cup fairytales, of course. He scored Wimbledon's goal that beat Liverpool in the 1988 FA Cup Final.

Joining Essandoh in the golden goals of the FA Cup campaign was Paolo Di Canio who kept his nerve, despite Fabien Barthez's hand-raised attempt to put him off, to score West Ham's winner at Manchester United in the Fourth Round.

RESULTS

FOURTH ROUND ONWARDS
Aston Villa 1 Leicester 2
Blackburn 0 Derby 0
Bolton 5 Scunthorpe 1
Bristol City 1 Kingstonian 1
Charlton 2 Tottenham 4
Crewe 0 Stockport 1
Everton 0 Tranmere 3
Gillingham 2 Chelsea 4
Leeds 0 Liverpool 2
Man City 1 Coventry 0
Man United 0 West Ham 1
Middlesbrough 0 Wimbledon 0
QPR 0 Arsenal 6
Southampton 3 Sheff Wed 1
Sunderland 1 Ipswich 0
Wycombe 2 Wolves 1

REPLAYS
Kingstonian 0 Bristol City 1
Derby 2 Blackburn 5
Wimbledon 3 Middlesbrough 1

FIFTH ROUND
Arsenal 3 Chelsea 1
Bolton 1 Blackburn 1
Leicester 3 Bristol City 0
Liverpool 4 Man City 2
Southampton 0 Tranmere 0
Sunderland 0 West Ham 1
Tottenham 4 Stockport 0
Wycombe 2 Wimbledon 2

REPLAYS
Blackburn 3 Bolton 0
Tranmere 4 Southampton 3
Wimbledon 2 Wycombe 2
(Wycombe won 8-7 on pens)

QUARTER-FINALS
Arsenal 3 Blackburn 0
Leicester 1 Wycombe 2
Tranmere 2 Liverpool 4
West Ham 2 Tottenham 3

SEMI-FINALS
Arsenal 2 Tottenham 1
Liverpool 2 Wycombe 1

NATIONWIDE LEAGUE

FULHAM UP AS CHAMPIONS, ROVERS JOIN THEM

CLASS OF COTTAGERS SHOWS

FULHAM returned to the top flight of English football for the first time in 33 years after leading the First Division from virtually the first kick of the season.

Buoyed by the ambition and bank balance of chairman Mohamed Al Fayed and managed by the astute Jean Tigana, the Cottagers were among the favourites to step up to the Premiership when the season began in August.

And they never looked like letting their fans – or the bookies – down, finally lifting the title with a 1-1 draw against Sheffield Wednesday at a packed Craven Cottage in April, their eventual winning margin 10 points.

Tigana, brought in by Fayed to replace Paul Bracewell in the summer of 2000, spent wisely and his move to link up Frenchman Louis Saha and Southampton loanee Luis Boa Morte in

attack was the catalyst for a victorious season, the pair sharing 45 of Fulham's 90 League goals during the campaign.

Saha had a short spell at Newcastle on loan from Metz in 1998 but failed to make an impact and Boa Morte had similar disappointing fortunes at Arsenal and Southampton.

But Tigana turned them into a formidable partnership at the Cottage and the pair showed signs of what they could do in the Premiership with a stern test of Manchester United's defence in the FA Cup Third Round tie, won by the Reds 2-1 in January.

"That is one of the hardest games my defence has faced all season," said a relieved United boss Sir Alex Ferguson.

"Fulham were excellent, a real credit to the Nationwide League. They showed what they are capable of against a top side. To be honest, I thought we were very lucky to beat them."

When Fayed took over at Fulham he had a five year plan to take the club from the Second

Division to the Premiership, Tigana shaved a year off that and player-coach John Collins reckoned they were ready for the step up.

"Winning the First Division title with Fulham means as much to me as my international caps and the French Championship I won with Monaco," said the former Scotland midfielder.

"We deserved to win the Championship and we are ready for the challenge of the Premiership.

"We will need to strengthen the squad, no doubt, but we have proved we can match Premiership teams in the Cup, now we have to go out and do it week in, week out.

"I'm sure we are capable of that because this club is going places, on and off the pitch."

The only blemishes on their successful year were a serious car crash that put question marks over defender Chris Coleman's career and news of the death of former boss Alec Stock, aged 84, which was announced on the same day that Tigana's side clinched the Championship.

Rovers return as Matt Jansen scores at Preston

ROVERS RETURN

A CLOSE range header from Matt Jansen gave Blackburn a 1-0 victory at Preston in their penultimate game of the season, clinched their return to the Premiership and satisfied the dreams of Rovers legend Jack Walker.

The steel magnate's greatest wish on the eve of his death in August 2000 was for his beloved Blackburn to return to the top flight.

He had led the celebrations after his millions – and desire – had driven Rovers to the Premiership Championship in 1995, and shed more tears than most when they were relegated four years later.

Jansen's 23rd goal of the season saw the hopes of a return come true and it was Walker's name that echoed around Deepdale more than any other as Blackburn fans celebrated promotion, with skipper Garry Flitcroft revealing a T-shirt with the words 'this is for you Jack' under his Rovers top.

"It's a great shame that Jack is not with us to see this moment," said Ewood Park boss Graeme Souness after the game.

"For many, he was Blackburn Rovers, and I know how desperate he was for the club to get back in the Premiership.

"It was hard though because for most clubs, we were their biggest game of the season and they all wanted to beat us. It was like playing a Cup Final every week, so the lads deserve tremendous credit for achieving promotion."

DOUGIE DELIGHT

DOUGIE Freedman kept **Crystal Palace** in the First Division with a dramatic 87th minute winner at Stockport County on the final day of the season.

The Eagles were only three minutes from being relegated when Freedman, who had also scored twice in his club's crucial 4-2 win at Portsmouth only four days earlier, rifled a shot into the net.

Portsmouth beat **Barnsley** 3-0 to survive on the last day of the campaign for the third time in six years, leaving **Huddersfield**, beaten 2-1 at home by Birmingham, to fill the third relegation spot along with **QPR** and **Tranmere**, for whom manager John Aldridge resigned in March after 10 years at Prenton Park as player and boss.

QPR announced plans of a possible merger with **Wimbledon** in May but the idea was met with anger by fans from both clubs and was quickly dismissed.

Midlands rivals **West Brom** and **Birmingham** joined Bolton and Preston in the Play-Off places, relegated **Watford** finished a disappointing ninth and appointed Gianluca Vialli as their new manager after Graham Taylor's retirement. **Burnley** surprised everyone by finishing seventh while **Stockport** and **Grimsby** lived to fight another day after a season long battle against the drop.

For the rest there was mid-table anonymity and dreams of a better year in 2002.

Eagles still flying in the First Division

HOW THEY FINISHED

CLUB	P	PTS
Fulham	46	101
Blackburn	46	91
Bolton	46	87
Preston	46	78
Birmingham	46	78
West Brom	46	74
Burnley	46	72
Wimbledon	46	69
Watford	46	69
Sheff Utd	46	68
Nott'm For	46	68
Wolves	46	55
Gillingham	46	55
Crewe	46	55
Norwich	46	54
Barnsley	46	54
Sheff Wed	46	53
Grimsby	46	52
Stockport	46	51
Portsmouth	46	49
C.Palace	46	49
Huddersfield	46	48
QPR	46	40
Tranmere	46	38

TOP LEAGUE SCORERS

Louis Saha	Fulham	27
Matt Jansen	B'burn	23
Lee Hughes	W.Brom	21
Jonathan Macken	Preston	19
Tommy Mooney	Watford	19
Michael Ricketts	Bolton	19
Jason Euell	W'don	19
Luis Boa Morte	Fulham	18

FULHAM FORWARDS' VICTIMS

Club	Lge goals	
	Saha	Boa Morte
Barnsley	3	1
Birmingham	1	0
Blackburn	2	0
Bolton	0	2
Burnley	2	0
C.Palace	1	2
Crewe	1	1
Gillingham	0	1
Grimsby	1	1
Huddersf'd	2	1
Norwich	1	2
Nottm For	2	0
Portsmouth	1	0
QPR	1	0
Sheff Utd	0	1
Sheff Wed	1	0
Stockport	0	1
Tranmere	2	2
Watford	2	2
Wimbledon	2	1
Wolves	2	0

Neither scored against Preston or West Brom.

NATIONWIDE LEAGUE

LIFT OFF FOR THE LIONS WHILE BARNET DROP OUT

Neil Harris and Paul Moody celebrate promotion

ROARING LIONS

MAY 5: Millwall clinched the Second Division Championship in spectacular style on the last day of the season with a 5-0 win over Oldham.

The Lions went into the game neck and neck with Rotherham on points, but their superior goal difference had left them top needing a win to secure the title.

Goals from Neil Harris (2), Paul Moody (2) and Steve Reid certainly ensured that happened in front of a delirious crowd at the New Den.

Harris' double took his tally to 27 in the League for the season, giving him a share of the Golden Boot as top scorer along with Reading's Jamie Cureton.

"As a kid you dream about days like these," said the Lions hero as he toasted promotion with a glass of champagne.

"I always said that signing for Millwall was the biggest day of my life. That was overtaken by winning promotion and now to clinch the Championship in front of 19,000 fans is even better. Really special.

"Now we want to continue to progress and reach the Premiership. Our incentive is to follow the leads of clubs like Charlton and Ipswich, who have shown they can survive at the highest level," added Harris, who was turned down by Liverpool after having a trial with the club.

Sadly for the former Cambridge City frontman, his personal Premiership ambitions were put on hold within a month of Millwall's promotion party after he was diagnosed as having testicular cancer.

TORQUAY WIN RELEGATION SHOOT-OUT

MAY 5: The last day of the Third Division season, the two bottom clubs facing each other in a relegation decider, the loser goes out of the Football League, maybe never to return. Talk about pressure.

That was the situation at a packed Underhill, with 2500 fans locked out half-an-hour before

Barnet fans take relegation hard

kick-off, when Barnet played host to Torquay. Among the crowd inside the ground was Sky Sports presenter and Torquay fan Helen Chamberlain - and it was her beloved Gulls that were left to fight another day.

Torquay coasted in to a three-goal lead by half-time, with Barnet losing their goalkeeper, Lee Harrison, through injury and missing a penalty as well.

But a stirring fightback from the home side after the break reduced the arrears to 3-2 and Torquay were hanging on at the end for one of the most precious victories in their 74-year League history.

"I felt sick during the Soccer AM show

that I did in the morning because I was so nervous," said Chamberlain after the game.

"By half-time we were having a disco but as soon as Barnet scored I could hardly watch. Still we made it and I'm ecstatic."

For Barnet, their 10 year stay in the professional game was condemned to the history books.

SEAGULLS FLYING HIGH

MAY 5: Brighton coasted to the Third Division title, finishing 10 points clear of their nearest challengers Cardiff.

The party atmosphere at their last game of the season, a 3-0 defeat at Shrewsbury, was hardly dampened by the scoreline and in Bobby Zamora (pic below), they had the best striker in the division.

The 20-year-old was watched by a host of Premiership clubs as he led the Seagulls to the Championship, scoring 28 goals along the way.

But the Third Division season was marred by controversy surrounding Chesterfield's nine point deduction for 'financial misdemeanours'.

Many in the game felt the Spireites should have been relegated to the Nationwide Conference as punishment for allegedly making irregular payments to players, but they retained their status and won promotion in third place despite their points reduction.

DIAMONDS ARE FOREVER

MAY 5: Nine years after being formed, the 'Manchester United of the non-League world' finally made it to the big time.

Rushden and Diamonds, founded by millionaire Dr Martens owner Max Griggs in 1992 when Rushden Town and Irthlingborough Diamonds merged, finished six points clear of Yeovil in the Conference, confirming their place in the Football League with a 2-1 win over Chester on the final day of the campaign.

More than £23 million had been pumped into the club's Nene Park ground since their formation and Griggs announced after that victory over Chester that manager Brian Talbot, a former FA Cup winner with Arsenal and Ipswich, would be offered a lucrative new contract.

"Brian has done very well for us and deserves a reward. This club would not be the same without him," he said.

HOW THEY FINISHED

SECOND DIVISION

CLUB	P	PTS
Millwall	46	93
Rotherham	46	91
Reading	46	86
Walsall	46	81
Stoke	46	77
Wigan	46	75
Bournemouth	46	73
Notts Co	46	69
Bristol City	46	68
Wrexham	46	63
Port Vale	46	62
Peterborough	46	59
Wycombe	46	59
Brentford	46	59
Oldham	46	58
Bury	46	58
Colchester	46	57
Northampton	46	57
Cambridge	46	53
Swindon	46	52
Bristol Rovers	46	51
Luton	46	40
Swansea	46	37
Oxford	46	27

THIRD DIVISION

CLUB	P	PTS
Brighton	46	92
Cardiff	46	82
*Chesterfield	46	80
Hartlepool	46	77
L.Orient	46	75
Hull	46	74
Blackpool	46	72
Rochdale	46	71
Cheltenham	46	68
Scunthorpe	46	65
Southend	46	63
Mansfield	46	58
Plymouth	46	58
Macclesfield	46	56
Shrewsbury	46	55
Kidderminster	46	53
York	46	52
Lincoln	46	51
Exeter	46	50
Darlington	46	49
Torquay	46	49
Carlisle	46	48
Halifax	46	47
Barnet	46	45

(* Nine points deducted)

TOP LEAGUE SCORERS

SECOND DIVISION

Jamie Cureton	Reading	27
Neil Harris	Millwall	27
Martin Butler	Reading	24
Mark Robins	Rotherham	24

THIRD DIVISION

Bobby Zamora	Brighton	28
Robert Earnshaw	Cardiff	19
John Murphy	Blackpool	18
Brett Ormerod	Blackpool	18

PLAY-OFF FINALS

1st DIVISION PLAY-OFF FINAL
MAY 28
MILLENNIUM STADIUM
BOLTON 3 PRESTON 0

TROTTERS' DELIGHT

BOLTON finally made it through the lottery of the Play-Offs at the third attempt with a comprehensive victory over Preston.

Defeat by Watford in the 1999 Final and Ipswich in an amazing Semi-Final a year later had broken Wanderers' hearts but manager Sam Allardyce rallied his experienced troops and drove them over the finishing line this time.

The Bolton boss was forced to sell Claus Jensen, Mark Fish and Eidur Gudjohnsen among others after missing out on promotion in 2000, but victory over a young Preston side looking for their second successive promotion ensured a cash windfall worth around £40 million to the club and gave Allardyce the facility to buy in the summer rather than sell.

"Our Play-Off victory will have a massive financial effect on this club," he said after his victory jig around the Millennium Stadium.

"We are going into the Premiership at a time when the old television deal is being superseded by a new one and that will bring us millions of pounds.

"I just have to make sure I use some of the cash that is made available to me wisely in order to keep us up and enable Bolton Wanderers to build for the future."

Gareth Farrelly opened the scoring for Bolton in the 16th minute with a perfectly struck drive from the edge of the box.

Dean Holdsworth, Bo Hansen and Gudni Bergsson all went close to adding to that lead but Wanderers were made to wait until the final minute before Farrelly released Michael Ricketts to score his 24th goal of the season.

Seconds later Ricardo Gardner galloped past the tired Preston defence to settle matters with a third.

For Farrelly, in particular, victory was sweet. He scored for Everton in the 1-1 draw with Coventry on the last day of the 1997-98 season to send Bolton down from the Premiership on their last stay there.

"The fans took a while to forget that when I joined Bolton on a free transfer from Everton," admitted the midfielder.

"But Bolton gave me a chance when things were not going well for me at Goodison Park and scoring against Preston was a great way to thank them."

HOW THEY LINED-UP

BOLTON: Clarke, Barness, Bergsson, Hendry, Charlton, Frandsen (Elliott) Nolan, Farrelly, Hansen (Ricketts) Holdsworth (Whitlow) Gardner.
PRESTON: Lucas, Alexander, Edwards, Murdock, Kidd, Gregan, Rankine, McKenna (Cresswell), Macken, Healy, Cartwright (Anderson).

2nd DIVISION PLAY-OFF FINAL
MAY 27
MILLENNIUM STADIUM
WALSALL 3 READING 2

SADDLERS WELL

WALSALL'S roller-coaster ride over the last three years took another upward turn.

Relegated in May 2000 after only a year in the First Division, the Saddlers returned to that level again thanks to their extra-time heroics.

Don Goodman' second-half strike had taken the game into the extra 30 minutes, the Walsall striker cancelling out Jamie Cureton's 30th goal of the season for Reading.

Martin Butler put the Royals ahead in the first minute of extra-time but Tony Rougier's own goal

memories of another Play-Off extra-time heartbreak, their 4-3 loss to Bolton in 1995.

"Our fans probably think we are jinxed in the Play-Offs," said Reading boss Alan Pardew.

"It was not our destiny to win promotion this time but come May 2002 we have to make sure it is."

HOW THEY LINED-UP

WALSALL: Walker, Brightwell, Barras, Tillson, Aranalde, Hall (Gadsby), Keates, Bennett (Bukran), Matias, Goodman, Leitao (Byfield).

READING: Whitehead, Williams (Hunter), Viveash, Murty, Robinson, Harper, Igoe (Forster), Parkinson, McIntyre (Rougier), Butler, Cureton.

Don Goodman is on target against Reading

levelled the scores again before Darren Byfield rifled in a 25-yard drive 11 minutes from the end to give the Midlanders victory.

"We looked down and out a couple of times but the players forced their way back in to the game and showed great character," said Walsall boss Ray Graydon. "It was a fantastic recovery."

For Reading, defeat only brought back

Brett Ormerod celebrates scoring against Orient

3rd DIVISION PLAY-OFF FINAL
MAY 26
MILLENNIUM STADIUM
BLACKPOOL 4 L.ORIENT 2

POOL OF JOY

BOXING promoter Barry Hearn watched his Orient side suffer a knockout blow in the Play-Offs for the second time in three years.

Blackpool twice came from behind before easing ahead in the last 13 minutes.

"Blackpool were better than us in the second-half and the stronger side won," admitted Hearn, whose club also lost out to Scunthorpe in 1999.

For Blackpool, victory meant an immediate return to the Second Division after suffering relegation 12 months earlier.

HOW THEY LINED-UP

BLACKPOOL: Barnes, Hills, Hughes, Reid, Clarkson, J.Murphy, Coid, Wellens, (M.Milligan), Ormerod (Thompson), Simpson (J.Milligan), Parkinson.

L.ORIENT: Bayes, Joseph, Lockwood, Smith, McGhee, Downer, Harris, Ibehre, Walschaerts (Castle), Houghton (Martin), Tate (Brkovic).

SEMI-FINAL RESULTS

FIRST DIVISION
West Brom 2 Bolton 2
Bolton 3 West Brom 0

Birmingham 1 Preston 0
Preston 2 Birmingham 1
(Preston won 4-2 on penalties)

SECOND DIVISION
Wigan 0 Reading 0
Reading 2 Wigan 1

Stoke 0 Walsall 0
Walsall 4 Stoke 2

THIRD DIVISION
Blackpool 2 Hartlepool 0
Hartlepool 1 Blackpool 3

Hull 1 L.Orient 0
L.Orient 2 Hull 0

UP AND DOWN
Bolton were immediately installed as favourites to be relegated in 2001-2002. And a look at how the recent First Division Play-Off winners have fared in the Premiership the following season shows you why.

SEASON	PLAY-OFF WINNERS	FINAL POSITION
2000-2001	Ipswich	5th
1999-2000	Watford	20th (r)
1998-1999	Charlton	18th (r)
1997-1998	C.Palace	20th (r)
1996-1997	Leicester	9th

THE ODDS
Relegation odds the week after Bolton's Play-Off victory over Preston North End.

4-7	Bolton
10-11	Derby
11-8	Southampton
7-4	Leicester
11-4	Charlton, Everton, Middlesbrough
4-1	West Ham
8-1	Blackburn, Ipswich
10-1	Aston Villa
12-1	Newcastle
14-1	Fulham
20-1	Sunderland, Tottenham
66-1	Chelsea
100-1	Leeds
250-1	Arsenal, Liverpool
500-1	Man United

SCOTTISH PREMIER

Martin O'Neill salutes Celtic's title triumph

O'NEILL IS KING

CELTIC returned to their position as kings of Scottish football and there was no doubt who was sitting on the throne – Martin O'Neill.

The Irishman took over the Parkhead reins in the summer of 2000 after a disappointing spell under John Barnes and Kenny Dalglish had seen the Bhoys finish a staggering 21 points behind arch rivals Rangers at the top of the table.

And he never looked back from the opening day victory at Dundee United, leading Celtic to their second Championship in four years, 15 points clear of 'Gers.

Such has been the influence of O'Neill that Hoops fans feel confident the club can dominate the next few years in much the same way that Rangers ruled football north of the border through most of the 1990s.

Three League victories in four games with the Ibrox club during the season, including a 6-2 hammering, are testament to their faith.

Celtic won their first eight Premier League games and the title race was as good as over by Christmas with Tommy Johnson's winner against St Mirren in April finally clinching the trophy.

O'Neill rated the achievement as one of the highest points of his career both as a player and manager.

'I'm proud to be manager of a Celtic side that has lifted the Championship'

"I won the European Cup as a player with Nottingham Forest and skippered Northern Ireland when we beat Spain in their own backyard during the 1982 World Cup, both great memories," said O'Neill.

"And winning promotion from nowhere with Leicester and then going on to lift the League Cup twice with them was great.

"But winning the League with Celtic in front of 60,000 fans was a very special moment, as good as I have ever had in the game.

"We had some problems during the season but came through them all and it makes me feel very proud that I was manager of a Celtic side that has lifted the Championship."

And star striker Henrik Larsson, who bagged a staggering 53 goals for the club during the year, joined the queue of players at Parkhead ready to salute the manager's role in their success.

"Martin O'Neill has made a massive impact at the club," said the Swedish international.

"He's a talented coach, and brought in a number of quality players. He also restored the confidence of players who were already at the club.

"He didn't make huge changes in our style of play during the season, or the way we trained, but he created a positive feeling within the squad. He made it a great time to be a Celtic player."

SWEDE SUCCESS

HENRIK Larsson was the star of Scottish football in 2001, only a year after fearing his career might be over.

A double leg fracture in the early stages of the 1999-2000 season left him sidelined for eight months but he stunned the experts by recovering better than ever and his tally of 35 League goals played a significant part in Celtic's Championship campaign.

"He had a tremendous season and proved what a world class player he is," said Larsson's striking sidekick, Chris Sutton, who arrived at Parkhead in a £6 million deal from Chelsea at the start of the season.

"He is strong, fit, scores goals with both feet or his head and also works very hard.

"I love playing alongside him because he plays to my strengths and there is no doubt that he is the top player at the club.

"There would be a riot at Celtic if the club listened to any of the offers made for him because the fans love him – and so do the other players."

Henrik Larsson - top scorer in Scotland

HIBS HIBS HOORAY

RANGERS may have finished runners-up to Celtic, but it was **Hibs** that won all the accolades outside the Parkhead club.

Alex McLeish's side were the only team to compete with the blistering pace set by the Bhoys in the first three or four months of the season.

The pressure finally told in the latter stages of the campaign and they ended up in third place, 16 points behind Rangers, but a UEFA Cup spot was a well-earned reward for McLeish's small but talented squad, led by the experienced Finnish striker Mixu Paatelainen.

And thoughts of their 6-2 win over Edinburgh rivals Hearts still burn brightly in the memory of the Hibees.

Rangers paid out a Scottish record £12 million to take Tore Andre Flo to Ibrox from Chelsea in November and he made his debut in the 5-1 win over Celtic a few days later but that was as good as it got in a terrible, trophyless year for Dick Advocaat's side.

Kilmarnock secured the second UEFA Cup place with a 1-0 win over the Champions on the last day of the season, depriving **Hearts**, who had lost manager Jim Jefferies to Bradford in November, of fourth spot.

Promoted **St Mirren** lost out to **Dundee United** in the battle to stay up, finishing five points adrift at the bottom, the only side relegated after the Premier League maintained its year long format as a 12-team division.

Mixu Paatelainen

HOW THEY FINISHED

CLUB	P	W	D	L	PTS
Celtic	38	31	4	3	97
Rangers	38	26	4	8	82
Hibs	38	18	12	8	66
Kilmarnock	38	15	9	14	54
Hearts	38	14	10	14	52
Dundee	38	13	8	17	47
Aberdeen	38	11	12	15	45
Motherwell	38	12	7	19	43
Dunfermline	38	11	9	18	42
St Johnstone	38	9	13	16	40
Dundee U.	38	9	8	21	35
St Mirren	38	8	6	24	30

TOP LEAGUE SCORERS

Henrik Larsson	Celtic	35
Arild Stavrum	Aberdeen	17
Juan Sara	Dundee	15
Andy Kirk	Hearts	13
Colin Cameron	Hearts	12
Stuart Elliott	Motherwell	12
Tore Andre Flo	Rangers	11
Chris Sutton	Celtic	11
Mixu Paatelainen	Hibs	11

LARSSON'S VICTIMS

CLUB	LGE GOALS SCORED
Aberdeen	4
Dundee	0
Dundee Utd	3
Dunfermline	4
Hearts	6
Hibs	3
Kilmarnock	5
Motherwell	0
Rangers	4
St Johnstone	4
St Mirren	2

SCOTTISH CUPS

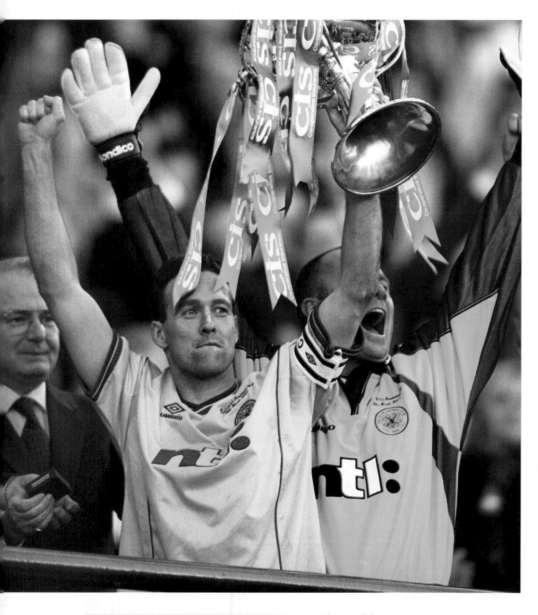

HOW THEY LINED UP

CELTIC: Gould, Lambert, Vega, Petta (Crainey, Boyd), Lennon, Valgaeren, Healy, Larsson, Moravcik (Smith), Sutton, Mjallby.

KILMARNOCK: Marshall, MacPherson, McGowne, Cocard (McLaren), Holt, Durrant (Reilly), Mahood, Dindeleux (Canero), Dargo, Innes, Hay.

RESULTS

THIRD ROUND ONWARDS
Celtic 4 Raith 0
Dundee Utd 0 Airdrie 0
(Dundee Utd won on pens)
Dunfermline 2 Motherwell 0
Falkirk 1 Hibs 2
Livingston 0 Hearts 2
Rangers 4 Aberdeen 2
St Johnstone 0 Kilmarnock 1
St Mirren 3 Dundee 0

QUARTER-FINALS
Hearts 2 Celtic 5
Kilmarnock 2 Hibs 1
Rangers 2 Dundee Utd 0
St Mirren 2 Dunfermline 1

SEMI-FINALS
Celtic 3 Rangers 1
St Mirren 0 Kilmarnock 3

FINAL
Celtic 3 Kilmarnock 0

CIS INSURANCE CUP FINAL
MARCH 18
HAMPDEN PARK
CELTIC 3 KILMARNOCK 0

HAT-TRICK HERO HENRIK

HENRIK Larsson's hat-trick gave Martin O'Neill his first trophy as Celtic boss.

The Swedish international struck all his goals in the second-half as the Bhoys overcame Killie despite being reduced to 10 men for the last half-an-hour after Chris Sutton was sent-off for a foul on Gary Holt.

Larsson's third was the pick of the bunch, beating 'keeper Gordon Marshall with lovely footwork before putting the ball in the empty net.

It was the striker's second League Cup triumph after victory over Dundee United in the 1998 Final. He missed the win over Aberdeen in 2000 because of a badly broken leg.

"I was obviously disappointed to miss out last year so this makes up for that," said a delighted Larsson after picking up the Man of the Match award for his efforts.

"Getting a hat-trick was a bonus really. The most important thing was to get our first trophy of the season."

Victory also marked a 'double' for Neil Lennon, who won the English League Cup with Leicester in 2000 before following his former Foxes boss Martin O'Neill to Parkhead and repeating the feat north of the border.

SCOTTISH CUP FINAL
MAY 26
HAMPDEN PARK
CELTIC 3 HIBERNIAN 0

HOW THEY LINED UP

CELTIC: Douglas, Mjallby, Vega, Valgaeren, Agathe, Lennon, Lambert (Boyd), Moravcik (McNamara), Thompson (Johnson), Larsson, Sutton.
HIBS: Colgan, Smith, Sauzee, Fenwick, Murray, O'Neil, Jack, Brebner (Arpinon, Lovell), Laursen, Libbra, Paatelainen (Zitelli).

RESULTS

FOURTH ROUND ONWARDS
Dunfermline 2 Celtic 2
Hearts 1 Dundee 1
Inverness CT 1 Kilmarnock 1
Livingston 0 Aberdeen 0
Motherwell 0 Dundee Utd 2
Stirling 2 Hibs 3
Ross Co 2 Rangers 3
Peterhead bye v Airdrie

REPLAYS
Aberdeen 0 Livingston 1
Celtic 4 Dunfermline 1
Dundee 0 Hearts 1
Kilmarnock 2 Inverness CT 1

QUARTER-FINALS
Celtic 1 Hearts 0
Dundee Utd 1 Rangers 0
Kilmarnock 0 Hibs 1
Livingston 3 Peterhead 1

SEMI-FINALS
Celtic 3 Dundee Utd 1
Hibs 3 Livingston 0

FINAL
Celtic 3 Hibs 0

BHOYS BAG TREBLE

CELTIC picked up the Scottish Cup for the first time in five years to round off an amazing year for the green and white hoops.

Victory for Martin O'Neill and his all-conquering side brought the Bhoys their first treble since 1969 and the great days of Jock Stein, with the Championship and CIS Insurance Cup trophies joining the Scottish Cup at Parkhead.

For Irishman O'Neill, it marked the end of his first season at the club after joining from Leicester. A season he could only have dreamed about back in August.

"It has been a remarkable year for this club and to win three trophies is more that I could have dared hope for when I arrived at Parkhead," said O'Neill.

"I'm privileged to be manager of such a great club, but our success is only the start. There is a lot of work to be done because our ultimate aim must be to compete successfully in Europe."

Jackie McNamara gave Celtic the lead seven minutes before the break and Henrik Larsson virtually ended the game as a contest with a brilliant strike early in the second-half.

And the sensational Swede took his goal tally to a staggering 53 for the season with a penalty after he had been brought down by Gary Smith 10 minutes from the end.

That spot-kick gave him his ninth goal in four matches at Hampden Park during the campaign, with two against Rangers in the CIS Insurance Cup Semi-Final, a hat-trick in the Final against Kilmarnock and two more in the Scottish Cup Semi with Dundee United.

"Hampden has certainly proved a lucky ground for me over the past year and beating Hibs was the perfect way to end what was pretty much a perfect season for me," said the striker.

SCOTTISH CHALLENGE CUP

FIRST ROUND
Airdrie 2 QoS 1
Albion 0 Clydebank 1
Alloa 2 Inverness CT 3
Brechin 3 Ayr 1
Cowdenbeath 2 Falkirk 1
East Stirling 3 East Fife 0
Elgin City 2 Dumbarton 4
Forfar 1 Peterhead 1
(Peterhead won on pens)
Partick 0 Livingston 2
Queen's Park 2 Montrose 0
Raith 0 Morton 4
Ross Co 2 Clyde 1
Stirling 2 Arbroath 3
Stranraer 4 Berwick 2

SECOND ROUND
Arbroath 2 Dumbarton 0
Clydebank 1 Peterhead 0
Hamilton 0 Airdrie 1
Inverness CT 1 Stranraer 2
Brechin 1 Queen's Park 1
(Brechin won on pens)
Cowdenbeath 1 Stenhousemuir 2
East Stirling 3 Morton 2
Ross Co 0 Livingston 3

QUARTER-FINALS
Airdrie 1 Clydebank 1
(Airdrie won on pens)
East Stirling 4 Stenhousemuir 0
Livingston 3 Brechin 1
Stranraer 3 Arbroath 2

SEMI-FINALS
Livingston 2 East Stirling 1
Stranraer 2 Airdrie 4

FINAL
Airdrie 2 (Prest 28, McGuire 78)
Livingston 2 (Crabbe 17, Anderson 50)
(Airdrie won 3-2 on pens)

HOW THEY LINED-UP
AIRDRIE: Broto, Armstrong (Capin), McCann, Brady, Forrest, Ireland, Elliott (McGuire), Moreau, Prest, Calderon (Garcia Sanjuan), Fernandez.

LIVINGSTON: Alexander, McManus, Fleming, Anderson, Coughlan, Deas, Wilson (Hart), McCulloch, Keith (McPhee), Crabbe, Bingham (Hagen).

TENNENT'S SCOTTISH CUP 2001 WINNERS 2001

UEFA CUP

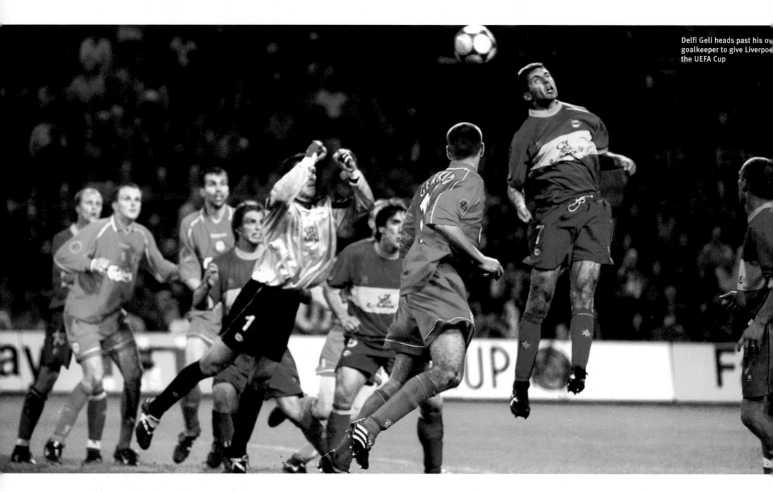

Delfi Geli heads past his ow
goalkeeper to give Liverpo
the UEFA Cup

UEFA CUP FINAL
MAY 16
DORTMUND
LIVERPOOL 5 ALAVES 4

REDS CLINCH TREBLE IN THRILLER

ONE of the most dramatic European finals of all time was settled by an own goal, gifting Liverpool the trophy and a place in the record books.

The Reds had already landed the Worthington and FA Cups when they kicked off their UEFA Cup Final clash with Spanish minnows Alaves and after 15 minutes they already had one hand on the treble.

Goals from Marcus Babbel and Steven Gerrard had taken Gerard Houllier's side into a commanding lead, but those two strikes were

only the first ascent of a dramatic rollercoaster ride at the Westfalenstadion.

Alaves, who had beaten Inter Milan and Kaiserslautern on their way to their first European final, made a desperate substitution after just 23 minutes and it paid immediate dividends with Ivan Alonso scoring with virtually his first touch.

From being outclassed, Alaves were the dominant force until the hapless Herrera hauled down Michael Owen for a penalty. Gary McAllister obliged from the spot and normal service seemed to have been resumed.

But six minutes into the second-half, the red half of the stadium was stunned into silence following a double strike from Javi Moreno: 3-3 and the Spaniards were in control.

Inexplicably Moreno was hauled off by coach Mane and the pendulum swung back Liverpool's way. McAllister released Robbie Fowler on the left and the England striker cut across the Alaves defence before firing into the bottom corner.

With the red ribbons out of their box and ready to be tied to the trophy, Alaves forced a corner in the last seconds of the game. One last chance and amazingly they took it, former Manchester United striker Jordi Cruyff heading past Sander Westerveld at the near post.

Extra-time brought even more drama. Both sides went close to claiming the golden goal winner, two Alaves players, Magno and Karmona, were sent-off and then the final twist.

Three minutes from the end McAllister floated a free-kick into the box, Delfi Geli got there first but the ball skimmed off his head and past Herrera into the net. The trophy was Liverpool's.

How they lined-up

LIVERPOOL: Westerveld, Babbel, Hyypia, Henchoz (Smicer), Carragher, Gerrard, Murphy, Hamann, McAllister, Owen (Berger), Heskey (Fowler).
ALAVES: Herrera, Contra, Eggen (Ivan), Karmona, Tellez, Geli, Cruyff, Desio, Tonic, Moreno (Pablo), Astudillo (Magno).

HOULLIER SALUTES HIS HEROES

LIVERPOOL boss Gerard Houllier hailed his side as 'immortal' after they clinched the club's first European trophy in 17 years.

"My players have had a lot to live up to after the success of the club under Bob Paisley," said the Frenchman.

"And maybe they will never repeat the achievements of the Anfield players of the past because in those days Liverpool dominated Europe and it is very hard for one club to do that now because there are so many big teams around.

"But they have become the first English team to win a Cup treble and they have written their own names into the history books of Liverpool Football Club.

"The team played for immortality against Alaves and I think every player will be remembered for a very long time."

EARLY EXITS

ENGLAND'S other participants in the UEFA Cup, Chelsea and Leicester, both suffered First Round exits in ties that were clouded in controversy.

Chelsea sacked manager Gianluca Vialli just before they did battle with little-known Swiss club St Gallen and their 1-0 first-leg lead was overturned in the return.

Defender Frank Leboeuf, who had spoken out against Vialli just prior to the first-leg, was booed by the Blues faithful, while Italian midfielder Roberto Di Matteo suffered a double fracture of his left leg, a career-threatening injury, in the second game.

Leicester's problems were even more acute, with their tie against Crvena Zvezda on the verge of being called-off at one stage because of arguments over the venue for the second-leg.

The game was scheduled to be played in Belgrade, but the political unrest in Yugoslavia prompted UEFA to switch the tie to neutral Vienna, much to the relief of the Midlanders.

Crvena Zvezda ran out comfortable winners but not before Leicester's fans were on the end of some crowd violence with Ade Akinbiyi and Andy Impey also said to be victims of racist abuse.

Scotland's contingent fared little better than their neighbours south of the border.

Aberdeen fell at the qualifying stage, **Hearts** gave German giants Stuttgart a real test before losing out 4-2 on aggregate and **Celtic** suffered a 2-1 home defeat by Bordeaux after holding the French club to a 1-1 draw in the first-leg.

Rangers entered the competition at the Third Round stage after their Champions' League exit but Germans Kaiserslautern soon ended their stay, winning 3-1 on aggregate.

Leicester take on Crvena Zvezda

RESULTS

THIRD ROUND ONWARDS
Rangers 1 Kaiserslautern 0
Kaiserslautern 3 Rangers 0
Espanyol 0 Porto 2
Porto 0 Espanyol 0
Olympiakos 2 Liverpool 2
Liverpool 2 Olympiakos 0
Bordeaux 4 Werder Bremen 1
Werder Bremen 0 Bordeaux 0
Roma 1 Hamburg 0
Hamburg 0 Roma 3
Bruges 0 Barcelona 2
Barcelona 1 Bruges 1
Alaves 1 Rosenborg 1
Rosenborg 1 Alaves 3
Feyenoord 2 Stuttgart 2
Stuttgart 2 Feyenoord 1
Shakhtar 0 Celta Vigo 0
Celta Vigo 1 Shakhtar 0
PSV 3 PAOK 0
PAOK 0 PSV 1
Leverkusen 4 AEK 4
AEK 2 Leverkusen 0
Nantes 4 Lausanne 3
Lausanne 1 Nantes 3
Lokomotiv M 0 Rayo Vallecano 0
Rayo Vallecano 2 Lokomotiv M 0
NK Osijek 2 Slavia Prague 0
Slavia Prague 5 NK Osijek 1
Parma 2 1860 Munich 2
1860 Munich 0 Parma 2
Hertha Berlin 0 Inter 0
Inter 2 Hertha Berlin 1

FOURTH ROUND
AEK 0 Barcelona 1
Barcelona 5 AEK 0
Porto 3 Nantes 1
Nantes 2 Porto 1
Roma 0 Liverpool 2
Liverpool 0 Roma 1
Rayo Vallecano 4 Bordeaux 1
Bordeaux 1 Rayo Vallecano 2
Stuttgart 0 Celta Vigo 0
Celta Vigo 2 Stuttgart 1
PSV 2 Parma 1
Parma 3 PSV 2*
Alaves 3 Inter 3
Inter 0 Alaves 2
Slavia Prague 0 Kaiserslautern 0
Kaiserslautern 1 Slavia Prague 0

QUARTER-FINALS
Alaves 3 Rayo Vallecano 0
Rayo Vallecano 2 Alaves 1
Barcelona 2 Celta Vigo 1
Celta Vigo 3 Barcelona 2*
Kaiserslautern 1 PSV 0
PSV 0 Kaiserslautern 1
Porto 0 Liverpool 0
Liverpool 2 Porto 0

SEMI-FINALS
Alaves 5 Kaiserslautern 1
Kaiserslautern 1 Alaves 4
Barcelona 0 Liverpool 0
Liverpool 1 Barcelona 0
(* won on away goals. Liverpool beat Rapid Bucharest 1-0 on aggregate in the First Round and Slovan Liberec 4-2 on aggregate in the Second Round).

CHAMPIONS LEAGUE

PENALTY KING KAHN

BAYERN Munich ended a 25-year wait for the European Cup thanks to the goalkeeping heroics of Oliver Kahn.

The giant German international picked up the man of the match award based mainly on his performance in the penalty shoot-out.

A dour match between Bayern and the 2000 runners-up, Valencia, was locked at 1-1 after 120 minutes, both goals coming from the penalty spot courtesy of Spanish star Gaizka Mendieta and Munich midfielder Steffen Effenberg.

In fact, all the main action revolved around the white spot 12 yards from goal with Bayern's Mehmet Scholl seeing his spot-kick saved by Santiago Canizares only four minutes after Mendieta had given Valencia an early lead.

Bayern's Paulo Sergio blasted the opening penalty in the shoot-out over the bar before Kahn made the first of his three saves to deny Zlatko Zahovic and level the scores.

Canizares responded by saving from Patrik Andersson to put Valencia within touching distance of the trophy, but Kahn produced a breathtaking save from Amedeo Carboni's blaster, touching the ball onto the underside of the bar before turning to see it land on the right side of the line for the Munich fans.

Five more kicks were converted before the Bayern No.1 flung himself to his right to beat out a spot-kick from Mauricio Pellegrino, giving his club the trophy they had craved for so long.

And leading the celebrations was England Under-21 international Owen Hargreaves, the youngest player on the pitch at 20.

He had more than held his own against some of the best midfield players in the world and admitted he was in dreamland.

"To win the European Cup at my age is just amazing. I can't take it all in," admitted the dazzled youngster after dancing around the San Siro with the greatest club prize in European football.

HOW THEY LINED-UP

BAYERN MUNICH: Kahn, Kuffour, Andersson, Linke, Sagnol (Jancker), Hargreaves, Effenberg, Lizarazu, Scholl (Sergio), Salihamidzic, Elber (Zickler).
VALENCIA: Canizares, Angloma, Ayala (Djukic), Pellegrino, Carboni, Baraja, Mendieta, Kily Gonzalez, Sanchez (Zahovic), Aimar (Albelda), Carew.

Oliver Kahn lifts the Champions' League trophy

KEANE: UNITED NOT GOOD ENOUGH

MANCHESTER United skipper Roy Keane admitted that his team did not deserve to progress past the Quarter-Final stage.

The Reds were beaten home and away by Bayern Munich, who gained revenge for their last minute defeat by the Old Trafford club in the 1999 Final.

"We have not performed well enough in Europe this season," said the Republic of Ireland international (pic below) after United's 3-1 aggregate defeat.

"And I don't just mean against Bayern. We struggled in the earlier rounds as well and could easily have gone out at the first stage.

"Great teams go back to the Final time and again and win the competition. We have not done that and that shows we are not a great team. We are only average."

United's demise in Munich came four days after they had clinched their third successive League title but their runaway success in the Premiership did not help their form in Europe.

They suffered away defeats against Anderlecht and PSV in the first group stage and needed a last minute Paul Scholes equaliser against Panathinaikos to earn them a point in Greece in the second qualifying section.

Their performances belied their pre-tournament odds of second favourites to lift the crown and were a million miles away from the team that swept Europe in 1999.

IT'S CAREW ON GUNNERS

VALENCIA striker John Carew ended the Champions' League hopes of Arsenal with a powerful header in the closing stages of their Quarter-Final tie. Arsenal, like Man United, were never at their best. They needed two late goals from Martin Keown to beat Shakhtar Donetsk 3-2 at Highbury and only qualified for the last eight because Lyon failed to beat Spartak in the last of the Second Round qualifiers.

Their best performances came against Lazio, a 2-0 win at home and a 1-1 draw away, but comprehensive defeats in Moscow and Munich provided evidence that the Gunners were well off the pace.

DAVID AND GOLIATH

DAVID O'Leary could hardly believe it, the Elland Road faithful could hardly believe it, the cream of European football refused to believe it.

Leeds were meant to be in the Champions' League to make up the numbers and gain some experience before returning to their normal routine in the Premiership.

Grouped with Barcelona, AC Milan and Besiktas, they were given no chance of progressing past the First Round and following a 4-0 drubbing in the Nou Camp in their opening fixture, those forecasts seemed accurate.

But no one told David O'Leary's players they were mere stage hands to the Champions' League show. Victory over Milan with a last minute winner and four points taken from the Turks, including a 6-0 win at Elland Road, left them needing a home win against Barcelona to qualify for the second stage.

Rivaldo denied them that with an injury time equaliser so Leeds went out and got the point they needed with a 1-1 draw at AC Milan.

Their Second Round campaign started with a comprehensive home defeat by Real but that just inspired the Leeds players to step up another level and they responded with victories over Lazio in Italy and then against Anderlecht, home and away. Nine points that ensured the fairytale would continue at least until the Quarter-Finals.

O'Leary's braves in fact reached the last four after a 3-0 blitz of Deportivo La Coruna in the first-leg left them enough breathing space in the return to set up a Semi-Final showdown with Valencia, before eventually bowing out 3-0 on aggregate to the 2000 runners-up.

David O'Leary takes the applause

RESULTS

SECOND ROUND		
GROUP A		
Man United 3 Panathinaikos 1		
Valencia 2 Sturm Graz 0		
Sturm Graz 0 Man United 2		
Panathinaikos 0 Valencia 0		
Valencia 0 Man United 0		
Sturm Graz 2 Panathinaikos 0		
Man United 1 Valencia 1		
Panathinaikos 1 Sturm Graz 2		
Panathinaikos 1 Man United 1		
Sturm Graz 0 Valencia 5		
Man United 3 Sturm Graz 0		
Valencia 2 Panathinaikos 1		
GROUP B		
AC Milan 2 Galatasaray 2		
PSG 1 Deportivo 3		
Deportivo 0 AC Milan 1		
Galatasaray 1 PSG 0		
Galatasaray 1 Deportivo 0		
AC Milan 1 PSG 1		
Deportivo 2 Galatasaray 0		
PSG 1 AC Milan 1		
Deportivo 4 PSG 3		
Galatasaray 2 AC Milan 0		
PSG 2 Galatasaray 0		
AC Milan 1 Deportivo 1		
GROUP C		
Bayern Munich 1 Lyon 0		
Spartak M 4 Arsenal 1		
Arsenal 2 Bayern Munich 2		
Lyon 3 Spartak M 0		
Bayern Munich 1 Spartak M 0		
Lyon 0 Arsenal 1		
Arsenal 1 Lyon 1		
Spartak M 0 Bayern Munich 3		
Arsenal 1 Spartak M 0		
Lyon 3 Bayern Munich 0		
Bayern Munich 1 Arsenal 0		
Spartak M 0 Lyon 0		
GROUP D		
Leeds 0 Real Madrid 2		
Anderlecht 1 Lazio 0		
Lazio 0 Leeds 1		
Real Madrid 4 Anderlecht 1		
Leeds 2 Anderlecht 1		
Real Madrid 3 Lazio 2		
Anderlecht 1 Leeds 4		
Lazio 2 Real Madrid 2		
Real Madrid 3 Leeds 2		
Lazio 2 Anderlecht 1		
Leeds 3 Lazio 3		
Anderlecht 2 Real Madrid 0		
QUARTER-FINALS		
Man United 0 Bayern Munich 1		
Bayern Munich 2 Man United 1		
Galatasaray 3 Real Madrid 2		
Real Madrid 3 Galatasaray 0		
Leeds 3 Deportivo 0		
Deportivo 2 Leeds 0		
Arsenal 2 Valencia 1		
Valencia 1 Arsenal 0		
SEMI-FINALS		
Leeds 0 Valencia 0		
Valencia 3 Leeds 0		
Real Madrid 0 Bayern Munich 1		
Bayern Munich 2 Real Madrid 1		

STAR OF 2001

GARY McALLISTER

YOU would have got long odds on a balding, 36-year-old midfielder who had been given a free transfer by Coventry becoming the most influential player of the last month of the season.

But that's exactly what Gary McAllister achieved in four weeks of football that provided him with the highlight of his career.

When his contract was up at Highfield Road in the summer of 2000, the Scottish international decided he wanted one last chance to add some silverware to the League Championship winners' medal he picked up with Leeds in 1992.

And much as he had enjoyed his time at Coventry, and in particular working with boss Gordon Strachan, a team-mate in that successful Leeds side, a move was his only option.

Liverpool boss Gerard Houllier offered him a year's contract at Anfield and McAllister duly accepted, but many felt that the veteran would be spending more time on the bench than dictating the Reds' midfield.

'To get three trophies with Liverpool was amazing. I wanted to win something else before my playing career finished'

And indeed he was absent from the early stages of the season, not that it had anything to do with his age or ability.

McAllister's wife, Denise, was diagnosed as suffering from breast cancer when eight months pregnant and the Scotman's life was thrown into turmoil.

"I had only been used to football-related problems so when the cancer was diagnosed, I didn't know how to cope with the situation," he recalled.

"But Denise was so brave about things and when she started to cope with the chemotherapy treatment, I started to think about football and Liverpool again."

After coming through some of the darkest moments in his life, McAllister was to be the shining light in the climax to an amazing season for his club.

With a Worthington Cup winners' medal already bagged, he came on as substitute in the FA Cup Final against Arsenal and helped turn the game around as the Reds won 2-1.

Four days later, he was named man of the match in Liverpool's amazing golden goal victory over Alaves, scoring from a penalty and then seeing his free-kick headed into his own net by the Spanish club's Delfi Geli for the winner in a 5-4 UEFA Cup Final thriller.

Throw in a last minute winner against Everton, the penalty that knocked out Barcelona in the UEFA Cup Semi-Finals and another brilliant strike at his old team Coventry

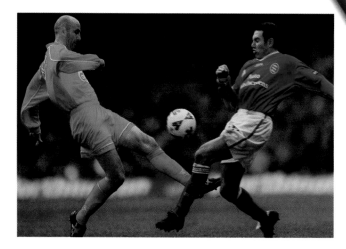

BORN: 25th December, 1964 in Motherwell
HEIGHT: 6ft 1in
WEIGHT: 11st 12lbs
PREVIOUS CLUBS: Motherwell, Leicester, Leeds, Coventry
CLUB HONOURS: Motherwell - Scottish First Division Championship 1985; Leeds - First Division Championship 1992, Charity Shield 1992; Liverpool – Worthington Cup, FA Cup, UEFA Cup 2001
INTERNATIONAL HONOURS: 57 Scotland senior caps, five goals

HIS 2001 HIGHLIGHTS

12TH NOV, 2000: Scored his first goal for Liverpool in a 4-1 win over his former club Coventry at Anfield.

25TH FEB, 2001: Scored in the shoot-out as Liverpool beat Birmingham on penalties to win the Worthington Cup Final at the Millennium Stadium. His first trophy in nine years.

16TH APRIL, 2001: Brilliant 30-yard free-kick in the last minute gave Reds a 3-2 win over Merseyside rivals Everton at Goodison Park to keep their hopes of a top three finish alive.

19TH APRIL, 2001: Put Liverpool into the UEFA Cup Final with a first-half penalty against Spanish giants Barcelona at Anfield in a 1-0 aggregate win.

22ND APRIL, 2001: Scored for the third successive game in the 3-1 win over Tottenham.

28TH APRIL, 2001: Another gem of a free-kick helped Liverpool to a 2-0 win at Coventry and put his old club on the brink of relegation.

1ST MAY, 2001: Macca made it five on the trot with another goal in the 2-0 win at Bradford.

12TH MAY, 2001: Played in his first FA Cup Final and his free-kick, after coming on as a second-half substitute, led to Michael Owen's equaliser in the Reds' 2-1 win.

16TH MAY, 2001: Man of the match in the UEFA Cup Final win over Alaves in Dortmund.

19TH MAY, 2001: Finished the season in the Champions' League after Liverpool booked a third place finish in the Premiership with a 4-0 win at Charlton on the last day of the season.

in a run of five goals in five successive games and you can understand why the former Leicester player found it difficult to take in his glorious end to the season.

"Winning three trophies really is amazing and it will take ages to sink in," he said after the UEFA Cup triumph. "It's a great achievement and one that everyone at the club can be proud of.

"For me, especially, it is wonderful because I wanted to win something else before my playing career finished.

"I don't know how long I can go on. Other players I have spoken to have said that you can feel fine one day, and the next it just hits you and you are struggling.

"I have signed another year's contract with Liverpool and when it comes to next May, I will sit down and see how I feel.

"I want to stay in the game when my career is over and I am taking the necessary coaching badges with the future in mind."

Many will hope the popular McAllister will stay in the game, Gordon Strachan for one.

"What matters more than having medals on your chest in this game is respect, and Gary has plenty of that in football," he said.

"What he achieved with Liverpool at the end of the season he deserved, because he works hard at football, and in his life.

"He is a lovely guy and I'm delighted the trophies came thick and fast for him at Liverpool."

But typically, in his finest hour, after being presented with the man of the match award by Dutch legend Johan Cruyff following the UEFA Cup Final, Gary's mind wandered back to those dark days when his wife was ill.

He donated the £2000 that came with the award to the Macmillan Trust and Christies Hospital in Manchester who helped Denise through her cancer battle.

"They helped Denise through a difficult time and if she had not coped the way she did, maybe the success I have enjoyed at Liverpool might never have happened," said McAllister.

ENGLAND

Keegan called it a day as England boss as his team said farewell to Wembley with defeat by Germany but the Swede smell of success was not far away...

Ray Parlour's shot hits the bar in Finland

FINLAND DRAW LEAVES ENGLAND BOTTOM

OCTOBER 11, 2000 England had to settle for a point in Finland in their second disappointing World Cup display in four days.

Howard Wilkinson took charge of the team following Kevin Keegan's shock decision to quit as national team boss after the home defeat by Germany.

But there was no improvement in the performance in Helsinki and David Seaman was the busier of the two goalkeepers, saving well from Jari Litmanen and Jonatan Johansson in the first-half.

England did come closest to getting on the scoresheet though when Ray Parlour's strike smashed against the underside of the bar and appeared to cross the line.

But Mr Ivanov, the Russian referee, waved play on and with it went any chance Wilkinson's side had of taking three much-needed points away from Helsinki.

The draw left England bottom of their qualifying group behind Germany, Greece, Finland and Albania with one point and no goals from two games. The World Cup finals looked a long way off.

KEEGAN QUITS

OCTOBER 7, 2000 Kevin Keegan quit as national team coach after England's World Cup campaign got off to the worst possible start with a home defeat by Germany.

Liverpool midfielder Dietmar Hamann struck the only goal of the game from a first-half free-kick as Wembley played host to its last game before being torn down.

And shortly after the final whistle Keegan announced live on Sky Sports that his two year stay as boss was over.

"I have not been quite good enough, it's as simple as that," said the former England skipper, with typical honesty.

"The Football Association tried to persuade me to stay but I feel now is the end of the road for me in this job.

"I know the timing is not the best but I am not the man to take the team that stage further. I have to be true to myself and that is why I have made the decision to go now.

"There is no one else to blame but myself. I have given it my best shot but I didn't think I could find that little bit extra at this level.

"A lot of the coaches at Euro 2000 who did better than me have gone so my run has probably been a bit longer than I initially expected. Now it's my time to move on."

Keegan's decision came after his team were jeered off following a poor display against a German team that were nothing more than mediocre at Wembley.

It was only three months earlier that an Alan Shearer goal had given Keegan his finest hour as England boss with a 1-0 win over the Germans at Euro 2000.

Keegan reveals to Sky Sports that he is quitting as England national team coach

FA CALL FOR ERIKSSON

OCTOBER 31, 2000 Football Association chief executive Adam Crozier revealed that Sven Goran Eriksson would be the new manager of England's national team.

The Swede had been number one on the FA's list of candidates since Kevin Keegan quit as manager after the World Cup defeat by Germany in early October.

Eriksson's appointment made history as he became the first foreign coach to be made head of the England national team and he was set to take over full time control from July 1, 2001 after the end of his contract at Italian club Lazio.

"To get the change England needed, we had to be dramatic," said Crozier, aware of the criticism that appointing a foreign coach would bring.

"We have to move forward. This country has to make a leap in the right direction and I am sure that will happen with this appointment.

"It does not matter that we have a foreign manager. We had to get the best man for the job and we have done that.

"There may be those who are against someone from outside England being in charge of the national team but it is a global game now, a world game and we should stop thinking about what it used to be like. We have to move on from there."

Eriksson's credentials were impressive enough and with many of the top English coaches making themselves unavailable for the job, Crozier had limited options in finding an English-born boss anyway.

BECKHAM - CAPTAIN MARVEL

NOVEMBER 15, 2000
David Beckham was handed the England captaincy for the first time in the friendly against Italy as caretaker boss Peter Taylor gave youth a chance to shine.

A brilliant goal from Gennaro Gattuso gave the Italians victory in Turin but England's young side coped well against experienced opponents and for the skipper, it was a memorable occasion.

"Leading England out was the proudest moment of my career," said the Manchester United midfielder.

"It's something that you dream about as a kid and it's just amazing that it has come true."

OCTOBER 6, 2001 Almost a year after being handed the England captaincy, Beckham produced a skipper's performance if ever there was one to guide his side in to the 2002 World Cup finals.

The midfielder capped an awesome display with a brilliant 93rd minute trademark free-kick to give England a 2-2 draw with Greece at Old Trafford and guarantee a place in the finals.

"We played badly against the Greeks and the captain carried the team. It was Becks that got us to the World Cup with that performance," said Teddy Sheringham, England's other scorer on the day.

SOCCER SHORTS

Germany's win at Wembley was the fifth time they had won at the Twin Towers in 30 years. They also triumphed 3-1 in 1972, 2-1 in 1982, 1-0 in 1991 and won on penalties during Euro 96. Their only defeat in that time was 2-0 in 1975.

England's defeat in Turin maintained their record of failing to beat the Italians away since a 3-2 win in Rome in 1961.

Sven Goran Eriksson signed a five year contract that will take him through to the 2006 World Cup and he also has a two year option on that.

Arsenal chairman David Dein, one of the six members of the FA panel who chose the new England boss, revealed that if Arsene Wenger had not taken the manager's job at Highbury, he would have gone for Eriksson.

The average age of England's side in the 1-0 defeat in Italy was just over 23 and between them they had a total of 182 international appearances. Italian skipper Paolo Maldini won his 114th cap on the same night!

Eriksson immediately appointed Tord Grip as his assistant for England.

David Beckham leads England out in Turin

ERIKSSON'S ENGLAND

SVEN RESTORES NATIONAL PRIDE

OCTOBER 2000 and the England players made their way to the Wembley dressing-room, soaked from the rain that had engulfed the stadium, heads down from a World Cup defeat by Germany, beaten and dejected. Korea and Japan 2002 a million miles from their thoughts.

Less than a year later and six of that starting XI that miserable Saturday afternoon in London faced the Germans again. This time it was raining goals – five of them smashed in to Oliver Kahn's net in a game that will be talked about for years.

And that turnaround in fortunes can be attributed to one man – Sven Goran Eriksson. England were going nowhere until the Swede arrived as a controversial appointment to replace Kevin Keegan.

The honest and hard working former England supremo had struggled to combat the more tactical game that is played at the highest level and his side's sorry showing at Euro 2000 left many experts predicting a gloomy future.

Keegan's typically brave decision to quit after that defeat by Germany left the door open for the Football Association to break with tradition and appoint a continental boss for the first time, the man they considered the best available.

Eriksson arrived with an impressive CV. He began his coaching career in Sweden in 1976 with Degerfors before moving on to Gothenburg, steering them to the Championship and Swedish Cup in 1982 and finishing the season with a treble, adding the UEFA Cup crown to the other titles.

The following year he moved to Benfica, leading them to the Championship in both seasons he was there before joining Roma, and then Fiorentina.

'Managing England is one of the greatest jobs in football'

Eriksson returned to Portugal with Benfica and enjoyed more Championship success, with the club also finishing as runners-up to AC Milan in the 1990 European Cup.

He moved back to Italy with Sampdoria for five years before taking over at Lazio, with whom he won the European Cup-Winners' Cup in 1999 and the Serie A title in 2000, the first time he had won the Italian Championship.

So when the FA wanted a man who had a vast knowledge of the international game, had a proven track record as a top coach and wanted the challenge of leading England, Eriksson's name was very quickly at the top of the wanted list.

By the standard of the English national team

The dynamic duo - Sven Goran Eriksson and Tord Grip

after that memorable September night in Munich 2001, his appointment looks a pretty inspired choice.

The quietly-spoken Swede took up his post with the England team more than six months ahead of schedule.

He was due to take charge from July 1, 2001 onwards because of his commitments with Lazio but a Champions' League exit at the hands of Leeds prompted an earlier than expected departure from the Rome club.

And that early arrival has been to England's undoubted benefit. Together with his long term friend and coaching ally, Tord Grip, Eriksson took on an exhausting tour of Britain and Europe to familiarise himself with English players and the English game.

If there was a Premiership game on, or one of the top flight clubs were in European action, Eriksson, Grip or more likely both, were there in attendance.

"I admit that I do not know everything about the English players so I must find out as much as possible as quickly as possible," he said. "But that also means that everyone has a chance to impress."

And Eriksson certainly made an impression with his squad for his first game in charge, against Spain at Villa Park.

He gave debuts to Charlton full-back Chris Powell, Everton's Michael Ball and Sunderland midfielder Gavin McCann and each one contributed to the 3-0 win.

The Swede also chose to keep David Beckham as his skipper, insisting the supremely talented but sometimes temperamental Manchester United midfielder was the right man for the job.

He harnessed the understanding of the team-mates from England's top three clubs, Manchester United, Arsenal and Liverpool and built his side around those players, creating a club like atmosphere in the England dressing-room.

Crucial World Cup wins against Finland, Albania and Greece followed that victory over Spain along with a comfortable friendly defeat of Mexico.

The Dutch brought the Eriksson bandwagon to a temporary halt with a superb 2-0 win at White Hart Lane to end his 100 per cent run as national team boss.

But then it was Germany and that night to remember, the night when Eriksson's England announced their arrival as a team to be feared on the world stage once more.

"When I took over as England manager I knew there were some very good players in the country," said Sven.

"The standard is high here and with so many talented players around the future is very bright.

"It has been clear to see that since I have been in the job although I could not have known how well the boys would play against Germany. Winning 5-1 was like a dream."

And Eriksson has no doubt about his dream for his adopted country in his time as manager.

"Managing England is one of the greatest jobs in football. When the chance came along, it was not hard to say 'yes'," he said.

"I have signed a five year contract and in that time I want to become a world champion. That is the ultimate achievement as a coach and I believe England have the players to do it."

What a difference a year makes!

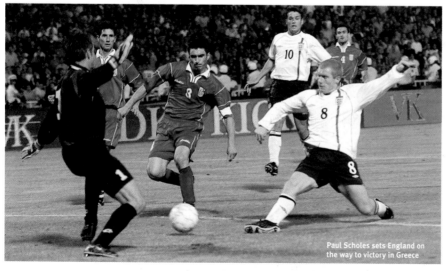
Paul Scholes sets England on the way to victory in Greece

WHAT HIS PLAYERS SAY

'You only have to look at our record under Sven to see what he has achieved as national team manager. On the training ground he leaves it mainly to the coaches but he is always watching and observing. Nothing escapes him in football.'
MICHAEL OWEN

'He has been great since he first came in as the manager. His knowledge of the game is excellent because he has done so much around the world and that comes out when he talks to you about the role he wants you to play.'
DAVID BECKHAM

'We are still learning under the boss but he is a great teacher and the results have been there for everyone to see. And the best thing is, we can still get a lot better. I am very confident of that.'
SOL CAMPBELL

'He has coached some of the top teams in Europe and commands a lot of respect in the game for that. And no one can deny he's done a magnificent job since he came in for England. He has proved he was the right man for the job.'
GARY NEVILLE

'He has come in and given everyone a role to play in the squad. We all know our jobs and what is expected of us when we go out on the pitch.'
PAUL SCHOLES

A NIGHT OF GLORY

FIVE STAR ENGLAND STUN GERMANS

WORLD CUP QUALIFIER
SEPTEMBER 1
MUNICH
GERMANY 1 ENGLAND 5

ENGLAND enjoyed their finest hour – well 90 minutes to be exact – since beating Germany to win the World Cup Final at Wembley in 1966.

Sven Goran Eriksson's rapidly improving side made the world sit up and take notice as they systematically took on and destroyed the Germans in their own backyard.

A goal down after only six minutes when Carsten Jancker toe-poked the ball past David Seaman, England, led by the brilliant David Beckham, forced their way back in to the game almost immediately when Michael Owen blasted the ball past Oliver Kahn after great work by Nick Barmby.

A Steven Gerrard piledriver rocketed into the bottom of Germany's net just before the break to give England the advantage and within three minutes of the restart, Owen had grabbed his second of the game to stun the home support.

The Liverpool striker made it 4-1 halfway through the second-half and his Anfield team-mate Emile Heskey completed the scoring 16 minutes from time to round off the most impressive England display in years.

The victory put England in pole position to qualify for the World Cup finals after seemingly having no chance following their home defeat by Rudi Voller's Germany at Wembley at the start of the campaign and then only taking a point from a goalless draw in Finland in the following match.

But the turnaround since Swedish maestro Eriksson took over had been sensational, culminating in that amazing night in Munich, a night the players and fans will not forget in a long time.

"Things have gone from strength to strength for me under the manager," said Owen, whose hat-trick was his first for his country.

"I wasn't having the best of times until Sven had a chat with me before his first game in charge, against Spain.

"He told me what he wanted from me, gave me a starting place and it has all gone on from there.

"Scoring a hat-trick in such an important game is the best moment of my career but it was a real team effort. All the lads played a part in a victory that we will remember for a long, long time.

"We were all confident that we could get a good result against Germany but to win 5-1 was just an amazing performance."

HOW THEY LINED UP

GERMANY: Kahn, Worns (Asamoah 46), Nowotny, Linke, Rehmer, Hamann, Ballack (Klose 67), Bohme, Deisler, Jancker, Neuville (Kehl 78).

ENGLAND: Seaman, G.Neville, Campbell, Ferdinand, Ashley Cole, Beckham, Gerrard (Hargreaves 78), Scholes (Carragher 83), Barmby (McManaman 65), Heskey, Owen.

SOCCER SHORTS

1-1 Owen latches on to Barmby's header to equalise in the 12th minute

1-2 Gerrard blasts in his first goal for England just before half-time

1-3 Heskey sets up Owen for his second straight after the break

1-4 Gerrard's pass puts Owen through for his hat-trick

1-5 Five goals for Liverpool and England as Heskey completes the scoring

The defeat was Germany's second at home in World Cup qualifying history. Their only other setback came against Portugal in 1985 when they had already qualified for the finals.

Steven Gerrard, making his sixth appearance for England in the game, maintained his 100 per cent record of being on the winning side in every international he had played in.

England also beat Germany 5-1 in Berlin in 1908.

Kurt Voller, the father of German manager, Rudi Voller, suffered a heart attack at half-time during the match and was taken to hospital. His son rushed to his bedside straight after the final whistle.

Any pundit wanting to put a bet on England winning 5-1 before the game could have got odds of 100-1.

It was Germany's heaviest defeat since they lost 8-3 to Hungary in the 1954 World Cup.

Germany were so confident that they would top the qualifying group that they arranged some friendlies on the dates set aside for the Play-Offs.

Michael Owen carried the hat-trick ball back to Britain in a plastic bag!

SCOTLAND

TIME FOR THE YOUNG ONES TO SHINE

Billy Dodds is shut out against Belgium as Scotland drop vital home points

SCOTLAND'S older heads reckon that the time is right to give youth a chance at the top level.

Defeat by Belgium in September all but sealed Scotland's fate in the World Cup qualifiers and left them staring at omission from the tournament's latter stages for only the second time in 28 years.

The pressure grew on national team coach Craig Brown to step down before his contract was up in December but the wise old heads of Paul Lambert and Tom Boyd reckoned it was changes on the pitch that were needed as much as anything else.

Boyd, 36, a veteran of over 70 appearances for the national team, said: "There are a lot of good young players around and I think it is time for them to be given a chance.

"I have really enjoyed playing for my country and the memory of playing in World Cup finals against the likes of Brazil will always stay with me but it is time for the new players now.

"I will still be available if Scotland want me but the time is right for us to make changes and move on."

Boyd's Celtic team-mate, Paul Lambert, announced his retirement from the international scene after the 2-0 defeat by Belgium and agreed it was time for a change.

"I have some special memories from my time with Scotland but that's it now. We need to give the youngsters a go," said the skipper.

Scotland's World Cup campaign started well enough although they left it late, the 89th minute to be precise, before Neil McCann grabbed the only goal of the game in Latvia.

Group whipping boys San Marino held Brown's side for 70 minutes before Matt Elliott and Don Hutchison ensured another three points in Serravalle and a 1-1 draw in Croatia made it seven points from nine on their travels.

But it was their home form that seriously dented their World Cup qualifying hopes with Belgium snatching an injury time 2-2 draw at Hampden in March and Croatia holding the Scots to a goalless draw in September, four days before that defeat in Brussels which is likely to spell the start of a new era in international football for the men north of the border.

But while Scotland look to the future they can still count on the brilliant support from their tartan army.

Despite watching their side go down to Belgium, 13,000 loyal fans stood to applaud their team off the pitch almost as fervently as if they had won the game, completely drowning out the home support.

Some things never change.

REPUBLIC OF IRELAND

MICK'S MARVELS

MICK McCARTHY finally laid to rest the 'ghost' of Jack Charlton on a Saturday afternoon in September.

The Republic of Ireland boss took over the daunting task of replacing Charlton in 1995 and during those six years there have been many people calling for his head as he struggled to return the Emerald Isle to the big time of international football.

Failure to qualify for the 1998 World Cup and Euro 2000 had put questions marks over McCarthy's position after the Irish had enjoyed almost 10 years of success under Big Jack.

McCarthy himself was the cornerstone of a green defence that became one of the hardest to break down in world football.

They went within 10 minutes or so of reaching the European Championship Semi-Finals in 1988 and it took hosts Italy to knock them out of the World Cup in 1990.

They got their revenge on the Italians in the 1994 World Cup, though, with a goal from Ray Houghton giving them arguably the country's finest hour in football.

Since then it's been a case of near misses and gloom and doom. But Jason McAteer changed all that on the first day of September.

The Blackburn midfielder struck a wonderful winner against the mighty Dutch to guarantee Ireland at least a Play-Off place.

Holland, with £60m of attacking talent in Ruud Van Nistelrooy, Jimmy Floyd Hasselbaink and Patrick Kluivert in the side at one stage, had destroyed England two weeks earlier at White Hart Lane.

But McCarthy's marvels wore their more illustrious opponents down in Dublin and even played the last 30 minutes with 10 men after Gary Kelly had been sent-off.

"Beating Holland was a famous victory because make no mistake, they are one of the best teams in the world," said a delighted McCarthy after the final whistle had sent Lansdowne Road in to party mode.

"We were beaten in the Play-Offs by Belgium for a place in the World Cup four years ago and were 12 seconds away from reaching Euro 2000 until Macedonia equalised out there and there were a few people who wanted my head after missing out on those two competitions.

"But the win over Holland has marked the coming of age for this team and has been the reward for six years' commitment."

Ireland, led by skipper Roy Keane, proved too good for mighty Holland

SOCCER SHORTS

Jason McAteer had only started one match for club and country in five months before his winner against Holland.

Holland's defeat in Dublin left them out of the World Cup for the first time since 1986.

Ipswich skipper Matt Holland blasted in his first goal for the Irish from 30 yards to give his country a 1-1 draw in Portugal in their second qualifying game.

Mick McCarthy's job was under threat before the win over the Dutch, with his contract up at the end of the World Cup campaign.

Ireland's top scorers in their qualifiers for Japan and Korea 2002, before the final match against Cyprus were midfielders Matt Holland and Roy Keane, who both had three goals.

Ireland's smallest attendance during their World Cup quest was the 5000 who watched the tie against Andorra in Barcelona. It was played in the stadium near the Nou Camp which is used by Barca's reserve team.

A Yorkshireman by birth, Mick McCarthy made 57 international appearances for Ireland and names the 1990 World Cup finals as his proudest time in football as a player.

NORTHERN IRELAND

Ireland were unlucky to lose at home to the talented Czechs

McILROY LOOKS TO THE FUTURE

NORTHERN Ireland were faced with an uphill task to qualify for the World Cup finals in 2002 as soon as the draw grouped them with the Czechs, Denmark, Bulgaria and Iceland.

The Czechs were very impressive during Euro 2000, qualifying in style and then not getting the rewards their football deserved during the finals in which they were unfortunate to lose to both France and Holland.

Bulgaria are always strong at home, Denmark have some talented players under the management of Morten Olsen and Iceland are

no longer the whipping boys they once were in international football.

Even Malta, the so-called make-weights in the group, gave England a real grilling in the summer of 2000 before going down 2-1 in Valletta.

So if Ireland's task was hard enough, it was made practically impossible by the loss of a number of their key players during the campaign.

Ipswich midfielder Jim Magilton, who finished the year as skipper of his country with 50 caps to his name, influential Celtic star Neil

Lennon and Blackburn winger Keith Gillespie were all absent at stages during the qualifying section.

They were also missing that important ingredient in any competition – luck. Last minute defeats in Iceland and the Czech Republic, a home defeat by the Czechs despite Phil Gray twice hitting the woodwork, and a home draw with Denmark, who spent the whole 90 minutes on the backfoot all cast a doubt over that famous 'luck of the Irish' tag.

Ireland went in to their 1-1 draw in Denmark on the back of six straight defeats but national team coach Sammy McIlroy had impressed his bosses enough to be rewarded with a new two year contract – with instructions to continue to build a side for the future.

"I was delighted to sign on for another two years, all I hope now is we get a bit more luck for our European Championship campaign," said McIlroy (pic below), who took over as boss in 2000 and will stay in charge until at least January 2004.

"Our World Cup bid was devastated by injuries in nearly every game but hopefully starting afresh for the next tournament, we can get all our players back.

"But I have taken the opportunity to give some of our younger players a chance to gain some experience and that will help us as well.

"That is the way forward for us. We still have a number of top professionals in our side and if I can find the right balance between that experience and the young players then I will be happy."

WALES

GIGGS FIRES RED DRAGON

RYAN Giggs is the man to lead Wales out of the international wilderness – and maybe as skipper.

The Manchester United winger led his national side in the absence of Gary Speed in the games against Armenia and Norway at the end of a campaign that had promised to bring some much needed cheer to Welsh football but ended in disappointment.

The boos that rang out around a near deserted Millennium Stadium after a goalless draw against little Armenia in September showed the frustration that the football folk from across the Severn Bridge were feeling.

Mark Hughes' side got some great results on their travels, a 0-0 draw in Poland, the group winners, and a 1-1 draw against highly-rated Ukraine were foundations to build on but they failed to capitalise at home and that dour draw with Armenia eventually put their campaign out of its agony.

But Hughes is confident that his side are on the right track and in Giggs he has a player that inspires others around him.

"With Gary Speed out injured Ryan was the obvious choice to take over the captaincy," said the former Manchester United team-mate of Giggs.

"He has a presence when he walks in a room and he has that aura about him. People notice him and the lads in the dressing-room certainly respect him.

"The captaincy doesn't worry him in any way. In fact when he skippered Wales for the first time, against Belgium a few years back, he played brilliantly and he was excellent for us against Armenia as well."

Giggs admitted that he revels in the responsibility of skippering his country.

"I've done the job a couple of times now and it's something that I really enjoy," he said.

"In football, there is no bigger honour than skippering your country but I am fortunate in that I have played under some great captains like Bryan Robson, Steve Bruce, Eric Cantona and Roy Keane at Manchester United, so I have had some good teachers."

Giggs, who was sent-off in the 3-2 defeat in Norway, believes Wales are heading in the right direction and has asked the fans to be patient.

"Under Mark Hughes we have improved as a team," said the flying winger.

"The supporters must keep their faith because we are on the right lines. We have some good players coming through and the team now has a lot of potential."

Ryan Giggs - future Wales skipper

Wales have not appeared in the World Cup finals since 1958.

The 18,000 attendance for Wales' goalless draw with Armenia at the Millennium Stadium was the lowest crowd ever to attend a game at the ground.

In his first two games as Wales skipper, Ryan Giggs was voted man of the match. He scored a brilliant goal against Belgium in October 1997 as Bobby Gould's side went down 3-2, then ran the Armenian defence ragged at Cardiff in September 2000 but couldn't make the breakthrough in a 0-0 draw.

Ryan admitted to one of the worst misses of his career in Wales' 2-1 home defeat by Poland in June 2001, when he failed to put the ball in the unguarded net from six yards out.

Wales drew six of their first eight World Cup qualifying games, holding the powerful Ukraine twice.

Giggs would have faced his Manchester United team-mate David Beckham in a World Cup Play-Off if England and Wales had finished in the runners-up spot in their respective groups. As it was they went in different directions!

ONE TO WATCH

JOE COLE

JOE COLE was a star before he had even kicked a ball at League level for West Ham United.

The skilful midfielder was the most talked about young teenager in the game since Ryan Giggs first burst down the Manchester United wing as a 16-year-old.

He was the player they all wanted. As a schoolboy no older than 14 he had every major club in the country chasing his signature. Cole was the child prodigy, the boy wonder, the next superstar of English football.

West Ham were the lucky ones. He decided they were the club for him, rather than Chelsea, the team he supported, Tottenham, Arsenal or even Manchester United.

"A lot of clubs came to see my parents and wanted me to join them but West Ham were very friendly and impressed me when I was down there," recalled Cole.

"It felt a really good place to be so I was happy to stay with them."

And stay he did, progressing from a youth player with undoubted talent to a Premiership player with proven class.

But such has been the hype surrounding the attacking midfielder that he was almost expected to arrive on the top flight scene and take it by storm. Well, football hardly ever works like that.

Yes, he's an established member of the West Ham first team, yes he's already an England international with one cap to his name, and yes he has already made a name for himself in the Premiership.

But he has not blitzed the game in the way everyone anticipated after he made his first team debut as substitute for Eyal Berkovic in an FA Cup Third Round tie at Swansea in January 1999.

And former West Ham legend Trevor Brooking believes that too much was expected from Cole too soon.

"He wasn't even a regular in the West Ham side and sections of the media were clamouring for him to be included in the England squad that went to Euro 2000," said the now TV pundit.

"Joe was going to be the flair player we needed, the player who was going to save the England side.

"But because of all that hype surrounding him it meant that when people went to watch him they were expecting a wizard, somebody exceptional that they had never seen the likes of before.

"That put a lot of pressure on the lad and was totally unfair. He needed a season or two to learn what football is like in the Premiership. He needed that time to make mistakes and learn from them. To gain the experience that you

A broken leg suffered in a 2-1 win at Derby in the closing weeks of the 1999-2000 season put paid to any hopes Cole might have had of fulfilling some of the media calls for him to be included in England's squad for Euro 2000.

And that injury carried over to the start of the 2000-01 term with him starting the season on the substitutes' bench.

He made 30 Premiership appearances in the Premiership that season, six of them as substitute as West Ham endured a nightmare campaign.

There were fears from those inside and outside Upton Park that the silky skills of Cole and Paolo Di Canio could not work in the same side and it was the youngster who was left out of the team by then manager Harry Redknapp on a couple of occasions.

"Obviously I was disappointed to be dropped a couple of times but the manager explained to me why," he said.

" I know I still have a lot to learn in the game but I am a hard worker at training and will listen to any advice that comes my way."

As well as being a regular in the England Under-21 side, Cole has made the step up to senior level with an appearance as a substitute against Mexico.

Playing for his country is very important to him: "It was a dream come true to play for England and I hope I get another chance to show what I can do," he said after the 4-1 win.

Given time to develop in the Premiership and free of the pressure of being labelled a boy wonder, Joseph John Cole will surely get that chance - and plenty more of them.

need at that level. But he never got that because everything he did was being examined and that was always going to make it difficult for him."

Cole, himself, is aware of the pressure heaped on him at such a young age but has tried to take it in his stride.

"I just try and enjoy my football as much as I can, whether it be for West Ham or in the England Under 21s, or even the full side," said the youngster, who celebrated his 20th birthday on November 8, 2001.

"I have been in the papers since I was 15 so I have learnt to deal with it now and I think I have handled all the attention quite well.

"Fortunately I am surrounded by my family and some good friends who are very supportive. "There is no way they would let all the attention go to my head. If it did, and I started to get big-headed, they would soon let me know!"

FACTFILE

NAME: Joe Cole
DATE OF BIRTH: 8th November, 1981
PLACE OF BIRTH: Islington
HEIGHT: 5ft 7in
WEIGHT: 9st 8lbs
CLUB: West Ham United

• Made his England schools debut against Wales on February 3rd, 1997 and starred in a 3-2 win.

• In November 1998, he was called up to train with the full England squad even though he had not even played for the first team at West Ham.

• Old Trafford was the venue for his Premiership debut with the Hammers, coming on as sub for Trevor Sinclair. January 10th, 1999 was the date; 4-1 to Man United the score.

• His first senior goal was a last minute winner in a 3-2 Worthington Cup victory at Birmingham in November 1999.

• He made his England Under-21 debut in a 1-0 win against Argentina on February 22, 2000.

CRICKET
CRICKET
CRICKET
CRICKET
CRICKET

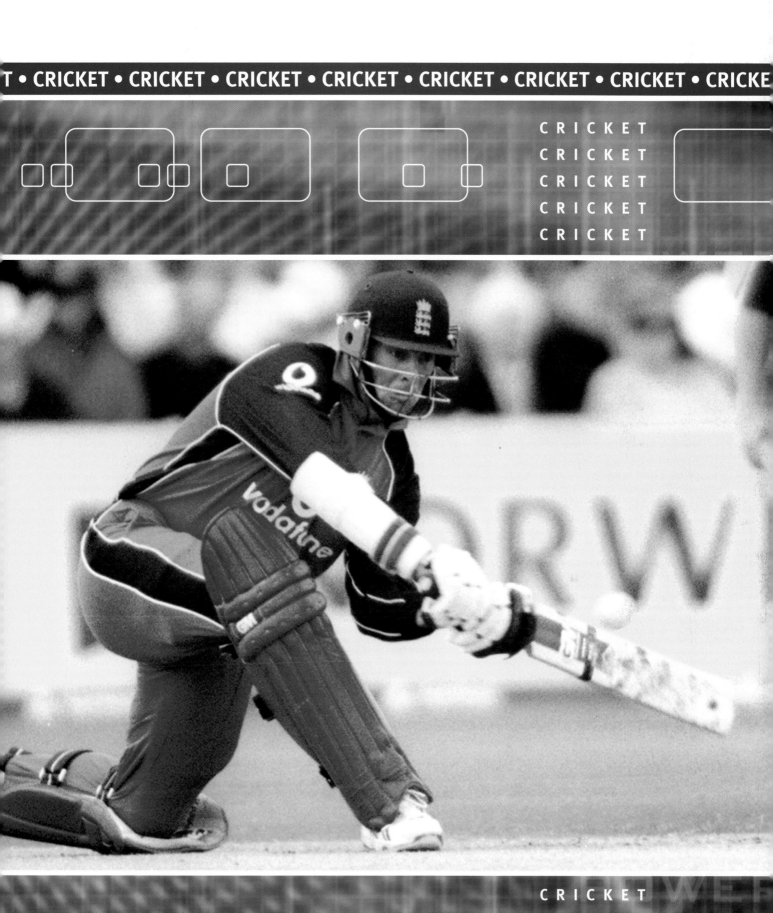

CRICKET
CRICKET
CRICKET

AUSSIES, ATHERS, ANGER AND AGONY

MIXED EMOTIONS IN SUMMER OF CRICKET

It was billed as potentially the greatest summer in cricket history and for drama, controversy and content the English season of 2001 was one of the best ever.

The Australian team were as awesome as everyone had forecast and England caught the backlash of the tourists' winter Test series defeat in India by losing the Ashes for the seventh consecutive time.

A seven wicket defeat in just three days at Trent Bridge gave the Aussies an unassailable 3-0 series lead, and they finally clinched the series 4-1 at The Oval after conceding a rare defeat at Headingley after England's Mark Butcher had plundered the innings of a lifetime.

Steve Waugh was so elated with his touring side's performances that he suggested that the famous Ashes urn should be released from the care of the MCC and flown from Lord's to Melbourne for safe-keeping.

npower, sponsors of the Ashes series, claimed they were prepared to risk the £5 million it would cost to insure the safe passage of the old urn but the ECB's new Test sponsor insisted their involvement would only happen if the MCC, custodians of the trophy, gave their blessing.

Despite vigorous lobbying, the notion received short shrift from the MCC overlords and Waugh's team flew home trophyless but undisputed world champions.

They left behind a host of golden memories for the bumper crowds and huge television audiences they had entertained.

Steve Waugh himself averaged 107 in the Tests, scoring an unbeaten 157 - his second ton of the series – at the Oval on possibly his final appearance in England as Australia finished the last Test as they ended the first, with a victory by an innings.

Mark Waugh, who also scored his second century of the series in the Oval Test, Damien Martyn and Adam Gilchrist battered England to defeat by their sheer weight of runs throughout the series.

And when the Aussie batsmen had inflicted maximum damage, their performances were complemented by Glenn McGrath and Shane Warne, England's executioners-in-chief, with the ball.

McGrath passed Dennis Lillee's 355 wickets, at the Oval, and leg-spin ace Warne moved past Curtly Ambrose's 405 to 407 victims, with only Courtney Walsh, Kapil Dev, Richard Hadlee and Wasim Akram ahead.

England captain Nasser Hussain offered some searing realism in his assessment of the series defeat and said: "We haven't progressed at all from any other series I have been involved in against Australia."

The absence of England's Graham Thorpe, Michael Vaughan and Ashley Giles through long-term injuries was never an issue Hussain chose to explore, though the subsequent inquest into the Ashes debacle led to some pointed

questions about the ECB's handling of injured players.

Sadly, the Ashes series drew the curtain down on Michael Atherton's outstanding career.

The best England batsman of the 1990s formally announced his retirement from cricket with a minimum of fuss.

He marked the final hooray with nothing more than a cursory wave of his bat to the crowd and attended a dinner given by team-mates in his honour.

"I have enjoyed 15 wonderful years in cricket and would like to thank all the players and staff I have been involved with at Lancashire and England," said Athers (pic below) after the Oval Test.

The warm-hearted relationship between the rival spectators in the Ashes series was in sharp contrast to the ugly crowd scenes that had marred the NatWest triangular one-day series between England, Australia and Pakistan at the beginning of the summer.

Unprecedented levels of security were set-up after crowd

Aussie destroyers Glenn McGrath and
Shane Warne celebrate their Ashes success

disturbances at Birmingham, Nottingham and Leeds, where a steward was attacked and taken to hospital (pic above).

The one-sided Final between Australia and Pakistan was also overshadowed by an incident at the presentation ceremony when Michael Bevan, one of the victorious Aussies, was struck by a beer can on the Lord's balcony.

"Unless crowds are controlled, a player will be killed," warned angry Aussie skipper Steve Waugh.

On the home front Yorkshire picked up their first County Championship in 33 years when David Byas, the captain, grabbed a catch out of the slate grey skies at Scarborough just before lunch on August 24th to leave Glamorgan defeated by an innings and 112 runs and the Tykes triumphant.

No player had done more than veteran skipper Byas himself to lift the title. Four Championship centuries had set the standard for others to follow.

Led by Ben Hollioake's match-winning innings, Surrey halted Gloucestershire's five-trophy run as the 'invincibles' of the domestic one-day game in a one-sided Benson and Hedges Cup Final at Lord's, winning by a comfortable 47 runs.

But only an estimated 18,000 of a capacity 30,000 turned up to watch, leaving questions over the future well-being of the once-popular competition.

Somerset wrapped up the Cheltenham and Gloucestershire Trophy at Lord's with victory over Leicestershire by 40 runs, their first trophy in 18 years.

The Foxes' brilliant Shahid Afridi had threatened to run riot with 20 runs off only a handful of balls at the start of Leicester's innings before launching another delivery in to the clouds and being caught.

It was a real crash, bang and wallop innings, full of excitement from first ball to last. Just like the whole summer of cricket.

TECHIE TALK

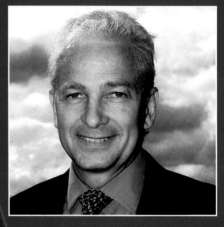

The call for more technology to be used in international cricket grew during the summer, with the no-ball fiasco during the Second Test between England and Pakistan providing the biggest argument yet for its introduction.

Four England wickets that fell in an amazing conclusion to the game were from no-balls that were not spotted by the umpires.

Sky TV cricket pundit David Gower (pic above) supports the use of technology in the game and wants to see the third eye ruling over more than tight stumpings and run-outs.

"If the third eye was used for lbws and bat-pad catches, then it would take the pressure off the umpires," said the ex-England skipper.

"Using something like SkyScope, which tracks the progress of the ball, a third umpire would be in a good position to judge lbw decisions and whether a ball has carried off the edge. All tools that can make the job easier for the umpires in the middle."

THE ASHES

JULY 5-8
EDGBASTON
FIRST TEST
AUSTRALIA WON BY INNINGS AND 118 RUNS

NASSER NIGHTMARE

NASSER Hussain got off to the worst possible start as England skipper in the npower Ashes series by suffering a broken finger for the second time in two months – and then watched as his side were taken apart by the Aussie bowling attack.

The Essex batsman, who was forced to miss the Second Test against Pakistan and the NatWest series after breaking a thumb in the First Test against Pakistan, was caught by a rising 90mph delivery from Jason Gillespie.

A brilliant 152 by wicketkeeper Adam Gilchrist, along with centuries from skipper Steve Waugh and Damien Martyn had put the tourists in a commanding position after the first innings and, following on, England collapsed after their captain's enforced retirement from the crease.

From being 117 for 2 as Hussain left the wicket, they crumbled to 164 all out inside 43 overs, with only Marcus Trescothick and Mark Butcher reaching double figures.

Pace bowler Andy Caddick did give England fans something to smile about though. The Somerset quickie's knock of 49 in the first innings was an Ashes record for a No.11 as he put on a century last wicket stand with Alec Stewart.

SCOREBOARD
Australia: First innings 576 (Gilchrist 152, S.Waugh 105, D.Martyn 105).
England: First innings 294 (Stewart 65, Atherton 57) Warne 5-71
Second innings 164 (Trescothick 76, Butcher 41) Warne 3-29, Gillespie 3-52.

JULY 19-22
LORD'S
SECOND TEST
AUSTRALIA WON BY 8 WICKETS

WAUGH ON THE MARK

AUSTRALIA snapped up their catches, England dropped their's and with them went any chance of winning the Second Test.

For the second successive match, the tourists won with more than a day to spare as England failed to recover from their disappointing first innings score of 187.

Mark Waugh, with 108, and Adam Gilchrist, who was dropped four times, with 90, guided the Aussies along to 401. Waugh also passed fellow Aussie Mark Taylor's world record number of Test catches when he caught Darren Gough in the second innings to take his tally to 158 in 113 matches.

SCOREBOARD
England: First innings 187 (Atherton 37) McGrath 5-54. Second innings: 227 (Butcher 83) Gillespie 5-53.
Australia: First innings 401 (M.Waugh 108, Gilchrist 90) Caddick 5-101
Second innings 14-2.

AUGUST 2-4
TRENT BRIDGE
THIRD TEST
AUSTRALIA WON BY 7 WICKETS

MAGNIFICENT SEVEN FOR AUSSIES

AUSTRALIA clinched the Ashes with a decisive 3-0 lead in a game that lasted less than three full days.

It was their seventh successive series win against England since they regained the Ashes in 1989 and was settled by a no-ball from Andy Caddick as the tourists eased to the chasing target of 158 with seven wickets in hand.

With Mike Atherton in charge again in the absence of injury victim Nasser Hussain, England collapsed to 185 all out in the first innings but a brilliant spell of bowling from Caddick and Alex Tudor, who claimed five wickets on his return to the Test arena, reduced the Aussies to 105 for 7 before Adam Gilchrist steered them to a slender first innings lead of five runs.

Faced with a realistic possibility of fighting their way back in to the series, England buckled again with only Atherton holding his end up for a lengthy time before controversially being given out caught behind for 51.

Shane Warne did the damage with six wickets after becoming only the 11th Australian to take 100 wickets in Ashes matches in the first innings.

England's second innings total of 162 was never going to really test a side of Australia's quality and Mark Waugh and Damien Martyn steered them home at a canter to clinch a 3-0 lead in the five match Test series.

Australia's victorious skipper Steve Waugh

SCOREBOARD
England: First innings 185 (Trescothick 69, Stewart 46) McGrath 5-49
Second innings: 162 (Atherton 51) Warne 6-33.
Australia: First innings 190 (Gilchrist 54) Tudor 5-44, Caddick 3-70
Second innings 158-3 (M.Waugh 42no, Hayden 42, Martyn 33no).

Mark Butcher celebrates his wonder innings

**AUGUST 16-20
HEADINGLEY
FOURTH TEST
ENGLAND WON BY 6 WICKETS**

BUTCHERED

MARK Butcher produced one of the best innings in Ashes history to give England their pride back at Headingley.

The Aussies had extended their first innings lead of 138 to 314 when stand-in skipper Adam Gilchrist decided to set a brave declaration.

But he had not accounted for the brilliance of Butcher's unbeaten knock of 173 from only 227 balls as England reached their target with six wickets in hand.

"That has got to be one of the greatest Ashes innings of all-time," said a stunned Gilchrist.

SCOREBOARD
Australia: First innings 447 (Ponting 144, Martyn 118, M.Waugh 72) Gough 5-103
Second innings 176 for 4 dec (Ponting 72).
England: First innings 309 (Stewart 76no)
McGrath 7-76
Second innings 315 for 4 (Butcher 173no).

**AUGUST 23-27
THE OVAL
FIFTH TEST
AUSTRALIA WON BY
AN INNINGS AND
25 RUNS**

400 FOR WARNE

Shane Warne booked his place in the history books with a brilliant spell of bowling to give Australia victory and a 4-1 win in the series.

The spin wizard finished the game with figures of 11 for 229, picked up his 400th Test wicket along the way and the Man of the Match award for his Oval efforts.

"The Oval is a great place to play cricket and the pitch encourages both batsmen and bowlers," said Warne "and it's wonderful place to pick up my 400th Test wicket."

Warne and Glenn McGrath destroyed England in their second innings with nine wickets falling on the final day as England slumped to 184 all out.

Aussie skipper Steve Waugh marked his return to the npower series, after missing the Fourth Test with a calf injury, with a brave unbeaten 157, and Mark Waugh and Justin Langer both contributed centuries as the tourists amassed 641 for 4.

Mark Ramprakash top scored for England with 133 in their reply but they fell just short of avoiding the follow-on and Warne made them pay.

The longest applause of the series was reserved for Michael Atherton, who received a standing ovation all the way to the pavilion after being dismissed for nine in the second innings. The following day he announced his retirement from first class cricket.

SCOREBOARD
Australia: First innings 641 for 4 dec (S.Waugh 157no, M.Waugh 120, Langer 102).
England: First innings 432 (Ramprakash 133) Warne 7-165. Second innings: 184 (Gough 39no) McGrath 5-43, Warne 4-28.

Shane Warne takes another England wicket on his way to claiming 400 Test victims

EXTRAS

Shane Warne's match figures of eight for 100 in the First Test took him past Sky commentator and England cricketing legend Ian Botham to become the sixth most successful bowler in Tests with 384 wickets.

Adam Gilchrist smashed 22 runs from a Mark Butcher over at Edgbaston, an Ashes record for an Australian.

Damien Martyn's ton in the First Test was his first century after making his debut in international cricket 10 years ago.

Australia's win in the Second Test was the 11th time they had won with more than a day's play to spare in 18 matches.

Marcus Trescothick was dismissed in freak circumstances during the Third Test when his shot cannoned back off Matthew Hayden's heel and into the gloves of wicketkeeper Adam Gilchrist.

Mark Ramprakash's first innings dismissal at Trent Bridge was the fifth time in six innings against Australia that he had been out for 14.

England recorded the 13th highest successful run-chase in Test cricket with their magnificent display at Headingley.

Glenn McGrath was named Man of the Series. He claimed 32 wickets for a total of 542 runs with his best figures seven for 76.

ENGLAND TESTS

Drama and controversy throughout as England made it four Test series wins on the trot, in Sri Lanka, but had to share the spoils against Pakistan...

FEBRUARY 22-26 - GALLE
FIRST TEST v SRI LANKA
SRI LANKA WON BY AN INNINGS
AND 28 RUNS

UMPIRE CHAOS

CONTROVERSY raged at the First Test with England players struggling to hold on to their tempers as a stream of mistakes by umpires Peter Manuel and A.V. Jayaprakash played their part in Sri Lanka's comprehensive victory.

Nine England wickets fell in dubious circumstances, most of them in the second innings.

Sri Lanka always had control of the game from the moment they won the toss and rattled up 470-5 dec, Marvan Atapattu scoring an unbeaten 201 and Aravinda de Silva a stylish 106.

Marcus Trescothick held the England first innings together with a brilliant 122 out of a 253 total, but following on Hussain's side were undone by the spin wizardry of Muttiah Muralitharan – and those dodgy decisions.

Darren Gough - 200 wickets for England

SCOREBOARD
Sri Lanka:
First innings 470-5 dec
(Atapattu 201no,
de Silva 106).
England:
First innings 253
(Trescothick 122)
Jayasuriya 4-50
Second innings 189
(Atherton 44) Jayasuriya 4-44,
Muralitharan 4-66.

MARCH 7-11 - KANDY
SECOND TEST V SRI LANKA
ENGLAND WON BY 3 WICKETS

WHITE STEERS ENGLAND HOME

CRAIG White held his nerve to see England home in another game marred by poor umpiring and an ever-increasing friction between the two sides.

The all-rounder scored a priceless 21 and he and Ashley Giles combined for an eighth wicket partnership of 19 to reach the target of 161 and a three wicket win.

A mistake by Sri Lanka wicketkeeper Kumar Sangakkara, who broke the stumps before taking Muttiah Muralitharan's throw which would have seen Giles run out still four short of victory, helped England's cause.

SCOREBOARD
Sri Lanka: First innings 297 (Jayawardene 101, Arnold 65) Caddick 4-55, Gough 4-73
Second innings 250 (Sangakkara 95, Dharmasena 54) Gough 4-50.
England: First innings 387 (Hussain 109, Thorpe 59, Stewart 54) Muralitharan 4-127
Second innings: 161-7 (Thorpe 46, White 21no) Vaas 4-39.

MARCH 15-17 - COLOMBO
THIRD TEST v SRI LANKA
ENGLAND WON BY 4 WICKETS

THORPE TRIUMPHS

ENGLAND clinched their fourth successive series win with victory over Sri Lanka in a match that saw 22 wickets fall on the third day.

The majestic Graham Thorpe fought off dehydration and dizziness to give England a first innings lead of eight with a brilliant, unbeaten 113 in a score of 249.

But that was only the start of an amazing eight hours play with Ashley Giles snapping up four wickets for 11 runs as Sri Lanka crashed to 81 all out in their second innings.

A victory target of 74 seemed a foregone conclusion for Nasser Hussain's side but early wickets left them on 43 for 4 before Thorpe's undefeated 32 ensured victory.

SCOREBOARD
Sri Lanka: First innings 241 (Jayawardene 71) Croft 4-56
Second innings: 81 (Jayasuriya 23, de Silva 23) Giles 4-11, Gough 3-23.
England: First innings 249 (Thorpe 113no) Vaas 6-73
Second innings 74 for 6 (Thorpe 32no).

Graham Thorpe is congratulated by England fans after victory at the Third Test in Sri Lanka.

MAY 17-20 - LORD'S
FIRST TEST V PAKISTAN
ENGLAND WON BY AN INNINGS AND 9 RUNS

DEADLY DUO STAR

DARREN Gough and Andy Caddick combined to blow Pakistan away in the first npower Test match of the summer.

The pair took 16 wickets between them with Yorkshire paceman Gough reaching the 200 victims mark in Test cricket, only the eighth Englishman to do so.

England's first innings total of 391 was shared around the batsmen, Graham Thorpe top scoring with 80, but it was their fearsome attack that dominated the Test.

Gough took 5-61 from 16 overs in Pakistan's first innings but Caddick's dismissals of Saleem Elahi, Abdur Razzaq and Inzaman were the catalyst for the victory.

Waqar's side struggled to reach 203 and in their second innings failed to topple even that disappointing score, with the deadly duo ploughing through their batting order to ensure victory inside three days of play.

SCOREBOARD

England: First innings 391 (Thorpe 80, Hussain 64, Stewart 44, Atherton 42) Azhar Mahmood 4-50.
Pakistan: First innings 203 (Younis Khan 58) Gough 5-61, Caddick 4-52
Second innings 179 (Abdur Razzaq 53) Caddick 4-54, Gough 3-40.

MAY 31-JUNE 4 - OLD TRAFFORD
SECOND TEST v PAKISTAN
PAKISTAN WON BY 108 RUNS

NO-BALL NIGHTMARE

A STAGGERING second innings collapse by England brought an end to their winning run and gave Pakistan an amazing victory.

In one of the most exciting Tests played over the last 10 years, both sides went into the final day with a chance of victory.

England needed 290 to win with 10 wickets in hand after Inzamam had top scored in both Pakistan's innings and Graham Thorpe and Michael Vaughan had both notched 100s, the latter his maiden Test century, for England.

Mike Atherton and Marcus Trescothick took the score to 146 before Atherton was bowled by Waqar. His opening partner went on to score 117 and at tea a draw looked the only conclusion with England too far adrift of the run chase.

But eight wickets tumbled for just 60 runs in 23 overs in the final session, Saqlain the chief tormentor taking 4-74, as England minus skipper Nasser Hussain, ruled out of the match with a broken thumb, crashed to defeat.

Pakistan played some sparkling cricket and deserved their victory but they were assisted by the umpires with four of the last five wickets coming from clear no-balls as the tourists lay siege to the England batsmen at the wicket.

"It was an amazing match and an extraordinary end. I have never seen so many wickets off no-balls before," said Sky TV commentator David Gower.

SCOREBOARD

Pakistan: First innings 403 (Inzamam 114, Rashid Latif 71 Younis Khan 65) Hoggard 3-79
Second innings: 323 (Inzamam 85) Gough 3-85, Hoggard 3-93, Caddick 3-92.
England: First innings 357 (Thorpe 138, Vaughan 120) Abdur Razzaq 3-61
Second innings 261 (Trescothick 117, Atherton 51) Saqlain 4-74, Waqar 3-85.

Andy Caddick celebrates taking another Pakistan wicket in the First Test

SKY **SPORTS** A YEAR IN SPORT CRICKET

NATWEST SERIES

Australia won a controversial NatWest Series, while England's sorry form in one day internationals resulted in an 11th straight defeat...

PAKISTAN v AUSTRALIA

JUNE 23
LORD'S
AUSTRALIA WON BY 9 WICKETS

JUST like in the World Cup Final two years earlier, Pakistan crumbled against the dream machine that is Australia.

Aussie skipper Steve Waugh picked up the NatWest trophy after this easy nine wicket win, with only 26 of the 50 overs needed to surpass a target of 152.

As in 1999, the brilliant but inconsistent Pakistan batted first and were always struggling to score against the pace attack of Glenn McGrath, Jason Gillespie and Brett Lee, although it was spin wizard Shane Warne who struck the most decisive blow, trapping potential matchwinner Inzamam lbw.

Mark Waugh and the brilliant Adam Gilchrist made sure there was never any chance of a Pakistan revival with the ball, setting up an opening stand of 76 before Waugh was run out.

Gilchrist finished unbeaten on 76 with Ricky Ponting on 33 as Australia coasted home.

But their celebrations were marred when batsman Michael Bevan was struck on the head by a beer can thrown from the crowd at the after-match presentations.

It rounded off a series that had been dogged by pitch invasions and general crowd trouble.

"One person has ruined a great day for 30,000 people," said disappointed and angry MCC secretary, Roger Knight.

SCOREBOARD
Pakistan: 152 (Saeed Anwar 27, Abdur Razzaq 24) Warne 3-56.
Australia: 156-1 (Gilchrist 76no, M.Waugh 36, Ponting 35no).
Man of the Series: Waqar Younis, Pakistan.

ENGLAND v AUSTRALIA

JUNE 14
OLD TRAFFORD
AUSTRALIA WON BY 125 RUNS

All out: England's collapse is complete

ENGLAND recorded their lowest score in one-day cricket to slump to another embarrassing defeat in the NatWest Series.

Chasing a modest target of 212 in 44 overs under the Duckworth/Lewis method, they were fired out for 86, beating their previous lowest total of 93 against the Aussies in the 1975 World Cup Semi-Final.

Jason Gillespie did the most damage with 3 for 20, but all the Australian bowlers chipped in with wickets as England were dismissed in 32.4 overs.

England did have the worst of the conditions, batting second under floodlights in the day/night game, but Alec Stewart's side were having problems from the moment Nick Knight went with the score on 25. Stewart and Michael Vaughan both failed to add to the total and at one stage the home side were a nightmare 40-6.

Dominic Cork top scored with 17 as sorry England booked an unwanted place in the record books.

SCOREBOARD
Australia: 208 for 7 in 48 of the 50 overs (S.Waugh 64, Martyn 51no).
England: 86 (Cork 17) Gillespie 3-20.

Australia lift another trophy

ENGLAND v PAKISTAN

JUNE 17
HEADINGLEY
ENGLAND CONCEDED GAME

Waqar strikes again

ALEC Stewart conceded defeat to Pakistan following a pitch invasion that left a steward in hospital.

The England one-day skipper took the unprecedented step with Pakistan four runs short of victory.

Fans ran on to the pitch thinking that Pakistan had passed England's total of 156 and the players were forced to race for the pavilion.

Stewart refused to bring his players back on to the pitch because of the threat to their safety and informed Pakistan skipper Waqar Younis that victory was their's.

Waqar had done more than anyone to ensure his side's triumph with a brilliant spell of bowling, taking the first seven England wickets to finish with figures of 7 for 36 off 10 overs, the second best one-day performance in history.

And after Stewart's decision to forfeit the game, the Pakistan paceman joined the growing campaign for safety measures to be introduced at grounds.

He said: "I think the England authorities have to look at erecting fences at grounds here. Something has to be done because there are a number of Asian teams set to tour here over the next few years and the same problem could arise again."

SCOREBOARD
England: 156 all out (B.Hollioake 53, Gough 4ono) Waqar 7-36. Pakistan: 153 for 4 (Abdur Razzaq 75) Gough 2-39.

ENGLAND V AUSTRALIA

JUNE 21
THE OVAL
AUSTRALIA WON BY 8 WICKETS

ENGLAND suffered a record 11th straight one day defeat to end the triangular NatWest series with no points. And this was one of the worst displays in that nightmare run.

Pakistan and Australia had already booked their places in the Final and England performed like the situation suggested – with little to play for.

Only some gallant hitting from Andy Caddick to add to Nick Knight's early innings of 48 dragged their total up to 176.

But Australia stormed past that figure with some brutal strokeplay, finishing their prey off with 20 overs still left to bowl.

Adam Gilchrist top scored with 80, ably assisted by Ricky Ponting, who won his third Man of the Match award in five games with a majestic unbeaten 70.

SCOREBOARD
England: 176 (Knight 48, Caddick 36) Lee 3-63. Australia: 177-2 (Gilchrist 80, Ponting 7ono).

Alec Stewart fails to inspire England against Australia

NATWEST SERIES

THE OTHER SCOREBOARDS

JUNE 7: England v Pakistan, Edgbaston Pakistan: 273 for 6 (Inzamam 79, Saeed Anwar 77) Cork 2-44. England: 165 all out (Knight 59). Pakistan won by 108 runs

JUNE 9: Australia v Pakistan, Cardiff Pakistan 257 all out (Yousuf Youhana 91, Rashid Latif 66) Warne 3-52. Australia: 258 for 3 (Ponting 70, Bevan 56no, S.Waugh 54no). Australia won by seven wickets

JUNE 10: England v Australia, Bristol. England: 264 for 4 (Knight 84, Trescothick 69) Lee 2-55. Australia 272 for 5 (Ponting 102) Gough 2-44. Australia won by five wickets

JUNE 12: England v Pakistan, Lord's. Pakistan 242 for 8 (Yousuf Youhana 81, Younis Khan 41) Caddick 2-37, Gough 2-38. England 240 all out (Trescothick 137, Shah 62) Waqar 2-20. Pakistan won by two runs

JUNE 16: Australia v Pakistan, Durham No play because of rain

JUNE 19: Pakistan v Australia, Trent Bridge. Pakistan: 290 for 9 (Saleem Elahi 79) Lee 2-41. Australia 254 all out (Gilchrist 70, S.Waugh 56) Waqar 6-59. Pakistan won by 36 runs

How they finished

	P	W	L	N/R	Pts
Australia	6	4	1	1	9
Pakistan	6	4	1	1	9
England	6	0	6	0	0

STAR OF 2001

ADAM GILCHRIST

'He has handled the skipper's job like an old pro' Dennis Lillee

A DAM Gilchrist returned to Australia after the Ashes series acknowledged as not only a national hero but the best wicket-keeper-batsman in history.

This remarkable achievement for the strong, amiable gloveman has been achieved in two years since the Australian selectors spotted a deterioration in Ian Healy's batting and decided to promote a 'keeper who had made many one-day international appearances but had yet to grace the big Test stage.

Gilchrist scored 81 on his Test debut against Pakistan in Brisbane two years ago in the second match of a sequence of Tests in which Australia enjoyed a record 16-match winning run.

This powerful left-handed bat followed that with a match-winning undefeated 149 in the next Test in Hobart in which he shared a partnership of 238 with Justin Langer.

And by the time Australia reached India at the end of February 2001, Gilchrist had become a permanent fixture in Steve Waugh's side.

He lacks some of Healy's finesse but what is missing in artistic content is compensated by solid, safe glovework allied to a rampaging style of batting that makes him the most destructive left-hander in the world. The Indian tour taught the Aussies never to take cricket for granted. Gilchrist scored the second fastest century in Australian Test history, reaching three figures in 84 deliveries in the First Test, but followed that with two ducks - a king pair – and just two singles in the next two.

A sobering nightmare he later described as "an out of body experience. I really went down on myself and I became reserved off the field after that."

Australia lost the series and poor England copped the backlash of his disappointment on the sub-continent last spring.

In June's NatWest series, he flogged the England attack for 80 from 90 balls, and in the Final savaged Pakistan with 76 off 93.

Gilchrist admitted to an acute attack of nerves at the beginning of the Ashes battle. He dropped two catches before lunch on the first day but recovered from that temporary aberration to treat a full-house at Edgbaston to a run-a-ball 150 in Australia's first innings.

By the end of the series, won 4-1, he had scored 340 runs at an average of 68, taken 24 catches and made two stumpings.

His bull-like charges down the pitch to congratulate England's tormentors-in-chief, Glenn McGrath and Shane Warne, became a feature of a summer in which Australia finished the series as they began it, with an innings victory and another vivid demonstration of their formidable all-round talent.

His bold declaration in the Fourth Ashes Test, in his stand-in skipper role for the injured Steve Waugh, illustrated perfectly the way he plays the game.

Mark Butcher's brilliant 173 won the match for England but it was Gilchrist's desire to entertain and go for an Aussie victory rather than play not to lose that opened up the door for the home side's one win of the series.

Despite that loss, he is still the favourite to replace Waugh as skipper and an Aussie legend

'A rampaging style of batting that makes him the most destructive left-hander in the world'

"He is a strong character with a quick cricketing brain and he has earned the respect of the other players around him.

"He proved in the Ashes series what a brilliant batsman he is and he reminds me of players like Gary Sobers, Clive Lloyd, Viv Richards and Ian Botham in the spectacular way he plays the game."

Gilchrist showed that steely determination and supreme talent in his early days when he moved from New South Wales to Western Australia to take over as wicket-keeper from Tim Zoehrer.

The former Aussie Test player was a legend at the WACA and Gilchrist's arrival was greeted with anger by the state side's supporters.

'A strong character with a quick cricketing brain, he has won the respect of his team-mates'

But he won them over with his tidy wicket-keeping and sparking strokeplay and forced his way from there into the Australian Test side.

The son of a schools inspector, his passion for cricket was nurtured from the age of seven and on the day before his 16th birthday he made an entry in a friend's diary saying: 'I will play for Australia – keep this page!'

It has been to his country's undoubted benefit that Adam Gilchrist has been true to his word.

of the past reckons he will be more than up to the job.

"Adam is looking to skipper Australia when Steve calls it a day and on the occasions he has done it in the past he handled the job like an old pro," said former paceman Dennis Lillee.

Gilchrist at work behind the stumps

SKY SPORTS **A YEAR IN SPORT** CRICKET

GILCHRIST FACTFILE

BORN: 14th November, 1971 in Bellingen, NSW
CLUBS: New South Wales, Western Australia
TEST DEBUT: v Pakistan, Brisbane, 1999-00
ONE DAY INTERNATIONAL DEBUT: v South Africa, Faridabad, 1996-97
FIRST CLASS DEBUT: For New South Wales v Tasmania, Sydney, 1992-93

2001 HIGHLIGHTS

JUNE 19, 2001:
Hits a brilliant 70 to lead the Aussie run chase but they fall 36 runs short of Pakistan's 290 in the NatWest triangular tournament.

JUNE 21, 2001:
Leads from the front as his knock of 80 guides Australia to an eight wicket win over England in the one-dayers.

JUNE 23, 2001:
Scores 76 not out as the Australians win the NatWest series Final against Pakistan at Lord's.

JULY 6, 2001:
Smashes a brilliant 152, including an Aussie Ashes record of 22 in one over, in the First Test.

JULY 20, 2001:
Follows that up with 90 in the Second Test, although he was dropped four times.

AUG 3, 2001:
Helps Australia recover from 105 for 7 with a knock of 54 in the first innings of the Third Test.

AUG 16, 2001:
Skippers Australia in the Ashes for the first time in the absence of injury victim Steve Waugh.

COUNTY SCENE

Yorkshire ended their long wait for Championship glory, Somerset and Surrey upset the odds and Leicestershire lost the lot but found a real star...

Ben Hollioake on his way to 73 against Gloucester

JULY 14
LORD'S
BENSON & HEDGES CUP FINAL
SURREY WON BY 47 RUNS

BROTHERS IN ARMS

BEN Hollioake inspired Surrey's comfortable victory over Gloucestershire in the Benson and Hedges Cup Final at Lord's.

The all-rounder put on 88 for the sixth wicket with his brother Adam to guide Surrey to 244 all-out after they were struggling at one stage on 118-5.

His free-flowing knock of 73 in 76 balls included two sixes and was enough for him to pick up the Gold Award as man of the match.

Brother Adam was forced to play a supporting role, contributing 39 from 65 balls and admitted Ben's innings swung the game in the direction of Surrey.

"He played brilliantly and we needed it because we were under pressure when he came out to bat," said the Surrey skipper.

"Once he got going I was just the player at the other end and his knock certainly turned the game around for us.

"And our bowlers carried the game on from there. We knew that Gloucester were the best one-day team in the country but we could get at them if we put the ball in the right areas and it turned out perfectly."

Ed Giddins was the pick of the Surrey bowlers with three prized wickets in Kim Barnett, Aussie dangerman Ian Harvey and Matt Windows with wicketkeeper Jack Russell top scoring for Gloucester with 62.

SCOREBOARD

Surrey: 244 (B.Hollioake 73, Ward 54)
Harvey 3-43, Alleyne 3-51.
Gloucestershire: 197 (Russell 62, Alleyne 26)
Giddins 3-31, Tudor 3-28, Saqlain Mushtaq 3-37.

SEPTEMBER 2
LORD'S
C & G TROPHY FINAL
SOMERSET WON BY 41 RUNS

CIDER COUNTRY CELEBRATE AT LAST

SOMERSET picked up their first trophy in 18 years with victory over Leicestershire in the Cheltenham and Gloucester Trophy Final.

Jamie Cox's side set a daunting target of 271 in their 50 overs with Keith Parsons top scoring with 60.

England opener Marcus Trescothick was one of three victims for Leicester all-rounder Shahid Afridi, caught for just 18.

Vince Wells' team stayed in touch with the run rate throughout their innings after Darren Maddy and Trevor Ward put on 85 for the second wicket but lost batsmen at regular intervals after those two were dismissed and fell 41 runs short.

Parsons picked up the Man of the Match award, with two wickets adding to his runs.

SCOREBOARD

Somerset: 271 (Parsons 60, Cox 44, Bowler 42, Turner 37) Afridi 3-47.
Leicestershire: 230 (Ward 54, Maddy 49) Jones 3-40, Parsons 2-40.

Jamie Cox lifts the C&G trophy

AUGUST 24
SCARBOROUGH
COUNTY CHAMPIONSHIP

YORKSHIRE PRIDE

Yorkshire clinched the County Championship for the first time in 33 years when skipper David Byas held a skier from Steve Jones to dismiss Glamorgan for 245 and give his side victory.

The win at Scarborough and the 20 points that went with it thanks to their innings and 112 run margin took them out of reach of their closest challengers, Kent and Somerset, with two matches in hand.

It was fitting that Byas, who was born just down the road from the county ground at

Leicestershire's Shahid Afridi - arguably the best one-day player in the world

Scarborough, was at the centre of the decisive moment in the season.

He had led the team from the front all year, scoring four centuries along the way and cajoling his young side to maintain their impressive form over the six months.

The last time the White Rose county looked down from their lofty perch at the top of the Championship table in 1968, the team was Yorkshire through and through. If you weren't born in the county, you couldn't play for the county.

Nowadays the squad includes an Australian, Darren Lehmann, and whisper it to that side of '68, even a Lancastrian in Steve Kirby who was born and brought up in Bury.

Ray Illingworth, former England skipper and manager, was a member of that 1968 side that included Geoff Boycott, Brian Close and Fred Trueman and saw similarities between the current Yorkshire champions and his team.

"It has been a long time coming but they certainly deserved it this year," he said.

"They work very hard for each other and really steamroller sides when they get the

upperhand, just like we used to.

"They will take some stopping now and the future looks very bright for Yorkshire."

The county's success was achieved mainly without the services of one of their favourite sons, Darren Gough, who was involved in a summer of Test cricket and played in only two games for his county. Michael Vaughan was also on England duty, or injured.

But their year did end in controversy with doubts over whether Gough would stay with the County Champions.

SEPTEMBER 16
TRENT BRIDGE
NORWICH UNION LEAGUE

FOXES HUNTED DOWN

LEICESTERSHIRE blew their second trophy chance in a matter of two weeks when they went down by five wickets to Nottinghamshire at Trent Bridge.

After losing to Somerset in the C&G Trophy Final, the Foxes seemed certain of picking up the Norwich Union League title, holding a 10 point lead with only three matches to go.

But a combination of the rain and a loss of form prevented them picking up the extra four points they needed for victory and Kent sneaked up to win the title after beating Warwickshire by nine runs in their final game.

Missing from Leicester's last game was one of the stars of the season, Shahid Afridi, whose brilliant strokeplay and spin bowling put him in contention as the world's best one-day player.

"We have been amazed at what he has achieved," said Foxes' coach Jack Birkenshaw.

EXTRAS

Northants, Glamorgan and Essex were relegated from the County Championship Division 1 with Sussex, Hampshire and Warwicks coming up.

Gloucester suffered their first defeat in their fifth successive appearance in a Final when they were beaten by Surrey in the B&H.

Gloucester, Surrey and Northants were relegated from the Norwich Union National League Division 1 with Glamorgan, Durham and Worcester replacing them.

Leicestershire's Scott Boswell delivered nine wides and conceded 23 runs in his two overs at the C&G Final.

Shahid Afridi announced his arrival at Leicester with 70 off 32 balls against Kent in their Norwich Union clash, then followed that up with 67 off 44 balls against Worcester and 95 from 58 deliveries against Lancs to steer the Foxes through to the C&G Final, where he hit 20 in 10 balls before being caught.

Yorkshire's triumph in the County Championship was the 30th time they had won the title.

Four Yorkshire players were picked for England's winter tour of India and New Zealand. Michael Vaughan, Craig White, Matthew Hoggard and new boy, Richard Dawson.

Comic Michael Palin joined the Sky commentary team at the B&H Final.

ATHERTON
LEADING FROM THE FRONT

As England's top opening batsman over the last 10 years, Mike Atherton has been battered, bruised and blitzed by the cream of fast bowlers around the world – but he has never been beaten.

DID YOU KNOW?

MICHAEL ATHERTON, one of England's greatest post-War batsmen, has slipped quietly into retirement from the Test stage he strode like one of those knighted giants of the English theatre.

From the moment he made his England Test debut, against Australia in August 1989, to the day be bowed out, against Australia in August 2001, he provided newspaper headlines and rolls of video footage that seemed entirely alien to the way he preferred to conduct his public and private life.

Wise, thoughtful, taciturn, stoic, stubborn, reticent and averse to any public show for one of the world's most easily recognisable sportsmen, Atherton leaves behind a vast library of x-certificate rated material of his Test match batting that is guaranteed to thrill cricket lovers for many years during those breaks for rain when television producers struggle for material to fill the gaps.

If Wally Hammond, Len Hutton and Peter May left sepia-toned images of their batting magic for posterity, Atherton has bequeathed rolls of filmed action of himself in nose-to-nose confrontation with an army of fast bowlers intent only of pinning the Lancastrian's wiry body to the sightscreen if they are unable to uproot his stumps.

Who will forget his duel with West Indies fast bowlers Curtly Ambrose and Courtney Walsh in the Georgetown Test of 1993-94 when he scored a brilliant 144, or the 135 he produced against the same attack a few days later in the Fifth Test of that series in Antigua that brought his length of time at the wicket in that series to a staggering 28 hours?

Or the day he slugged it out with Allan Donald at Trent Bridge in 1998 when he stood on cricket's equivalent of boxing's ropes and

He loved a fight against the odds in a solid, old fashioned, straightforward approach that was perfectly moulded to tackle the harsh demands he faced during a brilliant career

absorbed punishment over a long period with much the same courage and endurance that Muhammad Ali took into the ring in that fight with George Foreman many years ago.

Breathing fire and snarling his fury after Atherton 'gloved' a catch the umpire failed to spot in England's second innings, South African hit man Donald had Atherton bobbing, weaving, ducking and diving in a 90mph assault that was as absorbing a battle between batsman and bowler as anything seen in Tests since the legendary 'Bodyline' tour more than six decades before.

Demonstrating extraordinary powers of patience and concentration, he batted 10 hours to play the fourth longest innings by an Englishman in Tests in scoring 185 not out at Johannesburg in 1995-96 to save another

Atherton was bobbing, weaving, ducking and diving in a 90mph assault

game, against Donald's South Africa, a feat that made front page news as well as dominating the back pages of the national newspapers.

But it is Atherton's eye-balling spats with quick bowlers and a refusal to back down under withering fire in some of his shorter innings that will continue to burn on the memory when England supporters have to grow used to new personnel walking out to face the new ball in future.

Michael Andrew Atherton, son of a headmaster, comes from a classic cricket background, Manchester Grammar School, Cambridge University, Lancashire.

He was given the nickname 'FEC' - future England captain - from the moment his pedigree for a career in the first-class game emerged so excitingly at university when the Cambridge attack would be flayed and Athers would make a game of it, against the odds, by batting sublimely.

True to form, he went on to become England's longest serving captain, leading the side in 54 Tests.

His misfortune was to skipper England at a time of struggle for the side. He had only just celebrated the award of a 2:1 history degree at Cambridge and was settling into a successful Lancashire team in 1989, aged 21, when he was pushed into an under-achieving England Test side.

Aged 25, and now established at Test level, the captaincy was thrust upon him ahead of the more experienced Alec Stewart.

A year into the job, he became involved in the 'dirt-in-the-pocket' affair. Atherton was spotted by television cameras rubbing soil from his pocket onto the ball. He maintained he was trying to keep the ball dry in sticky heat.

The opening bat was fined £2,000 by England's chairman of selectors. He resisted pressure to resign and two months later took the side to Australia, a maturer, wiser leader.

England's supporters rarely doubted Atherton's energy or commitment to the cause throughout a difficult reign when the standard of English cricket was questioned worldwide, but when he resigned the captaincy at the end of the 1997-98 tour to the West Indies, the loss of responsibility and the time he could now give to more selfish pursuits enabled his ability to make runs against the world's best attacks blossom again.

For long periods of leadership, he had shown frustration in the media spotlight. He looked hunted and haunted. He grew chin stubble on match-days, suffered fools badly, and made Test cricket a daily grind he appeared not always to enjoy.

Throughout his career of 114 England appearances, in which he overtook Colin Cowdrey's aggregate in the 2001 Ashes series to become the 10th heaviest run-maker in Test history, Atherton suffered from debilitating back trouble.

On almost every day of his cricket career, he was in some discomfort with cortisone treatment as regular part of his staple routine as net practise.

But it never affected his form. He was a pillar of reliability when opening the innings for England, unfortunately he suffered from a lack of regular support at the other end.

He had 13 opening partners in his Test career, but among them only three really stand out as successful.

Atherton with Graham Gooch and Alec Stewart always offered England the prospect of a sound start, and by the time he confronted the Aussies for the last time during the 2001 series in England, he had established a fine and productive partnership with Somerset's Marcus Trescothick.

His wicket, as Australia's captain Steve Waugh testified during Atherton's final summer, was always the prize England scalp for all bowlers. For more than a decade he was

He was unlucky to play his international cricket when England were at a low ebb

the toughest England batsman and the most difficult to remove.

Atherton believed in taking one day at a time. He rarely set himself targets. When asked for his goals, he would reply: 'I do have figures and records in mind, but I'll not say what they are because this game teaches you not to look too far ahead.'

He was unlucky to play his international cricket when England were often at a low ebb, well down the Test ladder behind Australia, Pakistan, South Africa and West Indies.

But struggle was fundamental to his make-up. He loved a fight against the odds in a solid, old fashioned, straightforward approach that was perfectly moulded to tackle the harsh demands of the responsibilities he faced in an outstanding career. In announcing his retirement from first class cricket, Atherton thanked everyone that had supported him down the years and then enjoyed a farewell meal with his England team-mates. They will miss him. The game of cricket will miss him. Even those fearsome quickies will no doubt miss him.

"He really annoys bowlers. Athers can defend so well, but he can also play wonderful attacking shots when it really matters. He is the toughest batsman in England and the most important to get out."
ALLAN DONALD, South African fast bowler (pic above).

"That was one of the greatest Test innings of all time."
RAY ILLINGWORTH, England tour manager, on Atherton's monumental 185 not out in the Second Test against South Africa at Johannesburg in 1995-96.

"Athers has been a good friend of mine for many years. But that means nothing to him when he is up against you. He is a fierce character, a determined character and England's top batsman over the last 10 years."
WASIM AKRAM, Pakistan all-rounder and Atherton's former Lancashire team-mate.

"We know that we have to get Atherton out to get at England. He has our total respect. He is the one we want."
GLENN McGRATH, Australian opening bowler and Atherton's chief tormentor.

THE GREATEST TEAM EVER?

WIZARDS OF OZ STAKE THEIR CLAIM

IF a cricket team is to be judged on the number of standing ovations it receives in a Test series, then Australia's victorious Ashes winning side of 2001 would win the title 'Greatest Team Ever' by a mile.

And supporting the warmth of the receptions they received on every English Test ground last summer came the cold statistics that backed the public's judgement.

Victory in the Trent Bridge Test made it a record seven Ashes triumphs in a row and by the time they had completed the rout of England at the Oval to win the series 4-1, they had retained the Ashes in record time, with just 11 days of cricket.

England had been overwhelmed by an infinitely superior side. But are Steve Waugh's wizards of Aus the best Test side in history?

The capacity Oval crowd took an eternity to leave the ground, knowing they had witnessed a

'We were positive and we played to win every day of the tour' Steve Waugh

level of sustained brilliance by a touring party they will be lucky to see again in their lifetimes.

The chasm in class between the two nations had never been greater in more than a century of

battle for the famous terracotta urn containing the Ashes. Such was the Australians' superiority that skipper Waugh suggested the old urn should be transported from Lord's to Melbourne and held by the winning team in future series.

Five Australian batsmen, Steve Waugh, Mark Waugh, Damien Martyn, Adam Gilchrist and Ricky Ponting, scored Test centuries in the one-sided series and four of them averaged more than 50.

Their bowling attack was just as awesome. Glenn McGrath took 32 wickets in the series, just one more victim than Shane Warne, whose 11 wickets in the Fifth Test enabled him to smash the 400-wicket barrier and join an elite set containing such names as Courtney Walsh, Kapil Dev, Richard Hadlee, Wasim Akram and Curtly Ambrose.

Given full fitness, good form, and an appetite still for the game, Warne promised to return to England for the 2005 Ashes series. Should he scale that mountain, Walsh's record haul of 519 Test victims will surely have been overhauled by the Aussie leg-spin wizard.

England never came close to bowling out Australia twice and only once did they dismiss Waugh's side for under 400.

Cricket men with long memories and sound judgment were convinced they were watching the greatest Test side ever long before Waugh had laid the foundations for that crushing Oval win by scoring an incredible 157 not out, the final 70 runs coming with the Australian

after Lance Gibbs' retirement, meant that they were short of the variety and adaptability that the 2001 Australian attack carries into every Test in all climates and conditions.

If McGrath doesn't get you on a lifeless track in India, the odds are that Warne will conjure some life from the most placid strip to give Australia a chance of winning the match rather than merely drawing it.

The secret of Australia's success is the fact that there is hardly a weakness. There is NO weakness. Michael Slater or Justin Langer, Matthew Hayden, Ricky Ponting,

Brothers Steve and Mark went to Waugh on England during the summer

captain limping on a leg damaged during the Trent Bridge Test.

By the end of the series the general consensus of opinion was that the 2001 Australians would have been good enough to defeat the chief rivals to their 'Greatest Ever' crown, namely Don Bradman's undefeated 1948 Ashes tour party and the great West Indies' sides of the late Seventies and Eighties, led by Clive Lloyd and Viv Richards.

Waugh said simply: "We were aggressive the whole time and positive and we played to win every day of the tour."

The argument is supported by the belief that there are few flaws in Waugh's team, whereas the other great outfits carried at least one or two journeymen in their ranks.

With due respect to Bradman's team, Sam Loxton, Doug Ring and Ernie Toshack would not have gained a place in Waugh's side, and even the great wicketkeeper, Don Tallon, would probably have been sidelined by Gilchrist's phenomenal batting feats.

Viv Richards maintains that only Shane Warne of the current Aussie team would have gained a place in his side. There lies the problem for the West Indies side, for their lack of a match-winning spinner in the Warne mould

Mark Waugh, Steve Waugh, Damien Martyn, Adam Gilchrist, Shane Warne, Brett Lee, Jason Gillespie, Glenn McGrath.

Never before in Test history has there been such a line-up. Those privileged to see them in action in the summer of 2001 will have little doubt of that.

The best team ever? Almost certainly.

Glenn McGrath - voted Man of the Ashes series

TEST MATCH TABLE

Australia are the best team in the world at the moment and are favourites to retain that title for years to come. But the introduction of a Test Match Championship table will provide evidence of who their closest challengers are. The top 10 Test nations will play each other on a home and away basis over the next five years with points awarded for winning each series.

A league table will be produced, along with world rankings and a trophy for the top team in a rolling league format, where the results of a Test series between two sides will replace the results of their previous meeting.

ENGLAND'S TEST PROGRAMME FOR THE NEXT FIVE YEARS:

2001-02 WINTER
v India & New Zealand (away)

2002 SUMMER
v Sri Lanka & India (home)

2002-03 WINTER
v Australia (away)

2003 SUMMER
v Zimbabwe & South Africa (home)

2003-04 WINTER
v Bangladesh, Sri Lanka & West Indies (away)

2004 SUMMER
v New Zealand & West Indies (home)

2004-05 WINTER
v Zimbabwe & South Africa (away)

2005 SUMMER
v Bangladesh & Australia (home)

2005-06 WINTER
v India & Pakistan (away)

RECORD BREAKERS

Craig McMillan - record score in an over

Andy Roberts (West Indies); Kapil Dev (India); Sandeep Patel (India), Ian Smith (New Zealand) and English legend Ian Botham.

New Zealand won the game by an innings and 185 runs to record their biggest ever Test victory and inflict Pakistan's heaviest defeat.

TENDULKAR TON MAKES HISTORY

MARCH 31 Sachin Tendulkar became the first player to score 10,000 runs in limited overs cricket with a brilliant 139 against Australia in Indore.

The Indian master batsman reached the milestone with a single in the 19th over on his way to a 199 partnership with Venkatsai Laxman that saw India reach an impressive 299-8 in their 50 overs.

SOUTH AFRICA MISS OUT

JANUARY 17 South Africa's bid to enter the record books with an 11th consecutive one day Test win was thwarted by Sri Lanka in Johannesburg. The tourists won by four runs but lost the limited over series 5-1 overall.

Courtney Walsh - 500 wickets to his name

500 UP FOR WALSH

MARCH 19 West Indies quickie Courtney Walsh became the first player to take 500 Test wickets when he trapped South Africa's Jacques Kallis lbw in the Second Test in Port of Spain.

Walsh, 38, was playing his 129th Test over 17 years and nailed Kallis for a duck.

"It has been a big drain thinking about the record from the start of this series and I'm happy to get it out of the way," he said. "But I don't think reaching 600 wickets is likely."

Earlier in the Test, Walsh had been run out without scoring, taking his tally of ducks in Test cricket to 42.

STEVE HANDS IT TO INDIA

MARCH 22 Australia lost their first Test series for two years after Indian spin wizard Harbhajan Singh took 15 wickets in the deciding Third Test in Madras and then hit the winning runs.

His match figures of 15 wickets for 217 runs left India needing 155 to win and they squeezed

home with two wickets to spare, Singh unbeaten at the end on three.

Earlier in the Test, Aussie skipper Steve Waugh became only the sixth batsman to be given out for handling the ball in Test cricket when he palmed the ball away from the stumps after he had miscued a sweep shot from Singh.

India ended Australia's record 16-match winning run by levelling the series in the Second Test, staging a remarkable recovery as Waugh's side became only the third team in Test history to lose a game after enforcing the follow-on.

MIGHTY McMILLAN

MARCH 30 Craig McMillan scored the highest number of runs in one over of Test cricket to help New Zealand to an easy win over Pakistan in Hamilton.

The Kiwi batsman smashed 26 runs off Younis Khan with five fours and a six to set the Test best.

In the first ball of the next over, from Surrey's Saqlain Mushtaq, McMillan hit the ball clean out of the ground to register another six.

The previous record in an over was 24 held by

ONE TO WATCH

JIMMY ORMOND

A PLACE on the England winter Test excursions to India and New Zealand and the one-day tour to Zimbabwe confirmed Jimmy Ormond's arrival as a player to watch next year.

He would not have been given a prayer of playing international cricket at the beginning of the 2001 season but by the end half the county captains were forecasting a bright England future for the Leicestershire pace bowler.

He received the ultimate tribute from the England selectors in August when they chose the strapping 24-year-old bowler to replace the injured Alex Tudor in the final Test against Australia at The Oval.

Ormond, born in Coventry and a late blossoming product of the England Under-19 squad, acquitted himself well in a Test that left the Ashes team he had joined 4-1 losers in the series.

He took only one wicket - Ricky Ponting - in a one-sided Test in which only four Australian wickets were taken but gained recognition for his pace, control and commitment on a pitch that only Glenn McGrath and Shane Warne could exploit.

He showed commendable all-round qualities, too, scoring 18 and 17 in two innings that had occupied almost two hours against the best attack in world cricket.

Many county captains had been shouting his praises all summer, including Somerset's tough Australian overseas leader Jamie Cox.

"Jimmy is a terrific bowler," said Cox. "He bowls well on a flat wicket. His pace is sharp, he swings the ball away and gets the ball in the danger areas for batsmen. That's the recipe for a bright Test future I think."

Ormond's Test call-up on August 20, his birthday, was the reward for his recovery from back and hamstring injuries that had interrupted his career since his debut for Leicestershire in 1995.

He went on an England A tour in 1997-98 before injuries blighted his progress, but 41 first-class wickets at 21 by early August 2001 was enough for the selectors to give him a belated international debut at The Oval ahead of Surrey's Martin Bicknell and Richard Johnson, the Somerset paceman.

And a week after he had made his Test bow, he was at Lord's to play for Leicestershire against Somerset in the Cheltenham and Gloucester Trophy Final with his performance against Lancashire in the Semis helping the Grace Road side book that date at Lord's.

Ormond couldn't inspire his county to victory over Somerset at Lord's but rewards are sure to follow if he continues to progress as he has done over the last year or two.

After being selected for the winter tour to Zimbabwe as a member of England's one-day squad, he was forced to pull out because of injury. But the Leicestershire paceman has put himself in Test contention with his displays in 2001 and a continued improvement is likely to see him win a permanent place in the England attack and selection for the 2003 World Cup squad.

FACTFILE

NAME: James Ormond
DATE OF BIRTH:
20th August, 1977
PLACE OF BIRTH:
Walsgrave, Coventry
HEIGHT: 6ft 3in
WEIGHT: 14st 7lbs
COUNTY DEBUT: For
Leicestershire, 1995

• Was on the England Under-19 tour to Zimbabwe in 1995-96 but returned home after one day because of injury.

• Also went as part of the England A tour to Kenya and Sri Lanka in 1997-98.

• Played for Sydney University Cricket Club in 1996, 1998 and 1999.

• Took six Australian wickets for 54 runs at Grace Road in 1997.

• Is a keen football fan and follows Coventry City.

• Took four wickets in six balls against Derbyshire in 2000.

• Enjoyed figures of 6-33 against Somerset in 1998, his best Championship display.

GOLF • GOLF • GOLF • GOLF • GOLF • GOLF • GOLF • GOLF • GOLF • GOLF • GOLF

GOLF 
GOLF
GOLF
GOLF
GOLF

GOLF
GOLF
GOLF

GOLF • GOLF • GOLF • GOLF • GOLF • GOLF • GOLF • GOLF • GOLF • GOLF • GOLF

THE MAJORS

Retief Goosen misses a simple putt on the last green to send the US Open in to a Play-Off

DUVAL PROSPERS FROM CADDIE CALAMITY

JULY 18-22 American David Duval picked up his first Major with victory in the The Open but his triumph was overshadowed by a major howler from Ian Woosnam's caddie that left the Welshman out of contention for the trophy.

Miles Byrne took the blame when it was revealed on the second tee that Woosnam had 15 clubs in his bag, one more than the rules allowed.

He was handed a two stroke punishment and admitted that the incident could have cost him the trophy.

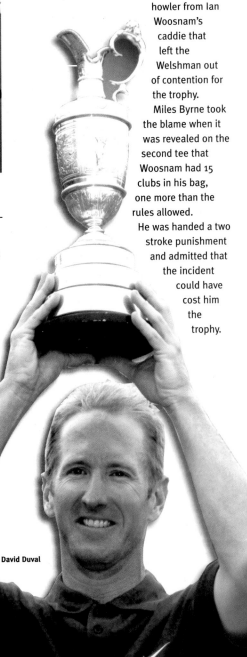

David Duval

WOODS IS THE MASTER

APRIL 5-8 Tiger Woods became the first man in golfing history to hold all four majors at the same time after his two-shot victory in the Masters at Augusta.

The 25-year-old superstar finished at 16-under, two clear of David Duval and three ahead of Phil Mickelson.

Woods' parents, Earl and Tida, were among the spectators around the 18th green when he sunk a birdie putt to complete his victory and take his place in history.

"It was very special to have them both there at a time which I shall always remember," he said, clutching the trophy.

"It was a hard competition and I was pushed to the end by David and Phil, but obviously I am very proud of what I have achieved."

Duval, who missed a five foot putt on the 18th to leave Woods needing a par on the last to triumph, was his usual gracious self in defeat.

"Tiger is a friend of mine and what he has achieved here will stand the test of time," he said.

It was the maestro's second Masters triumph, following his amazing success in 1997 when he stormed to a 12-stroke victory.

RETIEF'S RELIEF

JUNE 14-17 Retief Goosen became only the fifth non-American to win the US Open in 70 years after holding his nerve to win an 18-hole Play-Off with Mark Brooks.

But not before he had taken part in the most bizarre finish to the tournament in history.

On the last of his 72 holes, he was in the enviable position of taking two putts from 10 feet to win the title. His first rolled three feet past and the return never even went close.

His nightmare ending left him level with Brooks on 276, four-under par. It should have been a three way Play-Off but Stewart Cink amazingly missed a putt from 18 inches on the last green to miss out on the leaders by one shot.

South African Goosen dominated the Play-Off from the sixth hole, though, and finished a comfortable two shots clear of Brooks to lift the trophy on the fifth day in front of a packed crowd in Tulsa.

Ian Woosnam and Miles Byrne reflect on that extra club

TEE SHOTS

Of Britain's contingent at the Augusta Masters, only Northern Ireland's Darren Clarke beat the halfway cut, the worst performance by the Brits since 1986 and the first time no Englishman or Scot had played the final two days in 38 years. He finished on 284, 12 shots behind Tiger Woods.

Steve Stricker, lying in third place in the Masters after the third round, had his wife Nicki as his caddie and his father-in-law Dennis Tiziani as his coach.

The Masters' winning cheque of $1.08 million (£700,000) was the first time a million dollars had been paid out at a Major, with the total prize money distributed in excess of £4 million.

"It took me five holes to recover and I finished four behind David in the end, but who knows what might have happened if I had not lost those two shots," he said.

"I would have been two strokes nearer to David and that would have added to the pressure on him over the closing holes.

"I can't think of anything stupid like that which has happened to me before. It's a mistake in the biggest tournament there is in the game. I am going to give Miles some stick over it but I won't sack him."

For a jubilant Duval, who finished on 10-under, victory at Royal Lytham and St Annes was sweet after twice going close to winning the Masters.

"Now I have got one victory, I'm sure it will intensify my drive to win more Majors," he said after lifting the famous claret jug.

TOMS TRIUMPHS

AUGUST 16-19 David Toms sunk a 10ft putt at the last hole to clinch the US PGA Championship in a titanic finish with the unfortunate Phil Mickelson.

Mickelson, who lost out to Tiger Woods on the final green at the Masters, has still to win a Major but went down fighting in this one, leaving a monster 40ft putt on the 18th perched on the edge of the hole.

Toms still had plenty to do at the last but he held firm to land that 10-footer and finish on 265, one stroke clear of Mickelson, pocketing a cool £655,783 in to the bargain.

In a tournament dominated by the Americans, Japan's Shingo Katayama was the only player outside the host country to finish in the top 10.

Convinced that he would finish second in the US Open, Mark Brooks was packing his bags to go home while Retief Goosen was having his mare on the last green and had to rearrange his travelling plans to stay on for the extra 24 hours.

The putter that Retief Goosen used in the US Open was in massive demand after the tournament, despite his three putt finish on the final green. Manufacturers Yes! Golf from Denver claimed they had received a staggering 15,000 orders within a month of his triumph. The state-of-the-art putter has concentric circles on the front of the blade that are meant to give the ball a smoother roll.

David Toms (right) shakes hands with gallant loser - again - Phil Mickelson

TIGER FEAT

Tiger Woods made history in 2001 by becoming the first player to hold all four Majors at the same time. But that is only the beginning for the man who would be king...

DID YOU KNOW?

Earl Woods named his son Tiger after a Vietnamese friend Vuong Dang Phong with the same nickname.

He is the only player to win the prestigious US Amateur Championship three times, recording his hat-trick between 1994 and 1996.

Ever since he was a teenager, Woods has made it clear that his career goal is to top Jack Nicklaus' record of 20 Major Championship victories. He is already almost halfway there.

He had to withdraw from his first US Open because of a badly damaged hand.

In June 1997, at the age of 21 years, he became the youngest player ever to be ranked No.1 in the world.

He was also the fastest to achieve that position, landing the coveted No.1 status only 42 weeks after turning professional.

In 1999 he won 52 per cent of the total prize money on offer on the PGA Golf Tour.

At 21 years, three months and 14 days he became the youngest player ever to win the US Masters when he triumphed in 2000.

He became only the fifth player to achieve the Grand Slam of Majors when he wiped out the opposition to win the The Open in 2000, becoming the youngest player to land all four titles at the same time.

His scoring average of 68.17 in 2000 was the lowest in PGA tour history.

Tiger first held a club at six months old and reportedly shot 48 over nine holes at the Navy Golf Club in California little more than two years later

TIGER WOODS has been a phenomenon for far longer than he has been able to spell the word correctly, or even know what it means.

Ever since he was seen putting against comedian Bob Hope on the Mike Douglas show in America when he was just two-years-old and three years later demonstrating a perfectly honed swing on the TV programme 'That's Incredible', Tiger Woods has been a household name in the United States and tales of his incredible golfing feats have spread across the nation's clubhouses like wildfire.

Like many other sporting prodigies, Eldrick 'Tiger' Woods came from a relatively humble background and was encouraged to play golf at a very early age by his father, Earl, a retired lieutenant in the US Army.

Although Earl claims that he never once pressurised Tiger into playing, his son quickly demonstrated an aptitude for the game, gripping a club for the first time when he was just six months old and reportedly shooting 48 over nine holes at the Navy Golf Club, in Cypress, California, little more than two years later.

While there is probably a certain degree of poetic licence in some of the fantastic stories recounted by Earl concerning his immensely talented offspring, Tiger's prolific performances as a junior are well-documented.

In 1984, when he was just eight years old, he won the Optimist International Junior Championship and repeated the feat a further five times in the next seven years. In 1991, at the age of 15, he became the youngest ever winner of the US Junior National Championship, a title he would successfully defend for the next two years. In 1994, at age 18, he became the youngest ever player to win the prestigious US Amateur Championship.

With the burden of being touted as a future golfing superstar weighing heavily on his shoulders throughout the whole of his young life, perhaps the most impressive thing about Woods is not so much his mental resilience, his athleticism, natural talent or power, but his ability to continually meet and then exceed everyone's expectations of him.

While lesser mortals would probably have allowed the pressure to affect their performances, Tiger has flourished under the media spotlight and met every challenge head on.

As an amateur golfer, Woods won an unprecedented four consecutive US Amateur Championships, quite often clawing his way back from what appeared certain defeat in finals by holing a string of outrageous putts.

He played in a PGA Tour event - the Nissan Open in California - as a 15-year-old junior and although he didn't make the cut he still made a big enough impact on his fellow competitors during the week for them to tip him as a future mega star.

After playing college golf alongside fellow Tour Professionals Casey Martin and Notah Begay III at Sanford University, in California, Woods turned professional in 1996 on the very same day that he announced a $40 million endorsement contract with sportswear giants Nike as well as a highly lucrative deal with golf ball and equipment manufacturer Titleist. Once again, given the enormous price tag placed on his head, it would have been understandable had the 21-year-old Woods wilted under the pressure and faded into the background on Tour. Instead he immediately repaid a huge slice of his sponsors' investment when he won the Las Vegas Invitational and followed that up with victory in the Walt Disney Oldsmobile Classic in Florida.

Despite his quickfire start on the Tour, any lingering doubts as to whether or not Tiger was the real deal were dispelled for good the following season when he won his first Major Championship – The Masters at Augusta National – in spectacular style, finishing a record-breaking 12 shots clear of the field and turning in a four-round total of 18-under-par to clip one stroke off Jack Nicklaus' previous low score of 271.

What made the victory even more remarkable was the fact that Tiger was four-over-par after the first nine holes of the tournament, playing dismally and in danger of missing the cut. However, those who followed him over the remaining 63 holes witnessed some of the most sizzling golf ever played in a Major Championship arena.

After blitzing the field at The Masters, many people expected Woods to immediately increase his Major Championship haul, but the expected avalanche of victories failed to materialise.

Although he continued to win frequently enough on the PGA Tour to top the Money List and remain world number one, Woods spent a year making some adjustments to his swing under the watchful eye of his coach, Butch Harmon, and he didn't recover his best form until August 1999, when he held off a spirited challenge from Spain's Sergio Garcia over the closing holes to win the USPGA Championship, at Medinah in Chicago.

That victory seemed to kick-start his career again and after a top-10 finish in The Masters in 2000, Tiger went into overdrive, winning the remaining three Majors of the year together with the first Major of the 2001 season – The Masters – to become the only player in golf's illustrious history to hold all four Major Championships at the same time.

That feat alone surely places Woods right up there with Jack Nicklaus as one of the two greatest golfers ever to walk the fairways, and as long as he remains healthy, hungry and happy to hit it is surely only a matter of time before he overhauls Nicklaus' long-standing record of 20 Major Championships and puts the question of who really is the best golfer of all time beyond all reasonable doubt.

JACK AND ARNIE

If he continues to accumulate Major Championships at his current rate, Tiger Woods may well go on to become the world's greatest ever golfer, but in doing so he will have to supersede two sporting icons – Jack Nicklaus and Arnold Palmer. Nicklaus' record of 20 Majors, including two amateur titles, is held up as the pinnacle of golfing achievement.

While Nicklaus tops the record books, the game's most popular player has been Arnold Palmer (pic above, with Tiger). Even as a 70-year-old, the 'King' remains a huge attraction and continues to bank a substantial enough income in endorsements to regularly appear in the top-10 list of the world's highest paid sportsmen.

While Nicklaus had the power game and the mental resilience of a great champion, Palmer had the charm, the charisma and his own travelling gallery of fans, known around the world as 'Arnie's Army'.

Palmer's popularity kick-started corporate interest in golf back in the 1960s and he is widely regarded by his grateful peers as the man responsible for creating the huge prize funds that have created millionaires out of so many golfers – a certain Mr Woods included.

STAR OF 2001

PHIL MICKELSON

The icing on the cake for Mickelson's career, would be a Major Championship victory and, little by little, he is inching his way closer and closer to that elusive goal.

At the Masters this year, he went head-to-head with both Tiger Woods and David Duval in the last round only to see some wild tee shots and lapses of concentration on Augusta National's lightning-fast greens put him out of contention over the closing holes and relegate him to third place.

Two months later in the US Open, at Southern Hills, Oklahoma, Mickelson was right up there again just one shot behind the eventual winner Retief Goosen heading into the last nine holes on the final day, yet the very same faults returned to haunt him in the middle of his round and he retreated back into the chasing pack to finish well out of contention in a tie for seventh place by the end of the tournament.

In the Open

P HIL Mickelson has the unwanted tag of the greatest golfer never to have won a Major Championship.

The world number two added two more 'bridesmaid' medals to his growing collection in 2001, going close to winning in both the Masters and the USPGA in a familiar 'so near yet so far' tale.

His arrival on the PGA Tour as a fresh-faced 21-year-old back in 1992 attracted almost the same level of media hysteria as Tiger Woods' much-awaited debut in the pro ranks in 1996.

A highly successful collegiate player, Mickelson represented his country twice against Great Britain and Ireland in the Walker Cup and created headlines the world over when he won a PGA Tour event – The Northern Telecom Open – when still an amateur.

With his free-flowing swing, imaginative short game, silky-smooth putting stroke and clean-cut college boy looks, he was quite understandably touted as America's next superstar golfer.

However, during the early part of his career he made steady, if unspectacular, progress on the Tour, picking up the odd win here and there and posting plenty of top-10 finishes to bank huge earnings, but he never really played a part in the Majors.

Then along came Tiger Woods, who single-handedly raised the benchmarks of professional golf and, in dominating the sport to such an unprecedented level, took the media focus away from Mickelson.

No longer the only golden boy of American golf, the 30-year-old from San Diego, California, has responded to the challenge laid down by Woods admirably, winning no less than 14 times on the PGA Tour during the past five years (19 victories in total) while also emerging as a core member of the American Presidents' Cup and Ryder Cup teams and one of the PGA Tour's most experienced competitors.

Championship, at Royal Lytham, he produced four rounds of steady golf to comfortably make the cut and finish in the top 30, while only a birdie on the 18th hole by a rampant David Toms could pip him to the post in a final day shoot-out in Atlanta for the USPGA.

"I know I have yet to win a Major but I'm getting very close," he said after losing out to Toms.

"I'm not worried about it because I don't just want to win one Major. I'm confident I can go on and win a few of them. It's just the first one that is proving a bit difficult!"

ONE TO WATCH
ADAM SCOTT

FACTFILE

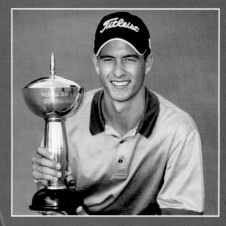

NAME: Adam Scott
DATE OF BIRTH:
July 16th, 1980
PLACE OF BIRTH:
Hope Island, Australia
TURNED PROFESSIONAL:
June 8th, 2000
HEIGHT: 6ft
WEIGHT: 12st 2lbs
INTERESTS: Reading, all
sports, clothes

• Originally coached by
his father, Phil, a PGA
qualified teaching
professional.

• Ranked world number
two amateur when he
turned pro in June 2000.

• Shot course record
63 as an amateur in
Greg Norman Holden
International.

• Won both the
Australian and New
Zealand Junior titles.

• Studied
Communications at
University of Nevada but
dropped out to focus on
golf after 18 months.

• Clinched his European
Tour card for 2001 season
in just eight starts as a
professional.

WHILE Jack Nicklaus always had the likes of Gary Player, Lee Trevino and Arnold Palmer snapping at his heels in the Major Championships during the 1960s and '70s, right now the game desperately needs at least one player to emerge as a serious rival for Tiger Woods.

David Duval, Sergio Garcia, Ernie Els and Phil Mickelson can all, on their day, challenge Woods and occasionally come out on top, but none appears to possess all the ingredients that are required to become a constant nuisance.

Garcia is young, immensely talented and fearless, but his feisty temperament and idiosyncratic swing can let him down in the heat of battle.

Mickelson has the power and the pedigree to match Woods, but he has proved on occasions to be mentally fragile over the closing holes of the Major Championships. Only time will tell if David Duval can use his Open Championship victory at Lytham earlier in the year as the catalyst for even greater things, while Ernie Els appears to have lost the desire for a fierce contest since recently becoming a father for the first time.

The world of golf is still waiting for that challenger to Tiger's crown and many believe Australian Adam Scott is that man.

The 21-year-old Aussie , who studied at the University of Nevada, shares the same coach as Tiger Woods in Butch Harmon and his powerhouse swing which regularly propels the ball over 300 yards off the tee is virtually identical to that of his illustrious stablemate.

After an exceptional amateur career which saw him ranked as the number two in the world before turning professional last year, Scott flew to Las Vegas shortly after turning pro to meet up with coach Harmon at his Rio Secco golf academy.

While he was there, he was invited to play a 'friendly' match by Tiger himself. After Woods comfortably won the match 5&4 on the 14th green, he extended his hand to the young Aussie and said "Welcome to the pro ranks!" The two have been good friends ever since.

Just like Woods, Scott immediately demonstrated his aptitude for pro golf when he clinched his full European Tour card for the 2001 season in just eight events as a professional. The following year, he won his maiden PGA European Tour event – the prestigious Alfred Dunhill Championship, in South Africa – in his first event of the season and he has played well on the few occasions he has competed on the PGA Tour in America.

At present, the only doubt over Scott's claim for golf greatness is his putting, which doesn't quite match the prowess of his long game. However, if he begins to sink a few on the greens, Tiger had better watch out.

SNOOKER
SNOOKER
SNOOKER
SNOOKER
SNOOKER
SNOOKER
SNOOKER

SNOOKER
SNOOKER
SNOOKER
SNOOKER

THE BIG TOURNAMENTS

NOVEMBER 26–DECEMBER 3
BOURNEMOUTH
LIVERPOOL VICTORIA
UK CHAMPIONSHIP

WILSHAW WIZARD WHIPS WILLIAMS

JOHN HIGGINS picked up his first rankings tournament success of the season with victory over Mark Williams in the Final.

The Scot stormed to a 10-4 win to take the title at the Bournemouth International Centre for the second time in his career and stop Williams becoming only the third player in the history of the tournament to retain the trophy.

He hit three century breaks in his victory over the Welshman, with 131, 105 and 115, after beating Stephen Hendry in the Semi-Finals.

It was Higgins' 14th ranking tournament win and put him third in the all-time winners' list behind Hendry and Steve Davis.

But it was to prove to be the Wizard of Wilshaw's only success of a disappointing season that saw him slip to third place in the world rankings behind Williams and Ronnie O'Sullivan.

FEBRUARY 4-11
WEMBLEY
BENSON & HEDGES MASTERS

HUNTER HOLDS HIS NERVE

PAUL HUNTER staged a brilliant comeback to snatch the Benson & Hedges Masters trophy from the grasp of Fergal O'Brien.

The 22-year-old clinched the deciding frame after a titanic 46 minute battle to win the Final 10-9.

A 10 minute game of safety play in the deciding frame left Irishman O'Brien with a matchwinning pot on the green but he missed it and Hunter held his nerve to take the frame 77-44 and with it his second ranking tournament win.

The Leeds-based player, who reached the Final after beating Peter Ebdon and Stephen Hendry at the Quarter-Final and Semi-Final stages, said: "This is the biggest win of my life.

"I made a slow start but the more I got in to the game, the more I was confident I could win the match.

"That last frame was a little bit of a nervy one though!"

Peter Ebdon

APRIL 5-14
ABERDEEN
REGAL SCOTTISH OPEN

PETER PERFECT

PETER EBDON picked up his second success of the 2000-01 season with victory in the Regal Scottish Open at the Aberdeen Exhibition and Conference Centre.

He beat Irishman Ken Doherty 9-7 in a closely fought Final to add to his British Open victory at Plymouth Pavilions at the start of the season.

It was a victory that clearly delighted Ebdon who said: "At the start of the season I set myself a target of winning two ranking tournaments and I'm thrilled that I have achieved that.

"I'm out to push my way back in to the top four ranked players in the world and the way I played in this tournament, I must have a good chance of succeeding."

Ebdon knocked out local favourites Alan McManus, Graeme Dott and Drew Henry along the way as well as recording a Third Round win over Mark Williams and an opening match victory over Jimmy White.

John Higgins - only one ranking tournament victory in 2000-01.

RONNIE ROCKETS TO THE TOP

RONNIE O'SULLIVAN clinched his first World Championship with an 18-14 win over John Higgins in the Final.

Rocket Ronnie played the best snooker throughout the tournament and was a deserving winner after keeping intact the temperament that has let him down so many times in the past.

After taking care of Peter Ebdon 13-6 in the Quarter-Final and then Irish battler Joe Swail 17-11 in the Semis, the Essex Exocet was always in control of the Final against Scotsman and former world champion John Higgins, although he did have a fright when his opponent won four frames in a row to reduce the arrears from 14-7 to 14-11.

O'Sullivan, who celebrated his triumph with his mother Maria and girlfriend Bianca at the Crucible, said: "This is what I came in to snooker for and I'm delighted for my family as well as me because we have come through some really hard times together.

"I am a good friend of Jimmy White's and feel gutted for him that he has never won this title. I wanted to make sure I wasn't in that position."

Beaten finalist Higgins conceded that O'Sullivan was a worthy winner and said: "He's got to be up there with the greats. He has so much natural talent and, when you add great safety play to that, he is one of the best that have ever played the game.

"He makes it look so easy and it is great for the game of snooker, with the way that Ronnie plays, that he has won the world title."

Rocket Ronnie rules the world

BREAKING OFF

Fergal O'Brien's missed opportunity to win the Benson & Hedges Masters means that no Irishman had won the competition since Dennis Taylor in 1987.

Ronnie O'Sullivan went on a brilliant point-scoring spree in the World Championship Final against John Higgins, amassing 362 points without reply at one stage.

Jimmy White was among the audience at the Crucible cheering on his good friend O'Sullivan and twice world champion Alex Higgins also sent his best wishes to the Rocket before the Final.

O'Sullivan had four of the six best rated shots in the World Championship tournament.

Peter Ebdon's victory over Ken Doherty at the Regal Scottish Open denied the Irishman a hat-trick of ranking titles.

The £78,000 first prize at the UK Championships came in handy for John Higgins. He was getting married to childhood sweetheart Denise Whitton a few weeks later and used the money to help pay for the honeymoon in Mauritius.

The top 10 world rankings for the 2001-02 season were: 1. Mark Williams; 2. Ronnie O'Sullivan; 3. John Higgins; 4. Ken Doherty; 5, Stephen Hendry; 6. Matthew Stevens; 7. Peter Ebdon; 8. Stephen Lee; 9. Paul Hunter; 10. Joe Swail.

STAR OF 2001

RONNIE O'SULLIVAN

RONNIE O'Sullivan started the snooker season with talk of retirement from the game, frustrated with his inconsistency that saw him fluctuate from the sublime to the ridiculous. He finished it as world champion after having his best year of his career.

The 25-year-old Essex Exocet, regarded alongside Jimmy White and Alex Higgins as the most naturally gifted snooker players of all-time, finally delivered what his talents had always indicated he was capable of doing – winning the Embassy World title.

His success in the Final over John Higgins at Sheffield rounded off a remarkable year for the Chigwell-based star who had turned professional in a blaze of publicity in 1992.

O'Sullivan opened his campaign with victory in the first tournament of the year, the Champions Cup in Brighton, before adding the China Open, the Irish Masters and the Regal Masters crown to his tally.

But it was the world title that he craved more than any other and the man dubbed the Rocket

'There were doubts in my mind last year about whether I really wanted to carry on playing'

because of the lightning quick way he flashes around the table, in the same way that Hurricane Higgins and Whirlwind White have entertained the crowds down the years, played like a champion from his First Round victory over Andy Hicks onwards.

Dave Harold, Peter Ebdon and Joe Swail were brushed aside as O'Sullivan set up a Final date with Higgins.

But the Scot was always playing 'catch up' in the showdown and the Rocket ran out an 18-14 winner to bring the Crucible to a crescendo.

"I can't describe what winning the World Championship means to me," said the number two ranked player in the game.

"There were doubts in my mind at the start of the year as to whether I wanted to carry on playing but wanting to experience this moment is one of the reasons why I did."

Now O'Sullivan, who can play left-handed as well as his more natural right, is looking forward to more success in the 2001-02 season.

"There are improvements that I need to make in my game," he said. "I don't think I played brilliantly last year, it's just that my head was right and a few things went well for me.

"But there is much more to come from me yet. I don't just think I can better, I know I can. That is what the challenge is for me now."

ONE TO WATCH
PAUL HUNTER

FACTFILE

NAME: Paul Hunter
DATE OF BIRTH:
14th October, 1978
LIVES: Leeds
TURNED PROFESSIONAL:
1995
HIGHEST TOURNAMENT
BREAK: 139

• Started the new
2001-02 season ranked
number nine in the world

• By the end of the 2001
campaign he had picked
up over £500,000 in prize
money.

• His main ambition in
the game is to win the
Embassy World
Championship at
the Crucible. "It's a
fantastic atmosphere
there," he said.

• He enjoyed his most
successful year in the
game last season,
winning £297,150, over
half the total winnings of
his career.

• A big fan of Leeds
United, he goes to Elland
Road as much as he can
to watch the team play.

• His good looks have
made him a pin-up
amongst female fans.

PAUL Hunter shot to prominence in 2001 with victory in the Benson & Hedges Masters after a titanic battle with Ireland's Fergal O'Brien.

The enthralled Wembley crowd watched the 22-year-old claw his way back into the Final from 5-1 and 7-3 down to win a 46 minute deciding 19th frame, 77-44.

He collected his highest ever prize money, £175,000, and included four century breaks in six frames with 129, 101, 132 and a tournament-equalling best of 136.

Stephen Hendry and Matthew Stevens were two of his victims along the way as Hunter enjoyed his finest hour in the game since turning pro in 1995.

It also marked the end of a barren run of three years since his first major tournament triumph.

Hunter first made his mark on the snooker world by winning the Regal Welsh Open at the age of 19, beating John Higgins in the Final.

"It was an amazing start to my career, something that I never really imagined would happen so early," he recalled.

Success seemed certain to follow quickly – but it didn't and he admitted that it took a change of outlook on the game to bring results.

"I was getting knocked out of tournaments when I knew that I should have been performing better," said Hunter.

"It was all very frustrating because I was spending hours and money travelling to competitions and staying in hotels and not making the impact I was hoping for.

"And I wasn't putting enough hours practising to make things change. So it got to the point where I sat down with people close to me and looked at why it wasn't working.

"That was a turning point for me. I cut out some of the late nights and got back to spending hours practising on the table."

And that practise has paid off. He is now ranked in the top ten in the world and has all the credentials to make a real impact on the snooker stage.

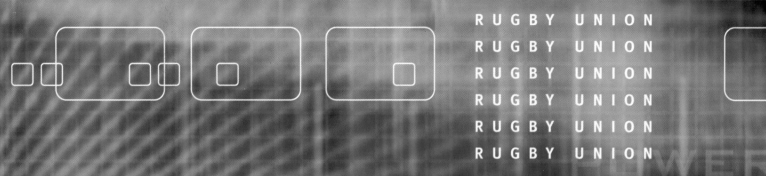

RUGBY UNION
RUGBY UNION
RUGBY UNION
RUGBY UNION
RUGBY UNION
RUGBY UNION

RUGBY UNION
RUGBY UNION
RUGBY UNION

LIONS TOUR

A captivating tour downunder saw the British and Irish Lions give Australia a mighty fright before the World Champions bounced back with a vengeance...

JUNE 30
FIRST TEST
BRISBANE
AUSTRALIA 13 LIONS 29

O'DRISCOLL LEADS LIONS CHARGE

THE British and Irish Lions produced a magnificent performance to win the first of the three Tests against the Australians.

And what made the display even more memorable was that hours before kick-off scrum-half Matt Dawson had hit out at the management of Graham Henry, Andy Robinson and Donal Lenihan, claiming they treated the players 'like kids'.

Dawson even suggested that such was the unrest in the camp that some of the players had contemplated walking out of the tour.

But the team certainly looked unified enough when they took on the World Cup winners in Brisbane and they turned in one of the best performances in Lions history to chalk up their highest ever score against the Wallabies.

Jason Robinson, who had switched codes from league to union only 10 months earlier, took just two minutes to make his mark,

ripping past Chris Latham to score with ease.

Brian O'Driscoll and Rob Henderson dominated at centre and Keith Wood led the forward charge as the Aussies were outplayed in every department.

Daffyd James added a second score just before the interval and then seconds after the restart, Irish flyer O'Driscoll scored a sensational try after opening up the Wallaby defence on halfway.

The rampant No.8, Scott Quinnell, completed the touchdowns for the Lions and only a late recovery from John Eales' side gave the scoreline some respectability.

"It's the best win of my career," said a delighted Lions skipper Martin Johnson.

HOW THEY LINED UP
Australia: Latham (Burke 41), Walker, Herbert, Grey, Roff, Larkham (Flatley 51), Gregan, Stiles, Paul (Foley 51), Panoho (Darwin 61), Griffin, Eales (Cockbain 65), Finegan (Lyons 73), G.Smith, Kefu. Tries: Walker, Grey. Penalties: Walker.
Lions: Perry (Balshaw 41), James, O'Driscoll, Henderson, Robinson, Wilkinson, Howley, Smith (Leonard 73), Wood, Vickery, Johnson, Grewcock, Corry, Hill, Quinnell (Charvis 62). Tries: Robinson, James, O'Driscoll, Quinnell. Cons: Wilkinson 3. Penalties: Wilkinson.

JULY 7
SECOND TEST
MELBOURNE
AUSTRALIA 35 LIONS 14

WILKINSON MISTAKE GIVES AUSSIES LIFELINE

THE Lions were only 40 minutes or so from clinching a decisive 2-0 lead in the series after dominating the first-half of the Second Test. Then the Aussies were handed a lifeline from an unexpected source – England's brilliant Jonny Wilkinson (pic above).

The stand-off tried an ambitious overhead pass deep inside the Lions' own territory and Joe Roff intercepted and burst clear to score a morale-boosting try.

That moment turned the game and the Wallabies, from being 11-6 down at the break, with fit again Neil Back going over the line for the Lions, cruised to a convincing 35-14 victory, their biggest winning margin ever against the tourists.

"The turning point in the game was Roff's try," admitted Lions coach Graham Henry after the defeat.

"We were the better side in the first-half but

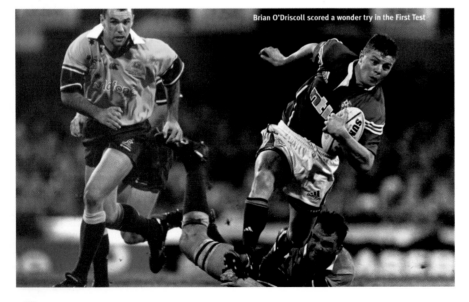

Brian O'Driscoll scored a wonder try in the First Test

once the Australians gained their confidence, they played very well."

Wilkinson's miserable match continued after his rare mistake when he missed chances to kick the Lions back into contention and was then stretchered off five minutes from time suffering from a leg injury.

HOW THEY LINED UP
Australia: Burke, Walker (Latham 47), Herbert, Grey, Roff, Larkham (Flatley 80), Gregan, Stiles, Foley, Moore (Cannon 80), Giffin (Cockbain 40), Eales, Finegan, G.Smith, Kefu. Tries: Roff 2, Burke. Cons: Burke. Penalties: Burke 6.
Lions: Perry (Balshaw 53), James, O'Driscoll, Henderson, Robinson, Wilkinson (Jenkins 75), Howley (Dawson 80), Smith, Wood, Vickery (Leonard 65), Johnson, Grewcock, Hill (Corry 40), Back, Quinnell. Tries: Back. Pens: Wilkinson 3.

JULY 14
THIRD TEST
SYDNEY
AUSTRALIA 29 LIONS 23

HEARTBREAK FOR HENRY'S HEROES

LIONS skipper Martin Johnson led his battle-weary troops off the Sydney pitch a beaten team – but their heads were held high.

Matt Burke's boot proved the difference between the two sides in the last 15 minutes, the Australian full-back nailing two high-pressure penalties to give his side a 29-23 win in an absolute classic.

Missing numerous players through injury, with at least two more suffering painful knocks

during the game, the Lions were still going strong at the final whistle, pushing the Aussies back onto their own line as they searched for the try and conversion that would give them victory.

"I can't speak highly enough of the lads," said coach Graham Henry after the game.

"We had hurdles to jump all tour, mainly through a string of injuries, but they showed huge resilience and can be proud of their achievements especially as they have been playing rugby for 11 months without a break."

A crowd of more than 84,000 packed into Stadium Australia - constructed for the 2000 Sydney Olympics - to watch the thrilling showdown, with Jason Robinson and Jonny Wilkinson for the tourists and Daniel Herbert for the home side sharing the tries, as the Wallabies beat the Lions for the first time ever in a Test series.

HOW THEY LINED UP
Australia: Burke, Walker, Herbert, Grey (Holbeck 78), Roff, Flatley, Gregan, Stiles, Foley, Moore, Harrison, Eales, Finegan (Cockbain 74), G.Smith, Kefu. Tries: Herbert 2. Cons: Burke 2, Penalties: Burke 5.
Lions: Perry, James (Balshaw 74), O'Driscoll, Henderson, Robinson, Wilkinson, Dawson, Smith (Morris 74), Wood, Vickery, Johnson, Grewcock, Corry, Back, Quinnell (Charvis 41). Tries: Robinson, Wilkinson. Cons: Wilkinson 2. Penalties: Wilkinson 3.

Keith Wood shows the pain of defeat

LINE-OUTS

Keith Wood had an unbeaten nine match record with the Lions until the Second Test defeat.

Lions' liaison officer Anton Toia died of a suspected heart attack in the week leading up to the First Test.

The Second Test in Melbourne's Colonial Stadium was played in front of a record crowd of 56,000, the first capacity attendance at the ground. It was also the first time that the Lions had played under a closed roof.

Aussie coach Rod Macqueen announced that he would be quitting his post after the Third Test regardless of the result. ACT Brumbies' coach Eddie Jones was revealed as his replacement. Macqueen's four years in charge of the Wallabies had been the most successful in their history.

Scotland's Andy Nicol was called up as emergency cover after Rob Howley was ruled out of the Third Test. Nicol was on holiday at the time and planned to watch the game as a spectator but ended up on the bench.

Injuries were the biggest problem for the Lions with at least seven players forced out of the tour. Among the worst casualties were Lawrence Dallaglio who suffered knee ligament damage and was ruled out for a year while Ireland's Rob Henderson, who played in all three Tests, had to undergo knee surgery on his return.

LEAGUE AND CUPS

Leicester flattened all before them to win an historic treble at home and in Europe, while Harlequins also flew the flag for Britain.

Dave Walder celebrates his late try

MAY 13
TWICKENHAM
ZURICH CHAMPIONSHIP FINAL
BATH 10 LEICESTER 22

TIGERS CONTINUE BURNING BRIGHT

THE Zurich Championship play-offs, brought in at the end of a long, hard season and played amongst the elite of the Premiership, only confirmed what the rugby world already knew: Leicester are the best in Britain.

The Tigers had already wrapped up the Championship before taking part in a series of play-off games that resulted in a Final with Bath.

In a dour game, tries by Leicester's England duo of Martin Johnson and Austin Healey guided the Tigers towards a comfortable win, although skipper Johnson did get a whack on the head in the closing stages and had to let Pat Howard lead the team up to pick up the trophy.

For Bath their bid to win a 12th trophy at Twickenham in 18 years always looked out of reach.

MAY 13
CARDIFF
PRINCIPALITY CUP
NEATH 8 NEWPORT 13

GLORIOUS GOODBYE FOR TEICHMANN

NEWPORT gave their South African star Gary Teichmann the perfect retirement present with a Principality Cup winners' medal.

The Newport skipper was returning to his homeland after the game and commented: "Winning this match was a wonderful way to end my career.

"The supporters have been magnificent to me since I arrived two years ago and it has been nice to give them something back."

Shane Howarth was Newport's hero with a penalty, dropped goal and conversion after Adrian Garvey had scored a try early in the second-half.

FEBRUARY 24
TWICKENHAM
TETLEY BITTER CUP FINAL
HARLEQUINS 27 NEWCASTLE 30

WALDER CLINCHES CUP FOR NEWCASTLE

FORMER Newcastle United schoolboy footballer Dave Walder achieved something his beloved Magpies couldn't – winning a Cup Final.

The Falcons full-back had dreamed of seeing Alan Shearer lift the FA Cup and was at Wembley in 1998 and 1999 as United twice lost the Final.

But he wrote his own chapter in cup fairytales in front of 70,000 – with the oval ball.

Newcastle were seconds away from defeat when Walder sprung through the Harlequins defence to score one of the most dramatic - and important - tries in the competition.

"I'd always dreamed of something like this," he said. "Watching Newcastle lose in two Cup Finals was heartbreaking and makes this moment all the more fantastic."

Quins' Paul Burke was the man of the match but left with nothing after Walder's late try.

MARCH 17
LEICESTER
ZURICH CHAMPIONSHIP
LEICESTER 51 NEWCASTLE 7

RICHARDS HAILS HIS LEICESTER HEROES

LEICESTER director of rugby Dean Richards hailed his side as the best he had seen at the club after they clinched their third successive League title with a 51-7 win over Newcastle.

"I'm pleased for the players, the coaches and everyone who puts the time and effort in at the club," said the Tigers boss, who has spent most of his career with the club in both playing and coaching capacities.

"I have to say this is the best side I've been involved with. I have played with some great players at Leicester but I don't think the teams of the past that I've been involved with would have been able to match this side.

"The players' willingness to learn, and the time they've spent at either the gym or in front of videos has been brilliant, and they fully deserve their prize as triple champions."

MAY 19
PARIS
HEINEKEN CUP FINAL
LEICESTER 34 STADE FRANCAIS 30

EUROPE MAKES IT THREE FOR LEICESTER

LEICESTER were crowned European Cup winners to complete a remarkable treble – but they left it late.

Leon Lloyd scored a dramatic last minute try in the corner to give the Tigers victory and add the Heineken Cup trophy to the Zurich Premiership and Zurich Championship crowns.

Leicester's triumph at the Parc des Princes made up for their bitter defeat in the 1998 Final when they were hammered by Brive 28-9.

It was the memory of that loss that drove Graham Rowntree, the only man to have featured in every one of their 29 European Cup matches, to push even harder for victory against Stade Francais.

"We had loads of fans in Cardiff for our first Final and we were embarrassed in the end," said the front row forward.

"Winning the European Cup was everything. It was the one trophy that we had not got. The one we all wanted and now it's ours."

Austin Healey picked up the Man of the Match award for his performance in France, highlighted by a brilliant run to set up Lloyd for his match-winning try.

It was the Leicester winger's second score of the game following a touchdown early in the second-half after a kick by Geordan Murphy.

Stade relied on Italian star Diego Dominguez's boot for all their 30 points while Leicester added a further try from Neil Back before Lloyd grabbed the winner.

"The lads were magnificent. This shows how immense they are," said delighted coach Dean Richards.

MAY 20
READING
EUROPEAN SHIELD FINAL
HARLEQUINS 42 NARBONNE 33

BURKE LEADS THE WAY FOR QUINS

HARLEQUINS booked their place in the 2001-02 Heineken Cup by making it an English double over the French in European competition.

Following on from Leicester's win over Stade Francais the day before, Quins took the glory but needed extra-time to do it.

Outplayed at times during the 80 minutes, they held on at 26-26 before their superior fitness showed in the extra period.

Irish stand-off Paul Burke was the star of the show, having a 100 per cent record from his 10 kicks.

Leon Lloyd and Austin Healey signal the treble for Leicester

Quins proved too strong for Narbonne

Leicester joined Bath and Northampton as the only English clubs to have won the European Cup.

Stade Francais' Diego Dominguez created a European Cup record with his 30 point haul in the Final, the best individual point scoring performance in a game.

Following his club's treble triumph Leicester skipper Martin Johnson announced that he was signing a new two year contract at Welford Road that would take him through to 2003.

Stuart Reid's last match for French club Narbonne ended in defeat in the European Shield before he returned to Scotland to rejoin the police force.

Newport's win in the Principality Cup Final was their first in 24 years.

Bath's defeat to Leicester in the Zurich Championship play-offs was their first defeat at Twickenham in 12 matches there.

JOHNSON
A GIANT AMONG MEN

Loved by his fans, respected by his team-mates, consulted by his management, feared by his opponents. When England and the Lions look for a skipper there is really only one candidate – Martin Johnson.

In a sport full of giants, one man stands head and shoulders above the rest: the Leicester and two-times British & Irish Lions captain Martin Johnson.

A veteran of three Lions tours, the Solihull-born lock has been there and done it all with club and country and his experience, never-say-die attitude and powerful displays make him one of the most valuable men in the oval ball game.

Memorably described by French centre Thomas Castaignede in 2001 as "not the kind of guy whose hand you'd want to shake in a dark street", Johnson has had several bust-ups with the game's authorities and his opponents during his years at the top, mainly due to his sometimes over-zealous determination to win. But he remains a powerful talisman for any side he represents.

Other nations may lay claim to players of greater match-winning ability - Australia's George Gregan, Christian Cullen of New Zealand and flying Irish centre Brian O'Driscoll, for instance - but in terms of raw drive and determination, and an utter refusal to accept defeat, it is hard to look beyond Martin Johnson.

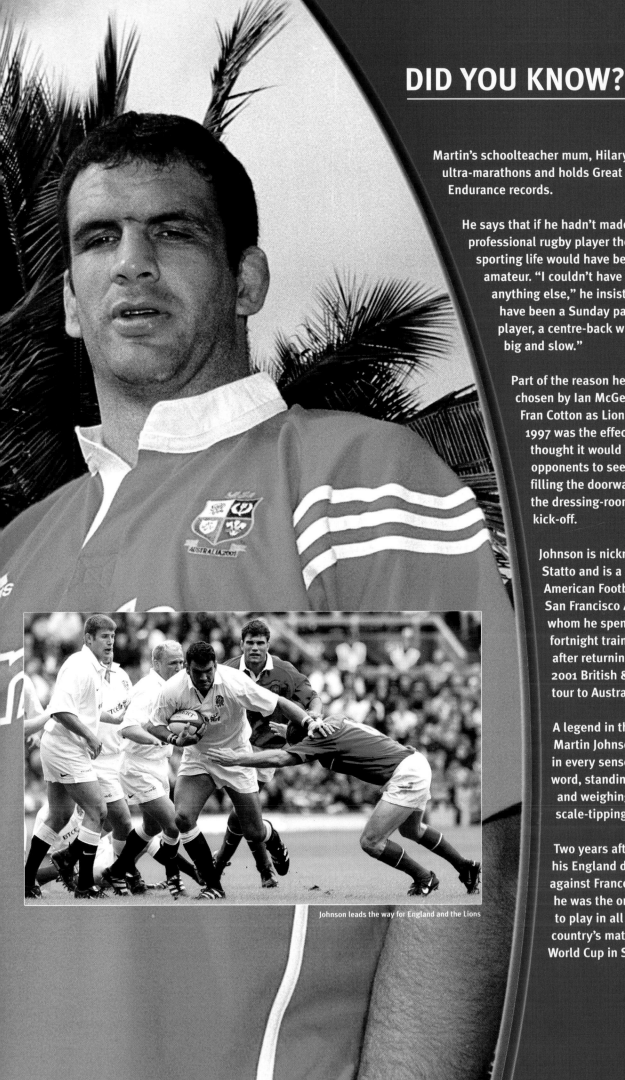

DID YOU KNOW?

Martin's schoolteacher mum, Hilary, has run ultra-marathons and holds Great Britain Endurance records.

He says that if he hadn't made it as a professional rugby player then his sporting life would have been strictly amateur. "I couldn't have been anything else," he insists. "I would have been a Sunday park football player, a centre-back who was too big and slow."

Part of the reason he was chosen by Ian McGeechan and Fran Cotton as Lions' captain in 1997 was the effect they thought it would have on opponents to see Johnson filling the doorway of the dressing-room before kick-off.

Johnson is nicknamed Statto and is a big fan of American Football side San Francisco 49ers, whom he spent a fortnight training with after returning from the 2001 British & Irish Lions tour to Australia.

A legend in the game, Martin Johnson is a giant in every sense of the word, standing at 6ft 7in and weighing in at a scale-tipping 18st 7lb.

Two years after making his England debut against France in 1993, he was the only forward to play in all five of his country's matches in the World Cup in South Africa.

Johnson leads the way for England and the Lions

119

'He tries so hard, his tackle count is always so high and he is a leader by example. He is a very inspirational captain, every game, every time'

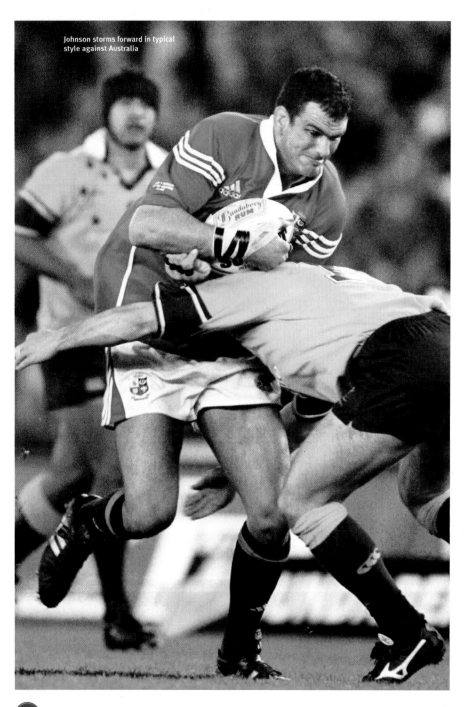

Johnson storms forward in typical style against Australia

A former bank official in Market Harborough, he had already represented England Schools when he travelled to New Zealand to continue his rugby education in one of the sport's most passionate and successful hotbeds.

He spent 18 months fine-tuning his game with Wigston and College Old Boys and also turned out for King Country in the highly-competitive Inter-Provincial Championship.

During that time, Johnson pulled off a rare feat, becoming one of very few foreigners to represent New Zealand in an international fixture. He turned out for the NZ U21 Colts against their Australian counterparts on a two-week tour of the island continent, alongside future All Black legends such as Va'aiga Tuigamala, John Timu and Blair Larsen.

"There was a lot of pressure on that tour," recalls Johnson now. "When they pick the New Zealand U21 team it's read out live at the end of the news. One of the things which struck me was how big a thing it was."

The initial plan had been to stay in New Zealand for twelve months, but a troublesome shoulder injury stretched his trip to a year-and-a-half before a return to England and his inexorable rise to international stardom and a position as the world's number one front-of-the-line jumper.

Already well known to his only senior club side, Leicester, Johnson quickly progressed to the England U21 side and from there to the 'B' set-up, making his debut away to France in February 1992.

But it was the following season, 1992-93, that he really shot to fame, emerging from the giant shadow of Wade Dooley to claim a place at full international level.

Johnson was expecting to play for England 'A' against France 'A' in mid-January 1993 when the call came to pack his bags and make his way to Twickenham as back-up after Dooley pulled out of the full squad with a thigh injury.

Less than 24 hours later, Johnson was sprinting out at the home of rugby union and into the boiling atmosphere of a crucial

Johnson celebrates another triumph with his Leicester side

Five Nations match against the French. A man who was to become an English rugby legend had taken his first steps on the international stage.

After a brief return to the 'A' team to gain more experience, Johnson's meteoric rise to the top continued when he was recalled from an England XV tour of Canada to join the British Lions for their series in New Zealand.

Again, it was an injury to Dooley which paved the way for Johnson's inclusion, and once again the big man grasped the opportunity with both hands, impressing in training and going on to play the final two Tests.

On the domestic front, Leicester continued to follow in the wake of all-conquering Bath, but Johnson was beginning to forge a reputation for himself at international level - albeit only in his home country.

His Leicester team-mate and Australian centre Pat Howard explains: "Coming from Australia I didn't really know much about Johnno. He's not as well known outside England as you might expect, but you soon learn to respect him as a player.

"He tries so hard, his tackle count is always so high and he's a leader by example.

"He is a very inspirational captain, every game, every time."

By the beginning of the 1996-97 campaign,

Johnson had established himself as an integral part of the England side - by its end he was celebrating glorious success as the captain of the Lions side that toured South Africa.

"If you'd told me at the start of 1997 what was going to happen I'd have laughed in your face," he says, before adding with classic understatement: "It was...very good."

For the record, Johnson led Leicester to a Pilkington Cup triumph over Sale, was awarded the RFU Player of the Year trophy, picked up the Team of the Year award and received the OBE.

But it was the Lions' achievement that really captured the public's imagination. Dismissed as no-hopers before the tour, Johnson led from the front as the Lions recorded a memorable 2-1 series win.

Four years later Johnson remains at the pinnacle of the game. Last season he captained a new look and one of the most highly spectacular England sides of all time, and in the summer of 2001 became the first man ever to be re-appointed as Lions captain.

In an injury-ravaged Australian tour, the men in red won the First Test handsomely in Brisbane but then capitulated in Tests two and three to lose a series to the World Champions for the first time ever.

"When I look back, not winning that series will be one of the big disappointments of my career," said Johnson.

"But these things happen, you can never get it back. It is not like playing for Leicester or England, when there is another match to focus on, but I am not the type of person who is going to mope around and worry about it. I just want to get on and meet the next challenge."

And that can only be bad news for the opponents of Leicester and England.

ENGLAND EXPRESS

Having long been criticised for the style of their play, England took last season's Six Nations tournament by the scruff of the neck and gave a thrilling display of open, expansive, attacking rugby.

Led by captain Martin Johnson they lived up to coach Clive Woodward's pre-series prediction that "we are going to give somebody a good hiding very soon" by crushing Wales in their opener.

Rampant England ran in six tries, with Will Greenwood touching down a hat-trick.

The winning score of 44-15 racked up a record loss for Wales to the English in Cardiff and left the rest of the countries in the Six Nations wondering how to stem the white tide.

Martin Johnson picks out the display as the highlight of the year.

"People were saying the new stadium was great and the crowd were awesome," he said. "But we had it won by half-time and there's a knowledge now that if we play our way we've got a good chance of winning any game we're in."

Johnson leads out the Lions in Australia

STAR OF 2001

BRIAN O'DRISCOLL

during the 2000 Six Nations Championship when he scored tries against Scotland, Italy and a devastating hat-trick of touchdowns against France to send them crashing to defeat against the Irish in Paris for the first time in 28 years.

He was injured in Ireland's game against the Barbarians at the end of that season and missed the summer tour of the Americas. But he returned to competitive rugby for Leinster in September 2000 and played against Japan and South Africa that autumn.

The flying centre missed Ireland's opening Six Nations game against Italy in Rome at the start of the 2001 Championship campaign but returned to the side to win his 15th cap against France in Dublin. And the French bogey-man struck again, scoring another try, the ninth of his short international career, to win the 'Man of the Match' vote at Lansdowne Road.

Another score in front of the Lions selectors on lucky Friday, 13th April, 2001 for the Rest of Ireland against Munster in Limerick merely confirmed the thoughts of the watching Lions

O'Driscoll leaves the Aussies spellbound with a brilliant try in the First Test on the Lions' tour

IN less than three years Brian O'Driscoll has shot from the obscurity of the Irish team's replacements bench to world superstar status.

Those rugby fans lucky enough to be packed into the Brisbane stadium that hosted the first Lions Test of the 2001 tour will corroborate the mounting belief that the Dubliner, born on 21st January 1979, is blessed with pure sporting genius.

He still lives at home with his parents, enjoys a quiet evening in front of the television, and takes kindly to an occasional invitation from his mates for a good night out.

He is quiet, undemonstrative, thoughtful and intelligent but any pretence to preferring a private life to a public one has been shot down

in flames by the sheer brilliance of this player when wearing either the green jersey of Ireland or the famous red of the Lions on tour.

The golden boy of Irish rugby is acknowledged already as the finest Irish centre since Mike Gibson, one of the greatest three-quarters of the post-war years.

Gibson was blessed with fierce mental and physical resilience, allied to a brilliant playmaking mind. He was a singular man who kept a determinedly low profile and Brian Gerard O'Driscoll, educated at Blackrock College and University College, Dublin, could have been cast from the same mould that carried Gibson to glory for Ireland and the Lions on five tours.

O'Driscoll's claim to greatness was fashioned

management, Graham Henry and Donal Lenihan, that in O'Driscoll they had a player capable of destroying the Wallabies.

And he justified that faith by scoring a wonder try from inside his own half and terrorising the Wallaby backs in the First Test at the Gabba on June 30, 2001.

Rob Henderson, his Lions and Ireland team-mate, says glowingly: "Brian is the most level-headed man you could ever meet.

"He rarely puts a foot wrong on the pitch, nor a word wrong off it. The way he's handled himself and all the exposure he's had, first in Ireland and now globally, shows a maturity beyond his years.

"That's the mark of a great player."

Few would disagree with those sentiments.

ONE TO WATCH

JASON ROBINSON

NAME: Jason Robinson
DATE OF BIRTH:
30th July, 1974
PLACE OF BIRTH: Leeds
CLUB: Sale Sharks
INTERNATIONAL DEBUT:
February 17th v Italy at
Twickenham

• Scored 184 tries in 302
league games for Wigan
before changing codes
and joining Sale Sharks.

• Also gained 12 Great
Britain caps and seven for
England in rugby league.

• Used only as a
substitute by England in
the 2001 Six Nations
Championship and did
not score in his three
appearances before the
delayed Ireland game.

• Made history by
scoring five tries on his
Lions debut in the 83-6
win over Queensland
President's XV.

• The only other time
he had scored five tries
in a game was for Wigan
against Oldham in 1998.

• Received hate mail from
rugby league fans when
he quit Wigan for Sale
saying he was a traitor
for switching codes.

JASON Robinson has illuminated the rugby union game with much the same electricity that Jonah Lomu gave to the 1995 World Cup in South Africa.

It took the dynamic wing, who renounced his rugby league background in favour of a future in the union game, just three minutes of his Lions debut in the Brisbane Test to open his try-scoring account and launch a career that could scale the heights even the legendary All Black has achieved.

Indeed, former Australia captain Michael Lynagh believes Robinson has the commitment, firepower and extravagant skills to rival everything Lomu has brought to rugby union.

"Jason is an extraordinary talent and if harnessed correctly could be a player capable of rivalling Jonah Lomu in terms of exhilaration on the field," said Lynagh, who was part of the Australian side that won the World Cup in 1991.

"He is still raw but with a little time and in the right environment he is going to be a matchwinner for England."

The ex-Wallaby captain made the startling assessment of the gifted Robinson moments after the dynamic pocket battleship had become only the eighth player to appear for the Lions without having started a Test for his country.

He was the highest individual try-scorer with 10 touchdowns by the end of the Lions tour and when England coach Clive Woodward chooses his 2002 Six Nations Championship squad, the Sale flier can expect to be one of the first names on the team sheet.

Robinson dabbled with a union career in 1996 when he spent four months at Bath but the timing was wrong and he returned to Wigan chastened by the experience.

But he returned to the 15-man code, making his debut for Zurich Premiership side Sale Sharks against Coventry in the Tetley's Bitter Cup in November 2000 after a glittering rugby league career.

Recognised as the fittest player on the union circuit within weeks of joining Sale but the least experienced in the game-plans and tricks of the union game, he became a quick learner and his skills were soon recognised at Twickenham when he made the England 'A' team against Wales at Wrexham.

It was onwards and upwards from there with Robinson rising from rugby union club rookie to Lions Test wing in just eight months.

Now there is no stopping the Robbo bandwagon as it gathers legendary pace in much the same way that Lomu's career gained superstar status after his first World Cup.

The next 12 months promise to be an exciting time for the wing wizard. He is set to join an already powerful Engand side that should provide him with plenty of opportunities to show what he is really capable of.

And by the end of 2002, even Jonah Lomu could be looking over his shoulder at the next megastar of rugby union.

Robinson celebrates his try on his Test debut against the Australians

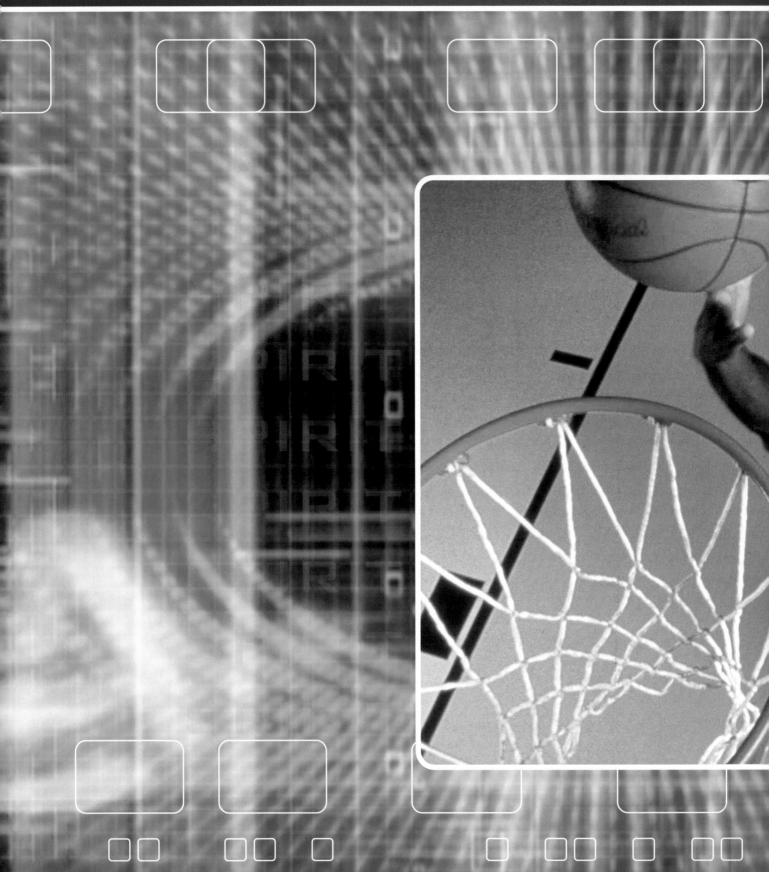

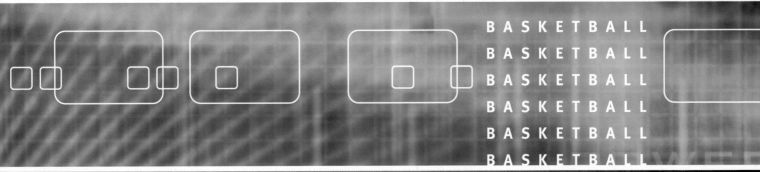

BASKETBALL
BASKETBALL
BASKETBALL
BASKETBALL
BASKETBALL
BASKETBALL

BASKETBALL
BASKETBALL
BASKETBALL
BASKETBALL

THE BBL YEAR

LEICESTER RIDING HIGH

JANUARY 7: Leicester Riders won the National Cup for the first time in their history with a sensational 84-82 win over London Leopards.

Local hero Karl Brown made the decisive basket for Leicester from a free-throw in the closing seconds.

"Things have not gone brilliantly for us in the League but we deserved the cup and now we can build on this success," said Brown.

Ralph Blalock, was voted Most Valuable Player in the game for his 26 point contribution.

SCANTLEBURY MAKES HISTORY

MARCH 4: Peter Scantlebury became the leading points scorer in British Basketball League history when he opened his account for Sheffield Sharks against Newcastle. He passed Russ Saunders' record of 8,945 points and went on to score another 16 points in the game. A presentation was made to celebrate his record.

JETS TAKE OFF

MARCH 24: Chester Jets clinched the Uni-ball Trophy Final with a comfortable 92-81 win over Newcastle Eagles at Birmingham's National Indoor Arena to record their first major trophy success in their history.

Newcastle made the running early on with Steve Ogunjimi, Donnie Johnson and Tony Windless all scoring from long range before the Jets starting to dictate the play.

Former NBA centre, Loren Meyer, caused problems for the Eagles defence and contributed 11 points to Chester's first-half advantage at 49-37.

And it was the big man who did the damage in the last two quarters, scoring successive three-pointers soon after the interval and then adding further baskets in the closing five minutes to stifle any hopes Eagles had of getting back in the game.

Meyer's final tally of 26 points proved decisive but the Most Valuable Player award went to Jets skipper, New Zealander Pero Cameron.

SHEFFIELD STUNNED

MAY 5: Sheffield Sharks were the final victims of an amazing run by Leicester Riders that gave the Midlands club the British Basketball League Championship trophy.

Leicester were not even considered as possible title winners at the start of the season but they rode on the crest of a wave under the coaching of Billy Mims.

Victory over the London Leopards in the National Cup Final in January launched them on the road to glory via the Play-Offs with wins over Chester Jets and Southern Conference champs London Towers setting up a showdown with Sheffield.

Sharks led 45-36 at the break but Leicester fought back quickly, driven on by their fans and going into the final quarter led by seven points.

The lead was cut to just two points with only a couple of minutes left but Ralph Blalock converted two free-throws to open up an eight point cushion before Riders ran out 84-75 winners in one of the most sensational upsets in the history of British basketball.

Leicester celebrate their historic season

FAULTY TOWERS

JULY 10: London Towers endured a nightmare time in the ULEB Euroleague in 2000-01 – and were then handed a terrible draw for this year's campaign.

After winning only one of their 10 matches in the competition last term and finishing one off the bottom in their group, they were stunned to find that three former European basketball champions had been drawn alongside them in Group B.

Reigning champions Kinder Bologna, Spanish giants Barcelona and formidable Lithuanians, Zalgiris Kaunas, present a severe test to Towers' prospects of qualifying for the Play-Offs from the eight team group.

Below: Towers and Barcelona meet again

BAD BOY BOB HEADS HOME

JULY 23: London Leopards lost their outspoken but brilliant coach Bob Donewald to the NBA.

The 32-year-old American agreed to return home and become assistant coach of the Charlotte Hornets in a two year deal that will net him £180,000.

Hornets, one of the top US basketball sides, had been negotiating with Donewald for a while before he made his move.

He becomes the first coach of a British team to take up a position in the American league, widely regarded as the best in the world.

Donewald had been coaching in Britain for five years, making a name for himself, good and bad, with Derby, Leicester and the Leopards.

"I have had a great time in Britain over the last five years and really enjoyed it, especially at the Leopards," he said.

"I have worked with some top players and learned a lot about the game."

Donewald had been in charge of the Leopards for two years and took them to the 2001 National Cup Final but he also had his run-ins with officials during his stay in Britain.

"Bob comes from a basketball family and has had some good coaching experience in England. He will be a valuable addition to our staff," said Charlotte head coach Paul Silas.

OFF THE BOARDS

Chester Jets' skipper Pero Cameron was watched in the Uni-ball Trophy Final by his parents who had flown over from their home in New Zealand for the occasion.

Jets' Robbie Peers became the first English coach since Mike Bett in 1995 to lead a side to Uni-Ball Trophy Final success.

Former London Leopards coach Bob Donewald was fined £300 after having a go at the line court judges during an after-match TV interview at the end of the 2001 season.

Donewald was so annoyed at Leopards' defeat by Leicester Riders in the National Cup Final that he refused to attend the after-match press conference.

Leicester became the first team seeded eighth in the Play-Offs to win the British Basketball Championship Trophy following their victory over Sheffield Sharks.

The Northern Conference won the 13th British Basketball League All Star game 161-148 at the Telewest Arena, Newcastle, in January. It was the first time the North had won the annual event in four years and left the overall score at 7-6 to the South. Newcastle Eagles star Tony Windless was named as Most Valuable Player after scoring 25 points.

STAR OF 2001

BILLY MIMS

YOU could have forgiven Billy Mims for wearing a wry smile after he had guided his Leicester Riders team to victory over the London Leopards at the National Cup Final in January 2001.

For it was the Leopards who dumped him as their coach in the early stages of the 1999-2000 season and left him wondering whether he still had a career in the game.

For the five years Mims had spent at Leopards, he had been ranked among the top coaches in the British game.

He guided them to successive Championships between 1996 and 1998 and picked up the Coach of the Year award in the 1997-98 season, as well as guiding Leopards to National Cup success in 1997.

But suddenly he was out on his backside, replaced by Bob Donewald, and it hurt.

"Fifteen months ago I was out of a job and didn't really know what I was going to do," he recalled.

"I didn't know whether I would stay in the game or what but then the opportunity came along to work with Leicester."

So revenge was sweet for the colourful Mims with that surprise 84-82 win over his old club at the Sheffield Arena in January.

"Taking the club that gave me back my life to their first trophy – against the team that stopped me coaching was very special to me," said Mims, who also worked for Sky TV as a commentator when not involved in the action.

"In fact it was the best moment in my career. That's how much it means to me."

While Leicester might have done Mims a favour in taking him on as their coach, he has more than repaid their faith in him.

The National Cup was the first trophy in their 33-year history and Mims didn't stop there, guiding his team on to their first British Basketball League Championship with an amazing victory over favourites Sheffield Sharks in May 2001.

Down at the break by 36 points to 45, his words of inspiration paid handsome dividends after the interval with Leicester running out 84-75 winners, recording one of the biggest fairytale stories in the competition's history.

"I said after we beat the Leopards that we had been the Cinderella club of British basketball and the fairytale certainly came true on that occasion," said Mims, who signed a three year contract in the summer of 2000.

"Now we are Champions and it feels great." From the moment he marked his first game in charge of Riders by stopping their 15 game run without a BBL victory with a win over, ironically, London Leopards, Mims has transformed Leicester in to the best offensive team in the country. And that's fact - not fairytale!

ONE TO WATCH

JOHN McCORD

FACTFILE

NAME: John McCord
DATE OF BIRTH:
26th February, 1972
BIRTHPLACE:
The Bronx, New York
HEIGHT: 6ft 6in
BBL CLUBS:
Thames Valley Tigers,
Edinburgh Rocks,
Chester Jets

• He attended Cornell
University in the
United States.

• The 29-year-old had
two spells at Thames
Valley Tigers, 1997-99
and then the 2000-01
campaign after spending
a year with the
Edinburgh Rocks.

• He has been a regular
in the All-Star game
since 1998.

• The top scorer in the
British Basketball
League in 2000-01, he
averaged 25.2 points
per game.

• He was named as the
Most Valuable Player in
the All-Star game in
1997-98, the annual
match played between
the cream of the players
in the Northern and
Southern Conferences.

CHESTER Jets showed their intention to be strong challengers for the British Basketball League in the coming seasons by signing one of the top players in the game – John McCord.

The Jets enjoyed the best campaign in their history last season with victory in the Uni-ball Trophy Final and a runners-up place in the Northern Conference.

Leicester Riders ended their participation in

the Championship Play-Offs at the Quarter-Final stage but they are determined to become a dominant force in the game and after losing BBL Player of the Year Loren Meyer, who returned to the United States at the end of last season, they decided that McCord was the man they wanted to lead the team forward.

"Loren Meyer is an excellent player and it was important that we brought in someone that matched his quality," said Jets' head coach, Robbie Peers, who was voted BBL Coach of the Year in 2001.

"McCord knows the league very well. He was the top scorer in the BBL with Thames Valley Tigers last season, has a lot of experience at the top level and we are delighted to have him at the club.

"John is very athletic and a real team player. His goals record is excellent but he only takes shots when he knows he has a good chance of a basket.

"We are building a team for the future. A championship team and John is going to be a big part of that."

If McCord's record is anything to go by, Jets are on to a winner. After joining the Thames Valley Tigers in 1997, he helped them to successive runners-up places in the Championship as well as landing the Cup in 1998, with the 6ft 6in New Yorker winning the Most Valuable Player award in the Final.

He spent a year at Edinburgh Rocks before going back to Tigers last season and in the last four terms, he has been selected every year for the All-Star clash between the two regions.

He did have his problems last season though and was involved in a bust-up during a game against Derby Storm at The Thunderdome. The power forward was accused of charging Storm's Hilroy Thomas, the two swapped several blows on court and were both dismissed, still arguing.

McCord was banned for a match but Jets will be hoping that he provides a few knock-out blows in front of the boards over the coming seasons to take them to the title they crave.

MOTOR SPORTS
MOTOR SPORTS
MOTOR SPORTS
MOTOR SPORTS
MOTOR SPORTS
MOTOR SPORTS

MOTOR SPORTS
MOTOR SPORTS
MOTOR SPORTS
MOTOR SPORTS
MOTOR SPORTS
MOTOR SPORTS

FORMULA ONE

Another season of drama in F1 with Michael Schumacher cruising to the Championship, his brother winning at last and lucky escapes for others...

APRIL 16
IMOLA
SAN MARINO

RALF WINS AT LAST

RALF Schumacher emerged from the shadow of his older brother Michael to win his first Grand Prix in 70 races.

The BMW Williams driver made his debut in F1 in 1996 with Jordan before switching to his current team two years later, but had rarely threatened to take top spot on the podium until the 2001 season.

He led from start to finish at Imola and ensured that the Schumachers became the first set of brothers to each win a Grand Prix.

"I have watched Michael win races many times and wished it could be me," said Ralf, seven years younger than his brother.

"So finally crossing the line first is a great experience. I have waited long enough for it, that's for sure."

Coulthard can't find a way past Bernoldi in Monte Carlo

Ralf Schumacher celebrates victory

APRIL 25
LAUSITZ
GERMANY

ALBORETO TRAGEDY

FORMER Italian Grand Prix driver Michele Alboreto was killed in a 200mph crash while testing his Audi R8 for the Le Mans 24-hour race in June.

The accident happened at the Lausitz circuit near Dresden in Germany when his car careered off the track and somersaulted several times before crashing into a barrier.

Alboreto finished second to Alain Prost in the 1985 World Championship, driving for Ferrari. He competed in 194 Grands Prix and also raced for Tyrrell, Lola, Arrows, Footwork and Minardi, winning three races with Ferrari and two with Tyrrell. He also won Le Mans in 1997.

Five months after Alboreto's tragic accident, another former Italian F1 driver, Alex Zanardi, had both his legs amputated after a crash on the same Lausitz circuit. He was leading the American Memorial 500 race when he spun in to the path of another car after exiting the pits.

MAY 27
MONTE CARLO
MONACO

LAUNCH CONTROL CHAOS FOR DC

DAVID Coulthard's Championship hopes stalled – literally – as his launch control system failed on the warm-up lap at Monte Carlo meaning he had to start the race from the back of the grid.

It was the second time his McLaren had suffered the problem in three races and left the Scot punching the steering wheel in anger.

Launch control was the latest hi-tech addition to the Grand Prix scene for 2001 and was brought in to stop wheelspin at the start of the race, allowing a cleaner getaway.

But for Coulthard, nicknamed DC, it proved a nightmare and from what should have been a pole position start, he ended up with no chance of winning although he did well to finish fifth, despite being held up by youngster Enrique Bernoldi for almost half the race.

"My over-riding emotion is one of total frustration," said Coulthard after the race.

JULY 29
HOCKENHEIM
GERMANY

WHEEL OF FORTUNE

THE world of Grand Prix racing breathed a huge sigh of relief after one of the most spectacular crashes in the recent history of the sport ended with no casualties.

Michael Schumacher's Ferrari crawled away from the start line suffering from gear problems. All the cars behind him managed to swerve around the scarlet machine apart from Luciano Burti, whose Prost catapulted over the rear of Schumacher's car and flew across the path of Enrique Bernoldi's Arrows.

By pure good fortune, the young Brazilian suffered no injury as his car was hit by wreckage from the stricken Prost.

"I was pretty lucky, I saw another car flying over my head and the wheel landed on my car and broke the engine cover and the rear wing. It was a shock," said Bernoldi.

Burti carried on in the spare Prost but damage to his right arm suffered in the crash forced him to skid off after the race had been re-started.

Schumacher, who switched to the spare Ferrari but was forced to pull out of the race with engine problems in the closing stages, added: "It was a scary situation for a few seconds and we were lucky because it could have been a lot worse."

A month later at Spa in Belgium, Burti was involved in another terrifying crash, heading straight in to the tyre wall at 180mph after a clash with Eddie Irvine's Jaguar.

He was air-lifted to hospital where a scan revealed bruising and concussion but no more serious damage, much to the relief of F1.

AUGUST 19
HUNGARORING
HUNGARY

TITLE AND HISTORY FOR SCHUMEY

MICHAEL Schumacher celebrated equalling Alain Prost's record of 51 Grand Prix wins in the best possible way – with the Drivers' Championship crown.

The German led from start to finish at the Hungaroring to take the chequered flag in 1 hour, 41 minutes and 49.675 seconds and with it his fourth world title.

Schumacher, who was followed home by his Ferrari team-mate Rubens Barrichello, had been in pole position in the race for the Championship since he comfortably won the first Grand Prix of the season in Australia.

"I wasn't optimistic that we would clinch the title here but the car went magnificently," said the delighted champion after the race.

"It is hard to believe that I have won the title again because when I entered F1 in 1991, I never dreamed I would be so successful."

His closest challenger all season was David Coulthard but a third place finish in Hungary left the Scotsman 43 points behind the Ferrari No.1 with only the Belgian, Italian, USA and Japanese Grands Prix left.

"There is no doubt that Michael deserves the Championship. He has made no mistakes and used the car to the best of his ability," conceded the McLaren driver.

Ferrari also clinched the Constructors' title with their first and second finish in Hungary.

RACING LINE

The first F1 race of the season in Australia was overshadowed by the death of a marshal, Graham Beveridge, who was hit by a flying wheel from Jacques Villeneuve's BAR after he hit a wall.

Jenson Button picked up points for the first time in the Benetton after finishing fifth in the German Grand Prix. It was the best performance at the time for the struggling Italian outfit with their other driver, Giancarlo Fisichella, taking fourth spot in the same race. Fisichella went on to finish third in Hungary.

Ken Tyrrell, the man who discovered Jackie Stewart and guided him to three World Championships with the Tyrrell team in 1969, 1971 and 1973, died in August after a long illness.

Eddie Jordan sacked Heinz-Harald Frentzen from his position as partner to Jarno Trulli in the Jordan days before the German driver was due to compete in his home Grand Prix. Frentzen had scored just six points and was 11th in the Championship at the time.

Two weeks later Frentzen joined Prost with Jean Alesi making the reverse journey.

Ralf Schumacher's win at Imola was the first F1 success for BMW Williams since Jacques Villeneuve won in Luxembourg in 1997.

Burti's Prost somersaults through the air at the start of the German Grand Prix

STAR OF 2001

MICHAEL SCHUMACHER

PUT the best driver in Formula 1 in the most reliable car in Formula 1 and the conclusion is almost inevitable – World Championship success.

Michael Schumacher has been arguably the best driver in the world ever since he stormed to his first F1 title in the Benetton in 1994.

Now he is driving a Ferrari car that is finally matching up to the reputation of the most famous car manufacturers in the business.

The 2001 season was a dream for the German ace. Already champion driver after taking Ferrari to their first title since 1979, in 2000 he wrapped up the campaign in Hungary in August with the 51st win of his career, equalling the achievement of Alain Prost.

With four races remaining you would have got short odds on Schumacher not only adding to that tally but also recording the highest number of wins in a season and the most number of points in a year.

He duly pocketed a record 52nd Grand Prix win at Spa, Belgium, in the next race.

And such is the professionalism of the Ferrari number one that it was clear that he was never prepared to just wind down the season after securing the Drivers' Championship.

"Winning the title is something that I find hard to put in to words other than to say it is very special," said Schumey after his start to finish victory at the Hungaroring.

"But it's a real team effort. We have some great people at Ferrari and we all get on so well, everyone is pulling in the same direction.

"Every race is a challenge to me. That is what I like about Formula One. And it does not matter whether I am racing for the Championship, have won the Championship or can't win the Championship, I go out to win every time I step into the car.

"That is my passion, that is what I went into the sport for."

Schumacher's fourth world title leaves him just one behind the all-time record held by Juan Manuel Fangio but the German refused to be drawn into whether he will be considered the best ever driver if he equals or goes on to beat Fangio's five.

"It would be an unfair comparison for anyone to make," he said.

"The cars in the old days were unbelievable compared to what we drive now so you can't

The Schumacher brothers - Ralf and Michael

make that choice. It would not be right."

But one of the leading voices in the sport, Patrick Head, technical director of Williams, had no doubts that Schumacher could go on to become the greatest of all-time.

"As an all-round driver, Michael is the best I have ever seen," he said.

'Every race is a challenge to me. That is what I like about Formula One'

"While he is still driving, he is always the man to beat and has it within himself to go on and win five, six or even seven titles if he wants to.

"If the motivation is there for him, then who knows what he can achieve. I could see him going on to win 60 or 70 races."

Schumacher, a keen footballer - he supports Cologne and plays for Swiss side FC Aubonne - led the title race from the first Grand Prix in

Australia in March and never really looked likely to be forced to hand over his crown.

He made the Monaco Grand Prix look like a lazy Sunday morning drive as he eased his scarlet machine around the twists and turns of Monte Carlo's streets while his nearest challenger David Coulthard was stuck at the back after launch control problems left him standing still on the grid on the warm-up lap.

A master in the wet weather, he used a combination of tactics and pure driving skill to win in Malaysia and his only real stroke of luck came in the Spanish Grand Prix in Barcelona when the clutch on Mika Hakkinen's McLaren packed up on the last lap allowing Schumey to steer his own sickly Ferrari past the chequered flag almost with embarrassment.

Ironically the strongest challenger to Michael completing his hat-trick next year is likely to come from someone very familiar to him – his brother Ralf.

As youngsters at home in Germany, where his father ran a karting circuit, the two would race relentlessly, neither willing to yield to the other. They have carried that mentality on to the F1 circuit and on three or four occasions during the 2001 Championship the two were locked together in racing combat. But while they are fierce rivals, they are also the closest of friends.

No one was more delighted than Michael to see his younger brother win his first Grand Prix, at San Marino in 2001, and follow it up with success in Canada.

But equally, no one will be more determined than the world champion that next time they race, it will be his scarlet Ferrari that comes out on top.

SCHUMACHER FACTFILE

BORN: 3rd January, 1969 in Kerpen, Germany
TEAMS: Jordan 1991, Benetton 1991-1995, Ferrari 1996-2001
HONOURS: German Formula Konig Champion, 1988; Formula 3 Champion 1990; Formula 1 World Champion 1995, 1996, 2000, 2001
FIRST GRAND PRIX: For Jordan at Spa in Belgium, 1991, when his brilliant performance persuaded Benetton to 'steal' him immediately after the race.
FIRST GRAND PRIX WIN: In Belgium, 1992

2001 HIGHLIGHTS

4th MARCH, 2001: Started from pole position in Melbourne, he picked up where he left off in 2000 by leading from start to finish.

18th MARCH, 2001: Came in to his own when it rained in Malaysia, got his tactics right and made it two wins out of two in the season and six on the trot.

27th MAY, 2001: Another start to finish drive on the most testing circuit of all at Monte Carlo.

1st JULY, 2001: A Schumacher double at Magny Cours as Michael won Grand Prix number 50, with Ralf second in France.

19th AUGUST, 2001: Hungary and a faultless drive from the front row of the grid clinched his fourth Championship, and with Rubens Barrichello making it a scarlet 1-2, the Constructors' title was secured by Ferrari at the same time.

2nd SEPTEMBER, 2001: Win number 52, at Spa, to take the Grand Prix victory record.

THE BIKE SCENE

RICKARDSSON MAKES IT A RECORD FOUR

TONY RICKARDSSON secured his place in speedway history with a record fourth World Championship crown.

The Swedish superstar chose the perfect venue to achieve his milestone, in front of 16,000 of his fans in his home stadium, the Olympic arena in Stockholm.

Rickardsson won the B-Final to clinch the 15 points he needed to take him out of reach of his nearest challenger, Jason Crump.

The 31-year-old finished the six-meeting series with 121 points, beating Greg Hancock's record tally of 118 set back in 1997.

Rickardsson, who rode for Poole Pirates in the Sky Sports Elite League during the season, won the Series' Finals in England (pic right) and Denmark, finished second in the Czech Republic and Poland and fourth in Germany.

Ironically, the only time he failed to reach the Final was in Sweden, but his fifth place finish was enough to spark some serious celebrations amongst the home crowd.

"My bike was perfect for the first heat, then I lost my focus a bit," said the new world champion after lifting the trophy. "But it was great to clinch the title in Stockholm. I could not have asked for anywhere better."

Rickardsson's fourth world title, his others were in 1994, 1998 and 1999, puts him level with the legendary Barry Briggs of New Zealand and Denmark's Hans Nielsen.

Britain's Mark Loram, who was world champion in 2000, finished in ninth place but was delighted that he has was handing over the crown to a worthy winner.

"Tony has the total respect of all the other riders and deserves the title," he said.

Australian Crump won the Swedish Grand Prix with Michael Karlson of Sweden in second place and another Aussie, Ryan Sullivan, third.

Crump finished eight points behind Rickardsson in the overall standings on 113 points with Poland's Tomasz Gollob third on 89, nine points clear of Sullivan with another Australian, Lee Adams, in fifth on 69 points.

SKY SIGNS UP FOR BRITISH SPEEDWAY

SKY SPORTS gave a massive boost to speedway when they signed a five year deal to cover all British events in the sport.

The contract to start in time for the 2001 season, included coverage of the Elite League, Premier League, Elite League Riders Championship, Premier League Riders Championship as well as Test matches and runs

alongside the existing deal to cover the World Grand Prix Series.

"The deal with Sky Sports is great news for the sport in this country," said British Speedway Promoters' Association president Terry Russell at the time.

TROY IS TOPS

AUSTRALIAN Troy Bayliss clinched the World Superbikes Championship with two victories at Holland's Assen circuit in September, 2001.

On board the Ducati, Bayliss (pic left) became only the second man behind Carl Fogarty to win both races at Assen and with it tied up the title with one round still to race.

World title holder and Bayliss' closest challenger, Colin Edwards, had mechanical problems in both races and could only finish 10th in the second leg, after collecting a podium place with third in the opening race.

Bayliss' joy was slightly tarnished at the end of the season after a crashing fall at Imola left him nursing a fractured collarbone.

ONE TO WATCH
MARK LORAM

FACTFILE

NAME: Mark Loram
CLUB:
Peterborough Panthers
HONOURS:
World Champion 2000
2001 WORLD
CHAMPIONSHIP POS: 9th

• Was excluded from the A Final at the end of the 2001 season in Sweden after touching the tape at the start.

• Became the first Briton to win the World Championship since Gary Havelock in 1992 when he clinched the title in Poland in September 2000.

• Is passionate about jet-skiing, snowboarding and skydiving and will often be found doing one of those dare-devil sports while out of the season.

• Has a reputation for moving clubs and his two-year stay (1999 and 2000) at Poole Pirates was the first time since 1996 that he had remained at a club longer than one year.

• Shortly before his World Championship success he was racing for England in an international meet with Australia. Trying to make an audacious move he crashed and handed the Aussies victory.

• Former World Champion Havelock regards Loram as one of the most exciting riders Britain has ever produced.

MARK LORAM has already tasted the delights of a World Championship - now he wants another bite.

Britain's speedway superstar finished as world champion in 2000 but couldn't retain his title last season and had to watch as Tony Rickardsson took over the mantle in front of his home fans in Stockholm in the final Grand Prix of the series.

Loram finished ninth in the standings after a dreadful start to the defence of his title but he warns he will be back next year looking to regain that number one position.

"Winning the Championship was a fantastic feeling and I'm determined to get to those heights again," he said.

"That is my number one ambition now. To be world champion again. But it will be hard because you have to maintain a high level throughout the series. In the year I won the title I was very consistent, which is what it is all about in six rounds. I didn't actually win a round but I was there or thereabouts all the time and it was that which gave me the edge.

"As far as racing goes I have a reputation as someone that can always win a race but it's that consistency that counts. That is what makes you world champion."

Loram clinched the title in the last Grand Prix of the season, in Poland, and admitted that it was a pressure-cooker atmosphere.

"I had a lot of pressure on me because British speedway desperately wanted another world champion," he recalled.

"I was ahead going in to the Poland round but was very nervous before the event. About as nervous as I have ever been in the sport.

"No one wanted to win the title more than me but there was a lot of pressure with the media as well so I was just glad I came through."

Loram, who moved from Poole Pirates to Peterborough Panthers for the Sky Sports Elite League 2001 campaign, has secured his place in the top 10 riders' list for the 2002 Grand Prix series and will probably indulge in some jet-skiing as he sets about gaining the right fitness levels for his assault on Rickardsson's title.

"Speedway is more of a sprint than endurance and you probably don't need to be as fit as an F1 driver. But you have to be very physically alert to win the World Championship and I intend to be just that."

OXING • BOXING • BOXING • BOXING • BOXING • BOXING • BOXING • BOXING • BOXIN

OXING • BOXING • BOXING • BOXING • BOXING • BOXING • BOXING • BOXING • BOXI

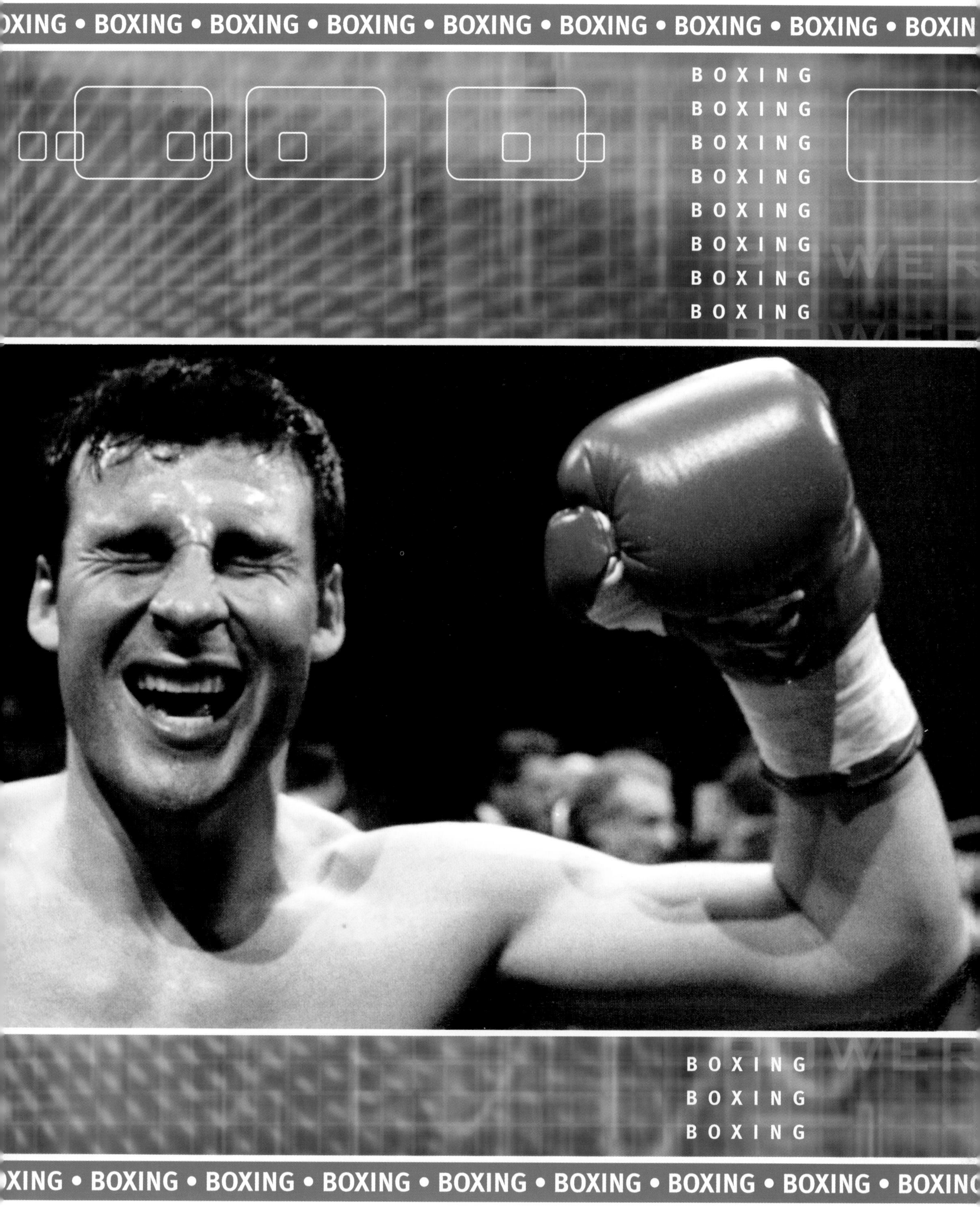

BOXING • BOXING • BOXING • BOXING • BOXING • BOXING • BOXING
BOXING
BOXING
BOXING
BOXING
BOXING
BOXING
BOXING
BOXING
BOXING
BOXING
BOXING
BOXING • BOXING • BOXING • BOXING • BOXING • BOXING • BOXING

BRITS IN THE RING

**APRIL 7
LAS VEGAS
PRINCE NASEEM v
MARCO ANTONIO BARRERA**

HAMED HAMMERED

PRINCE NASEEM Hamed suffered his first defeat in 36 fights as his world featherweight crown was ripped away from him by tough Mexican Marco Antonio Barrera.

The Sheffield-born Naz, regarded by many as the best pound for pound fighter in the world, was outclassed by Barrera over 12 rounds.

He was caught out by the Mexican's tactics of fighting in bursts instead of his normal gung-ho rampaging style. He was out manoeuvred by the lightning quick punches from Barrera and he was out-thought throughout the contest.

Barrera caught Naseem in the first round with a solid left hook that hurt the extrovert Prince more than he showed, acting defiantly by jutting out his jaw and dropping his arms in apparent mock surrender.

But Barrera was never going to be taken in by the showmanship that had entertained the public for years and simply pounded the 27-year-old at will.

To Naseem's credit, despite losing virtually every round, he was still standing when the bell signalled the end of the 12th and last round – but any chance of maintaining his unbeaten record had long disappeared by then.

Naz on his way to losing his unbeaten record and his world title as Barrera attacks

**APRIL 21
CARNIVAL CITY, JOHANNESBURG
LENNOX LEWIS v HASIM RAHMAN**

RAHMAN SHOCKS THE WORLD

THE WORLD of Lennox Lewis was turned upside down when a right cross from unknown American Hasim Rahman connected with the heavyweight champion's jaw in the fifth round.

Lewis crashed to the canvas and didn't even hear the count before Belgian Daniel Van De Wiele reached 10, then plucked the gum shield out of the prostrate ex-world champion's mouth before calling for medical attention.

It was one of the biggest shocks in recent boxing history with Lewis suffering only the second defeat of his professional career.

It also put on hold any hope he had of a mega bucks pay day against former world champion Mike Tyson.

"He caught me with a lucky punch," claimed Lewis after he had regained his senses.

"But I will be back. I have always said that I will go out at the top and I am determined to win back my belts and go out as champion."

Lewis may have blamed his defeat on a lucky punch but there were many who accused him of taking the fight too lightly and not spending more time acclimatising to the altitude and conditions in South Africa.

Michael Middleton is cornered by Audley Harrison as the British fighter makes his pro debut

Michael Middleton's defeat by Harrison was his 10th in 18 bouts.

Prince Naseem was approached about the possibility of fighting new world champion Juan Pablo Chacon for the WBC Featherweight title with the fight planned for 2002. If Naz agreed, the bout would be staged in Britain with Frank Warren the likely promoter.

Calzaghe's victory over Mario Veit in 1 minute 52 seconds was his first victory in the first round in four years.

Lennox Lewis was in line for the first £100 million fight against Mike Tyson if he had beaten Hasim Rahman. The bout had been pencilled in for late 2001 or early 2002.

Harrison was less impressive in his second fight and was taken the six round distance by Derek McCafferty before winning on points.

Prince Naseem faces a rematch with Barrera after a clause in their contract for the fight included an option for a return.

Lennox Lewis' manager Frank Maloney claimed Naz would be no great loss to the boxing world and said: "He was stripped of the WBO title because he wouldn't fight Istvan Kovacs and he gave up the WBA and IBF titles. He upset a lot of people and is now out in the wilderness. If he retires, boxing will not miss him."

**APRIL 28
CARDIFF
JOE CALZAGHE v MARIO VEIT**

CLASSY CALZAGHE

JOE CALZAGHE restored some pride to British boxing a week after Prince Naseem and Lennox Lewis both lost their world crowns.

The Welsh wonder held on to his WBO Super Middleweight title in thrilling style with a first round stoppage of Germany's Mario Veit in front of his home fans.

"Nobody was going to beat me tonight," said the 29-year-old after the fight.

"I looked in to his eyes and there was nothing there. He looked anxious and I was confident that I could finish it early.

"It was a great shame to see Naz and Lennox lose and I wanted to carry the honour of British boxing on my shoulders."

And Calzaghe's manager, Frank Warren, claimed that the Welshman was a better fighter than both Lewis and Naseem.

"Injuries have restricted Joe to fighting at say 50 per cent of his potential sometimes but he was still winning fights even then," said Warren.

"He can punch, has more skill than Naz and is a better fighter than Lennox. Joe has shown we still have one of the best champions in the world."

**MAY 19
WEMBLEY
AUDLEY HARRISON v
MICHAEL MIDDLETON**

NO JINX ON HARRISON DEBUT

AUDLEY HARRISON took just two minutes and 45 seconds of the first round to win his opening contest as a professional.

The Olympic Heavyweight gold medallist from Sydney 2000 made light work of Michael 'The Jinx' Middleton at the Wembley Arena as he took his first steps on the ladder to what he hopes – and many predict – will lead to a world title.

Middleton, at six inches smaller and over two stone lighter, was never going to seriously threaten Harrison's big debut.

The man from Florida was pushed back from the bell, although he did have the audacity to catch Harrison with a couple of right handers.

Two sharp jabs in to the face of the American did the trick and Middleton was forced to retreat into a corner before referee Dave Parris moved in to save him from further punishment.

A broken nose, the third of his career, was the end result for Middleton but at least he picked up a cheque for over £30,000 for two minutes' work.

The Welsh warrior - Joe Calzaghe

FIGHTING TALK

DID YOU KNOW?

Lennox Lewis became the first Briton to rule the world in 102 years when he grabbed the heavyweight boxing crown to become the undisputed No.1 in 1999. It marked the climax of years of blood, sweat and tears for the East Ender.

Widely regarded as head and shoulders above the heavyweight pack, Britain's Lennox Lewis saw his dreams take a serious blow early in 2001. But the man with the most destructive punch in boxing is used to knocks, and just like throughout his career, he came back fighting.

Lewis chose April 21st to take what he thought would be his final step towards the mega-bucks pay day of a showdown with former champ Mike Tyson. But in the event his lack of proper preparation and failure to acclimatise to the conditions in Johannesburg let unfancied challenger to his world crown, Hasim Rahman, steal a shock victory with a fifth round knockout.

A rematch in November gave Lewis the opportunity to once again return to the pinnacle of his sport.

But even while Rahman celebrated his surprise win, most in the boxing world still considered Lewis the best around.

He has had to deal with setbacks many times before in his lengthy climb to the top, from criticism of his 'plodding' style to opponents desperate to avoid him, to the fighter's own

143

'Lewis unleashed his big weapon, a booming overhand right seconds before the bell brought round one to a close and then sent Ruddock to his knees twice more in round two'

calm, relaxed personality that has left some accusing him of being too nice to succeed.

His supporters have never had any doubts that their man should be No.1 though, bringing honour and prestige to a sport that has been dragged through the gutter in recent years.

Born in Forest Gate in London's East End in September 1965, Lennox and his brother Denis stayed on in England with an aunt after their Jamaican mother, Violet, moved to Canada in search of a better life.

But when the 12-year-old Lennox started getting into trouble at school, it was decided that being nearer his mother would be better for his discipline, and he jetted across the Atlantic to join her.

Already developing into a tall, imposing

figure, Lewis soon took up boxing, carving out a name for himself in the amateur ranks and earning a call-up to Canada's national team to box at the 1984 and 1988 Olympic games, winning gold at super-heavyweight in Seoul in 1988.

That victory, knocking-out American Riddick Bowe in the final, tempted Lewis to return to the UK and embark on a professional career with up-and-coming promoter Frank Maloney.

His debut as a paid fighter came against one Al Malcolm in June 1989 and, in what was to become a familiar scenario, the challenger was battered into submission within two rounds as the newcomer announced his arrival in no uncertain terms.

Over the next three years, Lewis went quietly

and systematically about his business, improving and learning from every fight as he chased his dream of becoming the first Briton in 100 years to be crowned undisputed heavyweight champion of the world.

By October 1992 the under-rated Lewis had notched up an impressive 21 wins in 21 fights, 18 of them by knockout, with twelve of his victims unable to make it past round three.

But the big boys really began to sit up and take notice when Lewis went toe-to-toe with Donovan 'Razor' Ruddock later that month.

The winner of the bout, Lewis' toughest test to date, was set-up to meet the victor of the Evander Holyfield-Riddick Bowe title unification fight in what all four had agreed would be the next step forward for the heavyweight division.

The Briton had been primed for a fall, but the critics reckoned without his meticulous approach and cast iron will. Lewis unleashed his big weapon, a booming overhand right, seconds before the bell brought round one to a close and then sent Ruddock to his knees twice

Lennox proudly displays his world title belts

'Part one of Lewis' world title dream had been realised but in the most unsatisfactory of ways for the British fighter'

more in round two to force the referee to declare a technical knockout.

Lewis looked firmly on course for his longed for world title fight, but Bowe - still smarting from his 1988 Olympic defeat - had other ideas and refused to honour the pre-fight agreement after defeating Holyfield, famously throwing his champions' belt into a rubbish bin rather than agree to a showdown with England's finest.

Furious at being made a laughing stock, the World Boxing Council (WBC) stripped Bowe of his title and awarded it instead to Lewis. Part one of the dream had been realised, but in the most unsatisfactory of ways.

Lewis meets another champion for the world - Nelson Mandela

Three successful defences of his new title quickly followed before, on September 24, 1994 at London's Wembley Arena, Lewis suffered his first defeat as a professional, walking into a crashing right-hander from Oliver McCall and losing to a technical knock out in round two.

Having sacked trainer Pepe Correa, Lewis tore

'Despite an awesome display from Lewis the result was called a draw. Most neutrals at ringside had given it to Lennox'

back into action eight months later, battering Lionel Butler in five rounds and prompting WBC President Jose Sulaiman to say: "The position is very clear. The challenger to the winner of the McCall-Bruno title fight is Lennox Lewis."

Once again, though, the facts of the matter proved very different for Lewis, as his claims were ignored by fellow countryman Frank Bruno, who preferred to set up a predictably short-lived, but lucrative, encounter with Mike Tyson.

A series of by-now familiar changes of heart from boxing's authorities and promoters duly ensued, eventually resulting in Lewis being granted a title shot in a rematch with Oliver McCall in February 1997.

In one of the most bizarre fights of recent times, McCall suffered a nervous breakdown in the ring, refused to throw any punches and spent much of the bout sobbing before referee Mills Lane declared Lewis the winner in round five.

Four crushing defences followed as Lewis' desire to be known as the best finally started to make the world listen.

After Evander Holyfield won his two infamous battles with Mike Tyson in November 1996 and June 1997 it became increasingly obvious that Lewis-Holyfield was the fight that had to happen to return some credibility to a sport battered by corruption and greed.

But still the controversy would not go away. The fight was fixed for March 13, 1999, and despite an awesome display from the fired-up Lewis, after 12 brutal and tortuous rounds the result was called as a draw, even though most neutrals at ringside had given Lennox the verdict. Having steeled himself to climb Everest, Lewis would have to do it all again.

But do it again he did, and in fine style. Eight months to the day after the desolation of that draw, Lewis finally realised his dream and fulfilled his destiny by outpointing the great gladiator Holyfield in Las Vegas.

For the first time since Riddick Bowe in 1992, the heavyweight boxing world had one champion. And that man was Lennox Lewis.

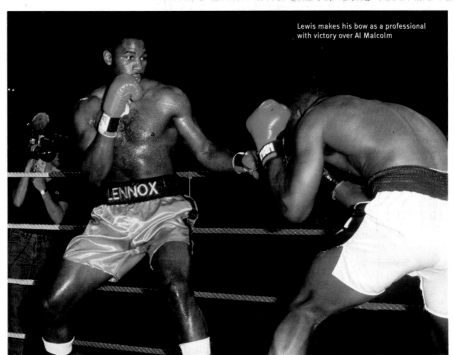
Lewis makes his bow as a professional with victory over Al Malcolm

FIGHTS IN FULL

LENNOX LEWIS' PROFESSIONAL CAREER UP TO THAT DEFEAT BY RAHMAN.

DATE	OPPONENT	RESULT
27.6.89	Al Malcolm	TKO2
21.7.89	Bruce Johnson	TKO2
25.9.89	Andy Garrard	TKO4
10.10.89	Steve Garber	TKO1
5.11.89	Melvin Epps	WDSQ2
18.12.89	Greg Gorrell	TKO5
31.1.90	Noel Quarless	TKO2
22.3.90	Calvin Jones	TKO1
14.4.90	Mike Simuwelu	TKO1
9.5.90	Jorge Descola	TKO1
20.5.90	Dan Murphy	TKO6
27.6.90	Ossie Ocasio	WDSQ8
11.7.90	Mike Acey	TKO2
31.10.90	Jean Chanet	TKO6
6.3.91	Gary Mason&	TKO6
12.7.91	Mike Weaver	TKO6
30.9.91	Glenn McCrory	TKO2
23.11.91	Tyrell Biggs	TKO3
1.2.92	Levi Billups	W10
30.4.92	Derek Williams@	TKO3
11.8.92	Mike Dixon	TKO4
31.10.92	Razor Ruddock	TKO2
8.5.93	Tony Tucker*	W12
1.10.93	Frank Bruno*	TKO7
6.5.94	Phil Jackson*	TKO8
24.9.94	Oliver McCall*	LTKO2
13.5.95	Lionel Butler	TKO5
2.7.95	Justin Fortune	TKO4
7.10.95	Tommy Morrison	TKO6
10.5.96	Ray Mercer	W12
7.2.97	Oliver McCall*	TKO5
12.7.97	Henry Akinwande*	WDSQ5
4.10.97	Andrew Golota*	TKO1
28.3.98	Shannon Briggs*	TKO5
26.9.98	Zeljko Mavrovic*	W12
13.3.99	Evander Holyfield*+	D12
13.11.99	Evander Holyfield*+^	W12
29.4.00	Michael Grant*^	KO2
15.7.00	Frans Botha*^	TKO2
11.11.00	David Tua*^	W12
21.4.01	Hasim Rahman*^	LTKO5

TOTAL

FIGHTS 41 WON 38 DRAWN 1 LOST 2

& = British title fight; @ = Commonwealth title fight; * = WBC title fight; + = WBA title fight; ^ = IBF title fight; KO Knock-out (2 denotes round); D = Draw; W = Won on points; TKO = technical knock-out; DSQ = disqualified; L = lost

STAR OF 2001

FELIX TRINIDAD

FELIX Trinidad has lit up the boxing world over the last few years in a one man mission that has crossed three weight divisions.

In that time, the Puerto Rican dynamo has soundly beaten some of the top fighters in the world, most of them a lot bigger than he is.

The 28-year-old has over eight years of top class boxing experience under his belt in a career that has seen him capture the IBF and WBC Welterweight Championships, the WBA and IBF junior middleweight titles and the WBA middleweight crown.

Unbeaten in the welterweight and junior middleweight divisions, he relinquished those titles to move up to middleweight, joining Don King's WBC, IBF and WBA tournament alongside William Joppy, Keith Holmes and Bernard Hopkins to unify the belts.

Along the way he blasted the top two junior middleweights in to oblivion. Olympic champion from 1996 and WBA title holder David Reid was smashed into a points defeat at the start of 2000 and Fernando Vargas was beaten sensationally at the end of the year.

Both men actually had Trinidad down during the fight but were made to pay by the speed, strength and skills of the fighter, nicknamed Tito, who also has bags of stamina, as proved by his victory over Mexican-American Vargas when Trinidad knocked him over three times in the last round before the referee stopped the fight.

A notorious slow starter, Trinidad, who also sandwiched a victory over the bulkier Mamadou Thiam between his comprehensive wins over Reid and Vargas, then moved on to a 'semi-final' in King's middleweight tournament, with William Joppy in May 2001.

Experts were predicting a close fight, with Joppy having held the WBA middleweight crown for over five years. Instead the awesome punching of the 5ft 11in Trinidad smashed his opponent all around the ring.

With over 18,000 Puerto Rican fans in the crowd, Joppy was up against it from the first bell and needed all his guile and bravery to last past the first round after hitting the canvas inside the opening three minutes.

He survived to the fifth before Trinidad landed him on his backside twice more, the referee calling a halt to his punishment with 30 seconds of the round left.

The victory took Trinidad's record to a perfect 40 wins in 40 fights, 33 of them inside the distance, gave him the WBA middleweight crown and set up a unification bout with IBF and WBC champion Bernard Hopkins.

That fight ended in Trinidad's first professional defeat, a last round stoppage by Hopkins in September 2001, but it couldn't detract from his place amongst the all-time boxing greats.

ONE TO WATCH

RICKY HATTON

RICKY Hatton has his eyes set firmly on landing one of the major world titles in 2002 and there are few in the British boxing game who would argue against him achieving it.

His impressive display against tough American John Bailey in Manchester in September 2001 illustrated his fighting credentials to the full, with the Hitman knocking his opponent to the canvas four times before stopping him at the start of the fifth round.

That victory extended Hatton's winning sequence to 25 fights and firmly installed the light-welterweight as the main challenger to WBO holder DeMarcus Corley.

The 23-year-old already holds the WBU crown but it's the main belts he wants around his waist and knows that time and ability is very much on his side.

"I am only young and the guys at the top at the moment are 27 or 28 and at their peak," said Hatton.

"I have a way to go yet but no one has seen the best of me. I have plenty of faith in my ability and know that my time will come."

Hatton's unbeaten career is littered with other impressive displays, victories over former British light-welterweight champion Mark Winters and Jason Rowland, in a defence of the WBU title, arguably the pick of the bunch.

His victory over Tony Pep to take the WBU crown at Wembley in March 2001, knocking out his opponent in the fourth round, was his 18th victory inside the distance in 23 fights since making his professional debut in 1997.

Since that first win over Kid McAuley in Widnes, a first round stoppage, he has been focusing on the world stage.

The WBU belt is a start - but only a start for the powerful hitter and a couple more impressive wins are almost certain to see him come face to face with Corley.

Britain has been looking for a new boxing superstar for a while. Ricky Hatton may just be closing in on that status.

NAME: Ricky Hatton
DATE OF BIRTH:
6th October, 1978
BASED: Manchester
HEIGHT: 5ft 7in
TURNED PRO:
September 1997
MANAGER: Frank Warren

• Won the ABA Light-Welterweight Championship in 1997.

• Voted the Boxing Writers' Young Boxer of the Year in 1998.

• Has picked up the nickname The Hitman following his powerful punching displays.

• Four of his first five fights ended with victory by technical knock-outs inside the first round. The only man to go past three minutes was Robert Alvarez who was beaten on points in a four round contest in New York.

• A big football follower, Hatton goes to Maine Road to watch his beloved Manchester City play as often as he can.

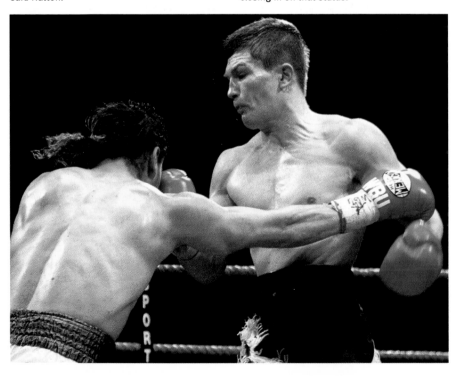

TENNIS
TENNIS
TENNIS
TENNIS

THE GRAND SLAM

Kuerten - almost unbeatable on clay

MAY 28-JUNE 10
PARIS
FRENCH OPEN

CLAY KING KUERTEN

GUSTAVO Kuerten clinched the French Open men's singles title for the third successive time.

The Brazilian's win over Spain's Alex Corretja 6-7, 7-5, 6-2, 6-0 was greeted with ecstatic applause from the Roland Garros crowd.

"I love this place, everything that happens to me here is quite special," he said after parading the trophy around the court. "It is a magic venue and all my dreams come true here. It is also the place where I have a great relationship with the fans. They make it so special to play here."

Kuerten needed four match points against Corretja before he took the title and promised he would be back in 2002 to try for a history-making fourth triumph.

Jennifer Capriati continued her amazing return to the pinnacle of the women's game with a marathon 1-6, 6-4, 12-10 win over Belgium's Kim Clijsters, which lasted two hours and 21 minutes.

It was her second Grand Slam win of the year and she became the first American to win the title since Chris Evert in 1986.

Fittingly Evert was there to make the presentation of the trophy to the winner.

She said: "I was delighted that Jenny won because I knew how much it meant to her. She hung in there and proved what a fighter she is."

JANUARY 15-28
MELBOURNE
AUSTRALIAN OPEN

CAPRIATI COMPLETES GLORIOUS COMEBACK

JENNIFER Capriati completed the most amazing comeback in the world of tennis to take the ladies' title at the Australian Open in Melbourne.

But her 6-4, 6-3 victory over Martina Hingis was no great fightback from the depths of despair during the game. It was much, much more than that.

Capriati's victory was comfortable enough – it was the very fact that she was on court at all that marked the great recovery.

Seven years earlier, tired of the sport that had made her a child star, the American was first arrested for shoplifting and accused of stealing jewellery, then caught allegedly in possession of drugs. The picture of the out-of-shape teenage athlete with the criminal case number against her name was flashed around the world.

A spell in a drugs rehabilitation clinic helped steer her back to tennis and former world number one Steffi Graf helped her further along the way with some words of encouragement when Capriati (pic right) was on the verge of quitting in 1996.

In 1999 she won her first tournament since returning to the game and completed her comeback in glorious style by lifting her first Grand Slam title with the win over Hingis.

"Who would have thought that I would be here a winner of a Grand Slam title," she said after holding aloft the trophy watched by her father Stefano, who is also her coach.

"It just shows that dreams can come true if you believe hard enough."

In the men's final, crowd favourite Andre Agassi retained his crown with a crushing 6-4, 6-2, 6-2 win over his French challenger Arnaud Clement.

VICTORY FOR VENUS AND GORAN

BRITAIN'S hopes of having a Wimbledon men's finalist for the first time since Bunny Austin in 1938 disappeared when Tim Henman was beaten in the Semi-Finals in a three-day thriller.

Goran Ivanisevic was his conqueror, winning 7-5, 6-7, 0-6, 7-6, 6-3 in a match much affected by the weather. After twice having the day's play halted by rain, the Croat finally reached his fourth final and this time it was to be a glorious one after three defeats.

The 125-1 outsider defeated Aussie Patrick Rafter 6-3, 3-6, 6-3, 2-6, 9-7 in arguably the greatest final in Wimbledon's 125-year history.

With the home support very much behind the 29-year-old Croatian, he held his nerve to serve out the deciding game after a cliff-hanger of a fifth set.

"That was the most fantastic atmosphere I have ever played in. There will never be anything like it again at Wimbledon," said the champion.

In a rather more sedate affair, the ladies' final was won by Venus Williams for the second successive year.

She beat Belgium's Justine Henin 6-1, 3-6, 6-0 in just over an hour to maintain her position as the best women's player on grass in the world.

27TH AUGUST-
9TH SEPTEMBER
FLUSHING
MEADOWS,
NEW YORK
US OPEN

SISTER ACT

VENUS and Serena Williams met for the first time in a Grand Slam final with big sister Venus coming out on top in straight sets.

Her 6-2, 6-4 victory was the first time siblings had played each other in a Grand Slam final since Maud and Lilian Watson, the daughters of a Midlands vicar, met in the Wimbledon showpiece in 1884 and it provided the world number four with her second successive major title of the year, following on from her Wimbledon triumph two months earlier.

In the men's final, 20-year-old Australian Lleyton Hewitt picked up his first Grand Slam in a one-sided encounter against Pete Sampras, winning 7-6, 6-1, 6-1 in 113 minutes.

Sampras entered the match on the back of a classic Quarter-Final win over Andre Agassi and hadn't dropped his serve in 87 games, stretching back over five matches. But he lost his opening service game against Hewitt and never recovered.

"The kid was awesome. So quick around the court. I had no answers in the end," said Sampras.

Venus Williams holds aloft the Wimbledon ladies' trophy

DROP SHOTS

Andre Agassi's Australian Open win put him level with, amongst others, John McEnroe, Mats Wilander and John Newcombe on seven Grand Slam titles.

Gustavo Kuerten's victory at Roland Garros put him alongside Ivan Lendl, Bjorn Borg and Mats Wilander as the only men to have won the French Open on three occasions.

Jennifer Capriati's success at the French Open came 11 years after she first reached the Semi-Final of the tournament as a 14-year-old.

Her beaten opponent in the 2001 Final, Kim Clijsters, is the daughter of former Belgian international footballer, Leo Clijsters.

Goran Ivanisevic became the first wild card entry to win the men's singles at Wimbledon. The previous best was Pat Cash who reached the last eight in 1986.

Ivanisevic hit 213 aces in the tournament, beating his previous record by seven.

More than 150,000 people turned out to greet Ivanisevic on his return to Croatia after his Wimbledon success.

The All England Lawn Tennis and Croquet club's Centre Court had its most raucous final day crowd ever for the 2001 Men's Final. Bad weather delayed the final until the Monday, meaning tickets went on general sale rather than being snapped up by members.

STAR OF 2001

GORAN IVANISEVIC

Goran celebrates Wimbledon glory with his dad, Srdjan

THERE are probably far more deserving recipients of the accolade 'Star of 2001' in the tennis world than Goran Ivanisevic.

After all, the Croatian left-hander had a pretty miserable time, dropped to 125th in the world rankings after a three-and-a-half year run without a tournament triumph, kicked off the year by losing in the qualifiers of the Australian Open and bowed out of the Stella Artois Championship, the warm-up for Wimbledon, in the First Round to unknown Italian Cristiano Caratti.

But for two weeks in the summer, Ivanisevic captured the heart of the British nation and achieved his ultimate dream – to win the Men's Singles title at Wimbledon.

He said it was his destiny to the win the crown he had been denied three times at the final hurdle, in 1992 by Andre Agassi in a five set thriller, and twice by the formidable Pete Sampras, in 1994 and 1998.

And maybe destiny did play a part in his success. The man from Split certainly played like he was on a mission, powering his way to the Final with a combination of blistering serves and thundering forehand drives.

Each victory was met with a jubilant Goran ripping off his shirt and throwing it into the crowd as bedlam broke out in London SW19.

Such was the effect the 29-year-old had on the crowd at Wimbledon, there were many who saluted his victory in the rain-affected match with local hero Tim Henman as though HE were the British player.

And despite a strong Aussie contingent supporting Patrick Rafter in the Final, you sensed the rest of the tennis world was urging Ivanisevic on to fulfil his date with destiny.

After throwing away three match points, another powerful serve was returned to the net by Rafter to end a classic Final, one of the best in history, with the Croat slumping to the floor as the tears flowed.

Then the first wild card entry ever to reach and then win a Wimbledon Men's Singles Final was climbing the steps to where his father, Srdjan, was watching, each unable to contain their emotions. It was one of the most dramatic scenes ever seen on the Centre Court and captured what it meant for the popular Ivanisevic to realise his dream.

"My father and I have come through many bad times together and I wanted to share the greatest moment of my life with him," said the delighted winner.

"He has seen me lose in the Final three times and it would have broken my heart, and his, if I had lost again.

"I have been waiting all my life to win this tournament and now I have done it. It does not matter what I do in the future, no-one can take away the moment I won Wimbledon."

ONE TO WATCH
ANDY RODDICK

FACTFILE

NAME: Andy Roddick
DATE OF BIRTH:
30th August, 1982
BIRTHPLACE:
Omaha, Nebraska, USA
HEIGHT: 6ft 1in
WEIGHT: 12st 8lbs
TURNED PROFESSIONAL: 2000

ANDY Roddick is being hailed as the new face of tennis after exploding on to the scene in 2000.

The World Junior No.1 has already made a big impression in his short career on the professional tennis circuit. He beat Pete Sampras in the Ericsson Miami Open during the summer, reached the Semi-Finals of his first tournament on grass, at Nottingham in June, and wowed the crowds at Wimbledon.

With America's superstars of the game, Sampras and Andre Agassi, passing the 30 mark, the States has been looking to the future and in 19-year-old Roddick they think they may have found it.

With a blistering serve that pushes Goran Ivanisevic and Greg Rusedski to the wire as the hottest service game in the world, he already has a powerful weapon. But there is more to his game than just that.

"He possesses a big serve, there is no doubt about that," said Sampras after being blown away by the teenager in that Miami defeat.

"It comes at you at 130mph and that is pretty hard to handle, especially when he is making so many first serves.

"His ground shots are strong as well and he looks to me as though he has got a good all-round game. I would say that if he carries on playing the way he has been, the future of American tennis is looking very bright."

And Sampras' main rival over the last five or six years, Andre Agassi, is full of praise for the new boy as well.

"He has a real presence on the court and certainly has the ability to have a great career in the game," he said.

Roddick, who is based in Florida, only got into tennis because his brother John took up the sport and joined an academy for promising youngsters.

"I tagged along with John and found I enjoyed playing the game," he recalled.

"I played a lot of baseball and basketball before that but when I was 10 we moved to Florida so John could enrol in a tennis academy there. I couldn't be bothered to find a new baseball and basketball team so started playing tennis more."

The young Roddick showed a mixture of talent and temper as he progressed to become world number one.

Now he is very much a star of the professional game. With a couple of titles under his belt on the ATP Challenger Circuit and the US Junior Open title also pocketed in 2000, he arrived for his first Wimbledon in June 2001, only his second tournament on grass.

A superb victory over Thomas Johansson brought a standing ovation and left Roddick the youngest player left in the Men's Singles before Ivanisevic beat him in the last 16.

- He is nicknamed A-Rod

- His hero as a youngster was Andre Agassi and Roddick would get up early to watch him play at Wimbledon.

- His older brother Lawrence was an accomplished springboard diver.

- Speed guns have already measured his serve at being around 140 mph.

- His greatest memory of the game as a child is seeing his two favourite players meet in the 1992 Wimbledon Men's Singles Final, with his number one hero, Andre Agassi, beating his number two, Goran Ivanisevic.

- Growing up in Omaha, the Roddicks were friends with top USA diver Greg Louganis and young Andy would copy his dives from the springboard at the local pool.

- His good looks and exciting style have made him a firm favourite with female fans.

RUGBY LEAGUE
RUGBY LEAGUE
RUGBY LEAGUE
RUGBY LEAGUE
RUGBY LEAGUE
RUGBY LEAGUE
RUGBY LEAGUE
RUGBY LEAGUE

SAINTS CLEAN UP

JANUARY 26
WORLD CLUB CHALLENGE
REEBOK STADIUM, BOLTON
ST HELENS 20
BRISBANE BRONCOS 18

MIGHTY BRONCOS BEATEN IN THRILLER

THE YEAR 2001 started with a bang. The World Club Challenge, the annual curtain-raiser to the season, saw English Champions St Helens take on the mighty Brisbane Broncos, Grand Final winners and a team packed with world-class stars despite losing seven players over the close season.

Saints were also without three of their Championship-winning side and few people outside their camp expected anything other than another defeat at the hands of the powerful Aussies.

What unfolded at the Reebok Stadium in Bolton on January 26 was astonishing. Just ten weeks after England were depressingly thrashed at the same ground by New Zealand in the World Cup Semi-Final, the domestic game bounced back in incredible fashion.

Not that you could have expected anything other than another home humiliation when Shaun Berrigan dived in to put the Broncos ahead after just eight minutes.

But Paul Sculthorpe, below his best for England in November, more than made up for it with a magnificent display, starting with an equalising try on 19 minutes and culminating an hour later with a field goal which put Saints 19-18 ahead with only seconds left.

As the Reebok erupted with glee, Sean Long slotted another drop kick over to confirm an amazing victory as the Merseysiders were crowned World Champions.

It was a tenacious display by Ian Millward's side, highlighting the ability in Super League.

What was most rewarding about the win was that the stars of the show were home-grown: England's Long, Sculthorpe and Paul Wellens, Ireland's inspirational Chris Joynt and Tommy Martyn, and Welshmen Anthony Sullivan and Keiron Cunningham.

"No-one gave us a chance," said Long, who, along with Joynt, had been at Central Park to see Wigan win the inaugural world title in 1987.

"The only people who believed we could win were inside the Saints dressing-room. But this puts the British game back on the map."

Brisbane coach Wayne Bennett admitted: "St Helens were very impressive in the last 20 minutes. They defended extremely well and played some wonderful stuff with the ball."

Saints celebrate their third trophy success - Challenge Cup Final victory over Bradford

**APRIL 28
CHALLENGE CUP FINAL
TWICKENHAM
ST HELENS 13 BRADFORD BULLS 6**

SUPER SEAN SEALS TREBLE

SEAN LONG inspired St Helens to victory over Bradford Bulls in the Challenge Cup Final at Twickenham to complete the treble.

With the World Club Championship and the Super League Grand Final safely tucked away before the encounter with the Paul brothers and Co., it was the Saints' scrum-half who dictated the game and with it the victory.

Long, who picked up the Lance Todd Trophy as man of the match, had a hand in both his club's tries - or rather a foot.

His grubber kick through the heart of the

Sean Long - winner of the Lance Todd trophy

Bradford defence put Irish stand-off Tommy Martyn in for the opening score.

And on the 30 minute mark it was Long's inventiveness that broke the Bulls defence again, his kick in to open space being picked up by the rampaging Keiron Cunningham who went over the line with ease.

Henry and Robbie Paul conducted proceedings for Bradford but they failed to bridge the watertight Saints defence and had to be content with three penalties as their only scores on the day.

The Merseyside-based club were always good value for their win and coach Ian Millward could hardly believe they had added another trophy to their impressive haul.

"This is a special time for the club," he said after hoisting aloft the trophy.

"To win three trophies is an amazing performance and I just want to savour every moment because it might not happen again.

"This team deserves all the praise that is heaped upon them. They are going to be talked about in the same terms as the great sides the club has had in the past."

For superstar Long, victory was also special.

"This was my first Challenge Cup Final and I was desperate for us to win the trophy," he said.

"I have always dreamed of playing in the Final and winning but it was very tense at the end and Bradford pushed us all the way.

"But we deserved it and to win the man of the match award just topped it all off for me really."

Saints had picked up the first trophy of their amazing treble back in October 2000 with victory over Wigan in the Super League Grand Final.

Tommy Martyn, Ian Millward and Chris Joynt with the World Club Championship

The 2001 Final was the 100th in Challenge Cup history with Saints losing in the first one back in 1897.

It was the first time the Challenge Cup Final had been played at Twickenham. In 2000 it was played at Murrayfield after the RFL decided to spread the game around the country while the Final's regular home, Wembley, was being rebuilt.

Ian Millward had only joined Saints in March 2000 but in the 13 months he had been at Knowsley Road he steered his club to that historic first treble.

Bradford and Saints fought out one of the greatest Challenge Cup Finals in history in 1997 with St Helens winning 32-22 at Wembley.

Bradford were the holders of the Challenge Cup before their defeat by Saints, winning the trophy for the first time in 51 years with victory over Leeds a year earlier.

WORLD CLUB CHAMPIONSHIP ROLL OF HONOUR

1987: Wigan
1989: Widnes
1991: Wigan
1992: Brisbane Broncos
1994: Wigan
1997*: Brisbane Broncos
2000: Melbourne Storm
2001: St Helens

* Aussie Champions Brisbane beat English title winners St Helens earlier in a 22-team Super League Championship.

SUPER LEAGUE

LAM LEADS INVASION FROM DOWN UNDER

THE salary cap restrictions in Australia's NRL meant some of the top antipodean stars were released by their clubs who simply could not afford to renew their contracts without losing half their teams.

English Super League clubs did not hesitate to pounce and 24 top quality new imports arrived in Super League VI from the NRL.

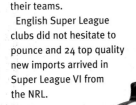

Of the new recruits, six were current internationals; Kiwis Richie Barnett (Sydney Roosters to London), Tonie Carroll (Brisbane to Leeds) and Joe Vagana (Auckland to Bradford); Papua New Guinea captain Adrian Lam (Roosters to Wigan) and Australians Jason Hetherington (Canterbury to London) and Jason Smith (Parramatta to Hull), although these last two were both omitted from the Kangaroos' World Cup squad once they'd signed for English clubs.

The biggest pre-season buzz was arguably at Wigan's JJB Stadium where Lam was joined by England's Harvey Howard (from NRL champs Brisbane), Kangaroo Matthew Johns (Newcastle) and David Furner (Canberra), with Irish winger Brian Carney (Hull) replacing Jason Robinson.

But Warriors made changes at the top, axing coach Frank Endacott and replacing him with Castleford's Stuart Raper.

He changed things immediately. Training a few mornings a week was replaced by full days at the club.

"It's like a job now," commented centre Paul Johnson. The improvement was rapid as Wigan leapt into the top two and stayed there to the end of the Super League season.

MANAGERIAL MERRY GO-ROUND

THE usual plethora of new coaches finally included a couple of Englishmen for the start of Super League VI, shortly followed by another as early defeats took their toll.

Former Great Britain captain Brian Noble stepped up to the hot seat at Bradford as his mentor Malcolm Elliott headed to Canberra Raiders, and he immediately encouraged his team of superstars to show more flair than Elliott's nearlymen.

He was rewarded with the post of assistant coach to Great Britain's new Australian boss David Waite and a thrilling first season holding the Bulls' reigns.

John Harbin, a proud Yorkshireman who moved to Australia when he was nine, took full control at cash-strapped Wakefield Trinity after a spell assisting.

And ex-Lion Darryl Powell, who only retired in 2000, emerged from Headingley's academy to take charge of Leeds Rhinos when Dean Lance was forced out after a poor start to the Super League season.

Lance was not the season's first managerial casualty though: Halifax parted company quickly with player-coach Gary Mercer, after just three games in fact.

Kiwi Steve Linnane took over and blamed Mercer for their lack of fighting spirit in subsequent defeats as Halifax continued to struggle to make an impact in the season.

Mercer returned to play for former club Warrington, who also changed boss mid-season; Steve Anderson moved across from Leeds to replace fellow Aussie Darryl van der Velde, who quit during a horrendous campaign.

The future for domestic coaches was certainly looking up though: Lee Crooks (Yorkshire) and Andy Gregory (Lancs) took charge of the Origin teams, Castleford Tigers' new coach Graham Steadman became Waite's right-hand man in the England set-up, in which World Cup coach John Kear took over the Under-21s, as the managerial merry go-round continued.

BRADFORD BLITZ

THE Bradford Bulls stormed to Super League Grand Final victory with a brilliant first-half display that left Wigan in tatters.

Led by the inspirational Henry Paul, playing his last game for Bradford before switching to rugby union with Gloucester, they opened up a 26 point lead at the interval and looked likely to whitewash their rivals until Adrian Lam scored a consolation try in the second-half.

Henry, the older of the two Paul brothers - Robbie was Bulls skipper at Old Trafford - picked up his second winners' medal in the competition after starring for Wigan in 1998.

But his old team were on the receiving end this time as he finished the season with 213 goals, a club record, with six of them coming in the Grand Final.

Michael Withers picked up the Man of the Match award after scoring a hat-trick of tries in front of the biggest crowd at the Final, 60,164.

MASTER McRAE

AUSTRALIAN coach Shaun McRae coped admirably with having to lose 10 of the foreign legion at the merged Hull-Gateshead club last winter by guiding his side to the Play-Offs for the first time in their history.

McRae, the only coach to have been employed throughout Super League's six seasons, held on to his best youngsters and added three internationals named Smith: Kangaroo Jason, Wales' Chris and England's World Cup star Tony.

When Scotland's Scott Logan arrived from Sydney Roosters midway through the season, he took the number of internationals at the club to 18 and reaped the dividends.

The new boys had an immediate impact with the club getting into the top five and staying there from start to finish.

Paul King's Great Britain call-up also showed how the youngsters had flourished under McRae, with Richard Horne and Gareth Raynor also coming on a storm in their second Super League campaigns.

Victory over London on August 19 put the Black and Whites in the Play-Offs and McRae said: "It shows just how far this club has come.

"When we all came down from Gateshead, we took one look around and said, this place has got talent and potential. But we knew we had to do some weeding and gardening.

"We had to go to work really quickly and in the space of two years we've seen a great turnaround. It's been very rewarding."

ON THE WING

The Welsh Rugby Union paid a world record £1.2m to take Iestyn Harris from Leeds Rhinos to Cardiff, cutting short an injury-blighted season for Harris. Kiwi Henry Paul also decided to return to 15-a-side, joining Gloucester in November.

The RFL formed Club GB to raise funds to keep Keiron Cunningham (wanted by Wales and Swansea RU) and Kris Radlinski (England) at St Helens and Wigan respectively.

Great Britain skipper Andy Farrell topped the 2000 points mark during the season, joining Salford scrum-half Bobby Goulding at passing that milestone figure. He also beat Sean Long's record for most points in a season – 352 – with three games left.

Salford City Reds had a wretched season but Malcolm Alker wasn't to blame. He passed the Super League record for tackles in a season – 985 with two games left.

Martin Offiah became the first Englishman to score 500 tries, in Salford's match at London Broncos.

After an incredible 400 appearances for Castleford, 'Diesel' Dean Sampson signed up for another year at The Jungle and also took a role as assistant coach to Graham Steadman.

Huddersfield were relegated after finishing bottom for the fourth straight season.

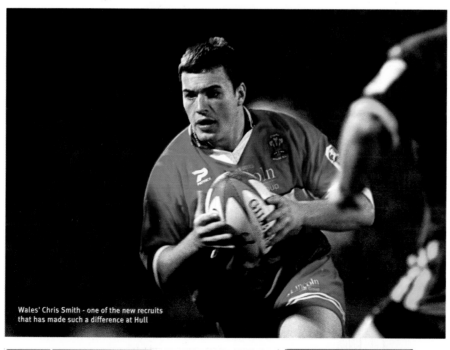

Wales' Chris Smith - one of the new recruits that has made such a difference at Hull

SAINT PAUL

Paul Sculthorpe is a one man rugby team. Whether it's a try saving tackle needed, a last minute burst through the defence or a nerveless penalty dropped between the uprights, the quiet man is THE MAN for the job as he proved time and again for St Helens.

Paul Sculthorpe is a man of steel – in more ways than one.

The St Helens loose forward picked up the Man of Steel award for 2001, a trophy given to top flight rugby league's player of the year.

His success completed a hat-trick of trophies for Saints with his team-mates, Tommy Martyn in 1999 and Sean Long in 2000, crowned the greatest player in the British game in their respective years.

And there is no doubting that Sculthorpe

deserved his award. Saints were far more inconsistent in Super League VI than in previous seasons, hanging on to a top four spot with little comfort, and the player who was responsible for keeping them in the Play-Off race was 'Scully'.

After his last minute try finished off Leeds in the Challenge Cup Semi-Final and capped a man of the match display, all done with a metal plate in his still broken jaw, Saints completed a unique treble by beating Bradford

at Twickenham in April. It was Sculthorpe's first Challenge Cup win, having joined St Helens from Warrington after their 1997 triumph.

But instead of using that Challenge Cup success as a platform to launch their Super League season, Saints were hit by one disaster after another.

Sean Long was ruled out for the season after a late hit at Huddersfield left him needing a knee reconstruction and Martyn missed three

DID YOU KNOW?

He was born on the 22nd September, 1977 in Oldham.

Scully played for Waterhead ARLFC as an amateur before making the break in to the professional game with Warrington in 1994, making his debut at the age of 17 a year later.

Paul scored his first point with a drop goal at Widnes on the 17th April, 1995.

His first try came two games later, ironically at St Helens, on the 7th May, 1995.

He joined Saints in December 1997 for a fee of £370,000, a record transfer for a forward.

He has since won the clean sweep of trophies with Saints; Super League Grand Final in 1999 and 2000, Challenge Cup in 2001 and World Club Challenge in the same year.

He made his England debut and scored a try in the record 73-6 win over France at Gateshead in June 1996.

He went on to make his Great Britain debut in September that year, on tour, coming off the bench in the win over Papua New Guinea.

He was a member of the England 2000 World Cup squad but injury ruled him out of all but the Semi-Final with New Zealand.

'He's one of the best young talents in the world, not just in this country, and a joy to coach.'
ST HELENS COACH IAN MILLWARD

months after Twickers because of a niggling hernia problem.

With their creative heart ripped out, coach Ian Millward turned to the versatile Sculthorpe to plug a gap here and a gap there, appearing in different positions week by week.

A loose forward by trade, he played games at stand-off in place of Martyn, and then scrum-half, filling in for Long. When other alternatives returned to the side, Sculthorpe merely moved to wherever he was needed most. Anywhere will do.

"He's a great player," said Millward. "He's one of the best young talents in the world, not just in this country, and a joy to coach."

Not only did Sculthorpe fill the huge gaps left by the absence of such international class performers as Long and Martyn, he matched the creative output they are rightly lauded for. After touching down in Lancashire's Origin win over Yorkshire in June, Sculthorpe, playing in the back row, was hit with a flailing elbow and was out for a couple of weeks with a badly gashed mouth.

When he returned, he went on a superb scoring streak which grabbed the headlines, including scoring three hat-tricks in eight games. Among them was an international triple. Playing at stand-off, he rescued England from a dire situation against Wales with two quick second-half tries to complete his hat-trick in a 42-33 win at Wrexham.

Not content with being in Super League's top five try-scorers with more than 20, Sculthorpe was also in the top ten for metres gained - nearly 3000 – and clean breaks – more than 30 – as he competed with the best forwards in the game.

To cap it all he even took over penalty kicking duties in Long and Martyn's absence with great success.

His five goals added to two tries which clinched a thrilling 38-26 win over Bradford were typical of his mid-season form. He ended the regular season with 70 goals – only Andy Farrell, Henry Paul, Jamie Rooney and Lee

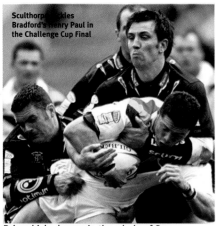

Sculthorpe tackles Bradford's Henry Paul in the Challenge Cup Final

Briers kicked more in the whole of Super League. All of which meant Sculthorpe was the third highest points scorer, beaten only by full-time kickers Farrell and Paul.

For a big man to step into the playmaking shoes of mini-maestros Long and Martyn is a tribute to his athleticism. Half-back pairings are normally far more Ronnie Corbett than Barker but Sculthorpe – tall, slim and muscular – has the nimble footwork to spin out of tackles, sidestep full-backs and outpace wingers, as well as the vision needed to know when and where to break the opposition's defensive line and when to offload.

It was the perfect preparation for taking on

the Aussies in the Ashes, a year after Sculthorpe had the most miserable of World Cups for England – missing all but the Semi-Final humiliation by New Zealand through injury.

After learning his trade with the Wolves of Warrington, Sculthorpe – shy by nature and not entirely comfortable with the superstar status Super League is trying to impose on him – is now in the winning habit at Knowsley Road. Two Super League Grand Final triumphs, the Challenge Cup and World Club Champions title have all come in a stunning 18 months.

And the awesome fact is that he is only mid 20s. Experienced at all but the very highest Test level, he would appear to have at least six years left in the game at the top.

Put him alongside Farrell, Long, Martyn and Kris Radlinski, plus the exciting youngsters Paul Wellens, Leon Pryce and Richard Horne, and the English game seems to have a small core of top class players who would not look out of place among the world's best.

And among the list of the world's brightest stars is where Paul Sculthorpe belongs.

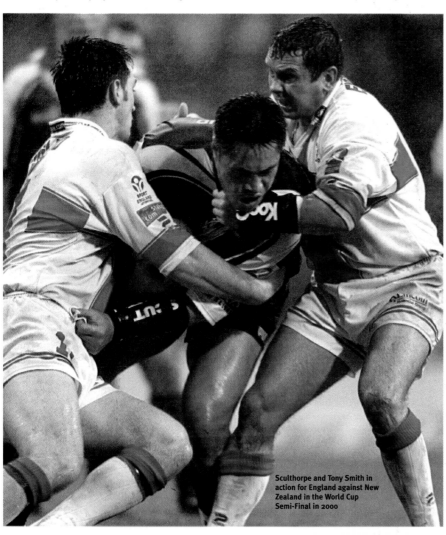

Sculthorpe and Tony Smith in action for England against New Zealand in the World Cup Semi-Final in 2000

HIGH FLIER

Sculthorpe was one of the leading points scorers in Super League rugby in 2001 with our tables showing the standings before the Play-Offs and Grand Final took place.

TOP TRY SCORERS

PLAYER	CLUB	T
Kris Radlinski	Wigan	2
Tonie Carroll	Leeds	2
Tevita Vaikona	Bradford	2
Paul Sculthorpe	**St Helens**	1
Francis Maloney	Salford	1
Steve Renouf	Wigan	1
Michael Withers	Bradford	1
Daryl Cardiss	Halifax	1
Keiron Cunningham	St Helens	1
Andrew Farrell	Wigan	1
Tony Smith	Hull	1

TOP GOAL SCORERS

PLAYER	CLUB	G
Andrew Farrell	Wigan	1
Henry Paul	Bradford	1
Jamie Rooney	Castleford	8
Lee Briers	Warrington	7
Paul Sculthorpe	**St Helens**	7
Steve McNamara	Huddersfield	6
Danny Tickle	Halifax	6
Matt Crowther	Hull	5
Danny Orr	Castleford	5
Martin Pearson	Wakefield	5

TOP POINTS SCORERS

PLAYER	CLUB	T
Andrew Farrell	Wigan	3
Henry Paul	Bradford	3
Paul Sculthorpe	**St Helens**	2
Lee Briers	Warrington	1
Steve Prescott	Hull	1
Danny Orr	Castleford	1
Matt Crowther	Hull	1
Danny Tickle	Halifax	1

STAR OF 2001

KRIS RADLINSKI

WHEN Kris Radlinski signed a new contract with Wigan Warriors at the end of August 2001, it signalled a new phase in his exciting career.

Having won the League title and been a Great Britain regular, the full-back could have been entirely forgiven for accepting the huge offer on the table from rugby union to play in the Zurich Premiership and progress to the England side.

Instead, he settled for less money, but more love.

"I am living my dream at Wigan," he said after signing a new five-year contract with the Warriors and helping them to yet another top two finish in Super League rugby.

'His re-signing is a great boost for Great Britain and rugby league in general' Stuart Raper

"I came pretty close to giving it up but that was wrong. I knew that Wigan could not offer me the money I was offered by union but the decision wasn't about that.

"I'm very lucky to be doing something I've always wanted to do. I wanted to help give young players the sort of start that I had at Wigan. This club has made me the player and person that I am."

The start Radlinski had was extraordinary. He came into an all-conquering Wigan side in 1995 and immediately took on a starring role himself, scoring 18 tries in 17 starts as the

Cherry and Whites completed a clean sweep in 1994-95, including scoring a hat-trick of touchdowns in the Premiership Final victory over Leeds at Old Trafford, just days after celebrating his 19th birthday.

"For the first few weeks that I was at the club I was pleasantly surprised by his ability," admitted Wigan coach Stuart Raper, who joined from Castleford.

"He was always a player I admired before I got here but perhaps had not watched as closely as I could have done.

"He's even better than I thought. His re-signing is a great boost for Great Britain and rugby league in general."

That new five year deal had to be partly funded by the newly-formed Club GB to enable Wigan to remain under the £2.3m salary cap they are limited to – already £500,000 more than everyone else.

It meant that Radlinski, who took over the full-back role at Central Park from Henry Paul, will now have to produce the goods for his country as well as his club if he is to keep critics and rival clubs' fans off his back.

But such is the all round skill of his game that the pressure will not faze him, whether it be at full-back or elsewhere on the park.

After playing at number one in the 20-2 defeat by Australia at Twickenham in England's opening game of the 2000 World Cup, he moved to the wing and scored in the thrashing

of Fiji and stayed there for the thrilling battle with Ireland.

He was on the end of the 49-6 humiliation against the Kiwis in the Semi-Final, which, coupled with the hammerings on the Lions' last trip Down Under led some to question his ability at the highest level.

But he responded to the challenge in typical blistering style in 2001 and that cash spent on keeping him in league will surely prove money well spent.

ONE TO WATCH

LEE RADFORD

L EE who? That was the question being asked not just by rugby league fans but by one of its finest players when the Great Britain training squad was announced in August 2001 ahead of the series with Australia.

Adrian Morley, starring for Sydney Roosters in the NRL, had no idea who Lee Radford was, and he can be forgiven for that.

After all, the Bradford Bulls youngster had made less than ten starts for the Bulls and former club Hull when he made his international bow for England against Wales in July 2001 just six years after turning pro.

The facts do not tell the whole story, however. Radford is one of the inventions of modern rugby league: the full-time replacement. When the going gets tough, he gets off the bench to storm in to the action in Bradford's second row, something he has done over 50 times.

He uses his pace and power when the starting 13 have worn the opposition down, but even then he still has the likes of Lee Gilmour, Jamie Peacock, Mike Forshaw and Shane Rigon to compete with for a place on the pitch.

And despite not being in the Bulls starting line-up, Great Britain & Ireland coach David Waite wanted to see him in action at a higher level, prompting a call-up to Lee Crooks' Yorkshire side for the Origin Game in June 2001. A month later he was making his England debut – and coming off the bench to touch down – in the narrow win over Wales.

"If someone had said at the beginning of the season that I would be selected for Yorkshire, England and Great Britain, I'd have laughed at them. It's a big thing for me, a goal I set as a kid," said Radford (pic below in white).

Going to a club full of internationals at Bradford was exciting for the youngster, who'd experienced the desperate last days of Hull Sharks, but it also meant biding his time. Having done that and received recognition of his ability with representative call-ups in 2001, he now hopes to fulfil his potential with a starring role in Super League VII in 2002.

"I want to get a regular starting spot at Bradford and push on from there," said Radford. "I'm on the verge of making it."

FACTFILE

NAME: Lee Radford
DATE OF BIRTH:
26th March, 1979
WEIGHT: 6ft 2in
HEIGHT: 15st 11lbs
POSITION:
Second row forward
CLUBS: Hull; Bradford

• Made history when he became Hull's youngest ever first team player, making his senior debut against Hunslet in the Challenge Cup in 1996.

• During two years of his time at Hull, he worked as a paint-sprayer in the day, employed by the club chairman, and trained at night.

• Is best mates with Hull's Paul King, the two travelling to Great Britain training camps together from their homes in Hull.

• Coaches his old amateur club, East Hull, formerly known as Mysons, in his spare time. Many of the players are his former team-mates from the Hull Academy who were released as youngsters.

• Coming from a family full of Hull KR fans, it was a big decision for Lee to sign for their bitter cross-city rivals. He still wants to play for Rovers at some stage in his career.

• His favourite meal is, appropriately enough for a Humbersider, fish and chips!

ATHLETICS
ATHLETICS
ATHLETICS
ATHLETICS
ATHLETICS
ATHLETICS
ATHLETICS
ATHLETICS

WORLD CHAMPIONSHIPS

GREENE LIMPS TO HAT-TRICK

AUGUST 5 Maurice Greene completed a hat-trick of World Championship sprint titles but crossed the line in agony.

The Olympic champion and world record holder equalled Carl Lewis' achievement of winning three world 100m titles, clocking 9.82 seconds – the fastest time of the year at that stage.

But he flinched in pain after 60m and was clearly struggling with the knee injury that had troubled him during the year as he plunged through the tape just ahead of his fellow American team-mates Tim Montgomery and Bernard Williams.

The Great Britain duo of Dwain Chambers and Christian Malcolm finished fifth and seventh respectively.

EDWARDS DELIVERS

AUGUST 7 Jonathan Edwards gave the British public a scare before producing his biggest jump in three years to take gold in the triple jump.

The Olympic champion only went through to the Final with his last jump in the qualifying round but made sure of his expected gold medal with a leap of 17.92m taking him well clear of the field, with Swedish jumper Christian Olsson and Russia's Igor Spasovkhodski his nearest rivals.

Edwards travelled further with his second jump than his winning one but received a red flag, indicating a no-jump, a controversial decision but accepted by the popular Brit.

"It was a really tiny mark in the strip and I have seen them given 'OK' before but I wasn't going to argue about it," he said.

"I felt relaxed, even though I was expected to win and just went out there and did my job as well as I could."

He completed his lap of honour, draped in the Union Jack, and suffering with cramp. There was no repeat of his world record leap from the World Championships in Gothenburg in 1995 but the reward was the same. Gold.

HERO MACEY TAKES BRONZE

AUGUST 8 British decathlete Dean Macey held his body together for one last push in the 1500m to take a well deserved bronze medal.

Dean Macey

The Essex-based athlete had five separate injections to ease the severe pain he was in over the 20 hours of competition.

Macey went in to the Championships with damaged hamstrings in both legs and then tore a groin muscle in the opening event, the 100m.

He admitted to almost quitting on at least two occasions but amazingly, led the field after the first day and was well in contention for gold until the javelin proved his undoing.

"I had so many injections I lost count but no-one was going to deny me a medal and getting bronze means all the hard work and pain was worthwhile," said Macey, after running the 1500m in under 4min 30sec to pass 8600 points for the first time in his career.

USA QUEEN JONES BEATEN AT LAST

AUGUST 7 USA's Marion Jones lost her first 100m sprint in four years, encompassing 54 races, in the Semi-Finals. Then two hours later she lost again and with it the gold medal.

The queen of American athletics suffered the biggest shock of the Championships, beaten by Zhanna Pintusevich-Block, who was quick off the blocks and never let go of the lead she built up over the first 50m to record a personal best 10.82 seconds.

Jones is beaten at last as Pintusevich-Block takes gold in the women's 100m

EDMONTON 2001 CHAMPIONS

MEN

100M	M.Greene (US)
200M	K.Kenderis (Gre)
400M	A.Moncur (Bah)
800M	A. Bucher (Swiss)
1500M	H. El Guerrouj (Mor)
3000M SC	R. Kosgei (Ken)
5000M	R.Limo (Ken)
10000M	C.Kamathi (Ken)
110M HDLS	A.Johnson (US)
400M HDLS	F.Sanchez (Dom)
4 x 100M RY	USA
4 x 400M RY	USA
JAVELIN	J.Zelezny (Cz)
POLE VAULT	D.Markov (Aus)
TRIPLE JUMP	J.Edwards (GB)
HIGH JUMP	M.Buss (Ger)
DISCUS	L.Riedel (Ger)
HAMMER	S.Zislkowski (Pol)
LONG JUMP	I.Pedroso (Cuba)
SHOT	J.Godina (US)
MARATHON	G.Abera (Eth)
20KM WALK	R.Rasskazov (Rus)
50K WALK	R.Korzeniowski (Pol)
DECATHLON	T.Dvorak (Cz)

WOMEN

100M	Z. Pintusevich-Block (Ukr)
200M	M.Jones (US)
400M	A.Mbacke Thiam (Sen)
800M	M.Motola (Mz)
1500M	G.Szabo (Rom)
5000M	O.Yegorova (Rus)
10000M	D.Tulu (Eth)
100M HDLS	A.Kirkland (US)
400M HDLS	N.Bidouane (Mar)
4 x 100M RY	USA
4 x 400M RY	Jamaica
JAVELIN	D.Menendez (Cub)
POLE VAULT	S.Dragila (US)
TRIPLE JUMP	T.Lesedeva (Rus)
HIGH JUMP	H.Cloete (SA)
DISCUS	N.Sadova (Rus)
HAMMER	Y.Moreno (Cub)
LONG JUMP	F.May (Ita)
SHOT	Y.Korolchik (Bir)
MARATHON	L.Simon (Rom)
20K WALK	O.Ivanova (Rus)
HEPTHATLON	Y.Prokhorova (Rus)

MEDAL TABLE (TOP 10)

Country	Gold	Silver	Bronze	Total
USA	9	5	5	19
Russia	6	7	6	19
Kenya	3	3	1	7
Cuba	3	1	2	6
Germany	2	4	1	7
Ethiopia	2	2	4	8
Romania	2	1	1	4
Morocco	2	1	0	3
Poland	2	0	2	4
Czech Rep	2	0	0	2

(Key: HDLS: Hurdles; SC: Steeplechase; RY: relay)

The Ukrainian had been beaten by Jones in a photo finish in the World Championships in 1997 and still believes she should have got the gold in that race, so victory was sweet.

"It's the happiest day of my life," said Pintusevich-Block after the race. "I have been dreaming of this moment ever since that race in Athens four years ago and I can't believe I have finally done it."

DRUGS SCANDAL TAINTS CHAMPIONSHIPS

AUGUST 11 World indoor 3000m champion Olga Yegorova won gold in the women's 5000m but came home to a chorus of boos as the Edmonton crowd left her in no doubt about their feelings towards her.

The abuse was directed at the Russian athlete because she had been allowed to compete despite being found to have taken the blood-boosting drug EPO in a meeting in Paris a month earlier.

Because the French authorities had failed to follow the proper procedure, the ban on the 29-year-old was lifted allowing her to compete in the Championships.

Britain's Paula Radcliffe, who narrowly missed out on a medal in the 10,000m, held up a banner in protest during the Semi-Finals of the 5000m and Romanian favourite Gabriele Szabo threatened to pull out of the Final before relenting but finishing out of the medals and 200m behind Yegorova, who had slashed a

staggering 10 seconds off her best time in the 3000m during the year.

"This is the worst thing that could have happened in these Championships," said former 1500m world record holder, Steve Cram.

"There has been some great athletics in Edmonton but the competition will be remembered for Yegorova's victory and that is very sad for the sport."

Yegorova - gold medal but no cheers at Edmonton 2001

TRACK AND FIELD EVENTS

Daniel Caines - a new British star

PAULA FINISHES IN STYLE

BRAVE Paula Radcliffe finally proved that when it comes down to a sprint finish – she can compete with the best.

A second place finish in the 10,000m World Championships in 1999 and fourth in the Olympics in Sydney added to the growing opinion that she might always be the 'bridesmaid and never the bride'.

And when Radcliffe and Ethiopian Gete Wami were locked in combat at the end of the prestigious 8km race through the muddy fields of Ostend, most would have backed the African to come out on top.

But Paula, who also took silver in the 4.1 km race, kicked again with 100m left and Wami had no answer to the extra injection of pace.

'I wanted to win in a sprint finish'

Victory, in 27 mins, 49 secs, fulfilled a lifetime's ambition for Radcliffe who finished runner-up twice in her previous eight attempts to win the prestigious event.

"Winning the gold medal is very special to me and I wanted to win the race in a sprint finish just because everyone said that I couldn't do it," said a delighted Radcliffe after her victory.

"And now I have cracked it I have the confidence to go on and win more – both on the track and cross country."

Paula's ambition to win the 10,000 metres in the World Championships later in the year ended in disappointment though, with Wami just beating her to the bronze medal. It led to an apparent on-track confrontation with her coach, Gary Lough, about her tactics in the race. They happen to be married as well!

GOLD FOR CAINES

BRITISH athletics found a new hero at the World Indoor Championships in Lisbon in young Daniel Caines.

The 21-year-old stormed to glory in the 400m, leading from gun to tape, crossing the line in 46.40 seconds.

American Milton Campbell took the silver with Jamaica's Danny McFarlane third but they were never going to catch Caines, who runs for Birchfield Harriers and clocked the fastest time in the world indoors in Birmingham a month earlier.

His success follows on from Jamie Baulch's triumph in the same event in 1999.

"I can't take in what has happened to me over the last year," said Caines, who narrowly missed out on a place in the 400m Olympics Final in Sydney.

"It's like I am in a fantasy world and winning the indoor title is just amazing for me really.

"Doing well at the Olympics has made me so much more confident and I am better equipped now to perform at a high level in races."

Fellow Briton, Mark Hylton, finished fifth in the race.

Paula Radcliffe and her coach and husband, Gary Lough, don't see eye to eye over her tactics in the 10,000m at the World Championships

Daniel Caines' mother, Blondelle Thompson, was British high-hurdles record holder in 1974 and the 400m runner is also the nephew of former Aston Villa and Coventry footballer, Garry Thompson.

Mark Lewis-Francis won bronze in the 60m dash at the World Indoor Championships and set a world junior record along the way. In his first senior event, the 18-year-old British star clocked 6.51 seconds to finish behind American duo Tim Harden and Tim Montgomery.

Paula Radcliffe became the first Briton since Zola Budd in 1986 to win the World Cross Country Championship. She is also the first British-born athlete to achieve that status since Ian Stewart in the mid 1970s. Budd hailed from South Africa.

The World Cross Country Championships were switched from Dublin to Ostend because of the Foot and Mouth epidemic which curtailed most international sporting events in Ireland over a three month period.

Paula Radcliffe added a silver medal in the 4.1km race at the World Cross Country Championships to her gold in the longer event. Gete Wami, who was second behind Radcliffe, took first place over the shorter distance.

Britain finished fifth out of eight in the men's European Cup table and the women were fourth from eight.

JUNE 23
BREMEN
EUROPEAN CUP

FLYER FRANCIS STUNS OLYMPIC CHAMP

Mark Lewis-Francis announced his debut for the British senior team with a brilliant display of running that brought him an unexpected gold in the 100m at the European Cup.

And among his victims in the sprint was Sydney Olympic 200m gold medallist, Kostas Kenderis.

The Greek was overtaken by the 18-year-old star from Wolverhampton in the closing 10 metres, the winner finishing in 10,13 seconds.

"I didn't even know he was in the race until we were warming up and then I saw him and the nerves set in," said Lewis-Francis after the event.

"I was told that Britain always win the 100m at the European Cup so that added to the pressure.

"But once the nerves calmed down a bit I loved it. This is my first big race in Europe and I'm delighted that it has gone so well."

SEPTEMBER 15
YOKOHAMA, JAPAN

LEGEND JOHNSON QUITS WITH VICTORY

Michael Johnson, one of the most gifted runners of all time, eased out of the world of athletics with a farewell tour of the globe during 2001.

Avoiding the US National Championships, World Championships and many other high profile events, the American 200m and 400m superstar (pic below) took part in meets at places like Gothenburg and Seville before dusting down his studs for one last hurrah in Australia and Japan in September.

"There are no more goals for me now," he said at the start of the track season.

"I have enjoyed my career and won many titles but the time has come to move on in my life."

Johnson, five times Olympic champion and world record holder at 200m and 400m, ended 10 years at the top by anchoring home his Dream Team to victory in a 100m to 400m relay in Japan.

STAR OF 2001

JONATHAN EDWARDS

IT MAY not have been a vintage World Championships, in fact it was a pretty average one at best, with so many class performers missing either injured or taking time out after the Olympics.

And it was certainly a dire one for Britain's athletes, with just two medals to show for their efforts. Dean Macey took a brave bronze in the decathlon but it was Jonathan Edwards who did more than anyone to lift the spirits of the 63-strong team.

The 35-year-old triple jumper went to the Edmonton games as the overwhelming favourite to lift the title and duly delivered with a winning jump of 17.92 metres.

It had none of the glamour of his world record leap of more than 18 metres in Gothenburg in the 1995 World Championships, when he received a standing ovation that nearly brought tears to his eyes.

But while the other Brits got their tactics wrong, dropped batons or carried injuries, Edwards produced it when it mattered again.

"He is awesome," said Swede Christian Olsson, who finished in the silver medal position.

"I was a high jumper in my teens and saw Jonathan record his world record jump in Gothenburg. He inspired me to take up the triple jump and all the jumpers still look up to him as the master."

Olsson, like bronze medal winner, Igor Spasovkhodski, from Russia, is among the new breed of young talent coming up in the sport, but Edwards is not afraid of their challenge. He is thriving on it.

"I don't know if I am regarded as a great uncle by the lads coming through but it's good for the sport that so many good young jumpers like Christian are around now," he said.

"But who knows how long I can go on for, or will want to go on for. There have been times when I have gone to a meet and asked why I am there and when that starts to become the norm, it will be time to call it a day.

"I have had a good run without too many injuries over the last three or four years though and that helps maintain the desire to compete.

"I'm enjoying my athletics at the moment and have not ruled out competing in the next Olympics in Athens 2004. It's a long way off but who knows, I could be there.

"For now I am just enjoying being world champion."

IT'S A FACT

- Edwards' winning jump of 17.92 metres was his best in three years.

- Jonathan jumped more than 18 metres with one mighty leap but it was ruled a 'no jump' because a fraction of his spikes had gone over the permitted area for take-off.

- He claims that the two really important things in his life are his family and his Christian beliefs.

- A motor enthusiast, he has spent some of his hard-earned money on his favourite toys, fast cars.

- He was suffering from cramp during the competition and pulled up on the approach to his final jump to avoid further injury, having already forfeited his fifth.

172

ONE TO WATCH
DEAN MACEY

FACTFILE

NAME: Dean Macey
DATE OF BIRTH:
12th December, 1977
SPORT: Decathlon

• Won the silver medal
in the Junior World
Championships in 1996.

• Injuries meant that the
2001 World Championships
was his first event since he
finished fourth in the
Sydney Olympics in 2000.

• Girlfriend Lucy gave him
a teddy bear with a Union
Jack waistcoat to wish him
luck before he set out for
the World Championships.
"I know it sounds daft, but
that bear really helped me
get through the second
day," he said.

•He set personal bests in
three events during the
competition, the 110m
hurdles, the 400m and the
high jump.

• A former lifeguard,
he lives in Canvey Island,
Essex.

• He picked up £13,000 for
winning bronze in Canada.

BRITISH team performance director in the 2001 World Championships, Max Jones, called it 'the bravest performance I have seen in my life'.

And Daley Thompson, Britain's greatest ever decathlete and arguably the most supreme athlete of the 1980s, predicts he will become the best in the world.

Dean Macey's bronze in Edmonton was the most deserved medal of the games, with the Essex lad shedding blood, sweat and tears as he overcame a series of hamstring and groin injuries to complete the 10 events to the amazement of his colleagues and rivals.

He added the third place prize to the silver medal he won in the Seville World Championships in 1999 and now he is determined to complete the set with a gold in the Commonwealth Games in 2002 and then push on for the Athens Olympics two years later.

"I am still only 23 and take it from me, I will win gold one day," he said after returning from Edmonton.

"I have proved that I can challenge for gold at a major competition and it will not be long before I am standing on the rostrum with the number one medal around my neck."

And Daley Thompson echoed those sentiments saying: "Dean scored 8605 points in Canada and that is his best ever tally.

"If he can stay clear of injuries over the winter, he will have a real chance of winning the Commonwealth Gold.

"Technically he is very good in a number of events. There are no glaring weaknesses in his make-up and he just needs to keep improving.

"If he does that I'm sure he will beat my British record points score of 8847 and go over the 9000 barrier. And that would make him the best decathlete in the world."

And that is the target Macey has set himself – to be the best.

"There are still a couple of events that I need to improve on – mainly the pole vault and the javelin, which really let me down in the World Championships, but I will get there," he said.

"It's there in my mind that I can beat Daley's record and by the next Olympics in 2004, I reckon I should be up near the 8900 points mark."

And that will give him a great chance of winning the gold medal he so richly deserves.

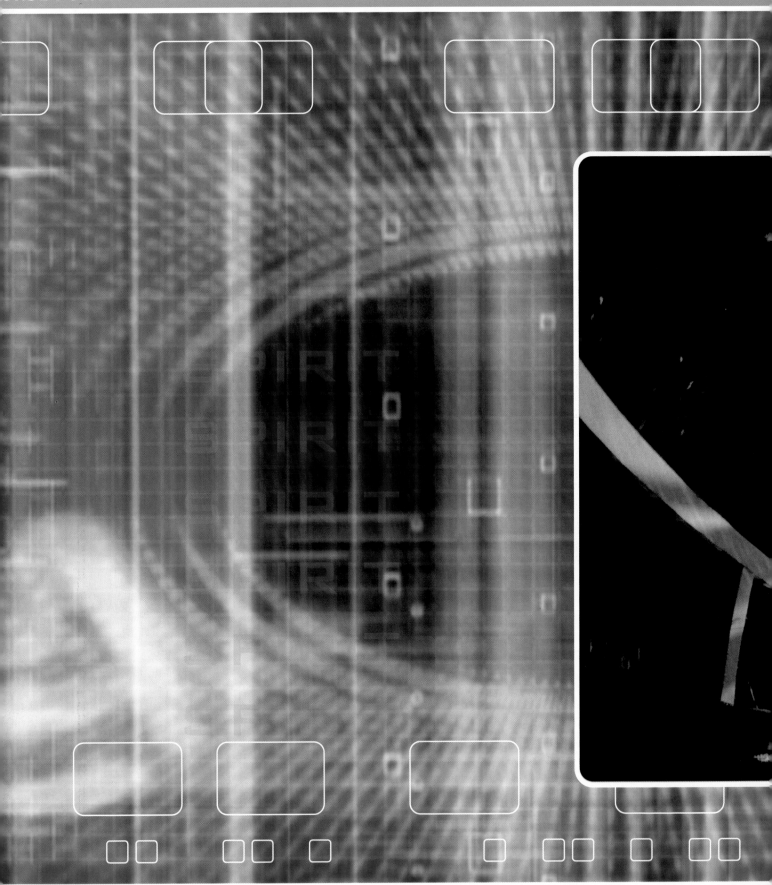

E POWER • HORSE POWER • HORSE POWER • HORSE POWER • HORSE POWER • HORS

HORSE POWER
HORSE POWER
HORSE POWER
HORSE POWER
HORSE POWER

HORSE POWER
HORSE POWER
HORSE POWER

E POWER • HORSE POWER • HORSE POWER • HORSE POWER • HORSE POWER • HORS

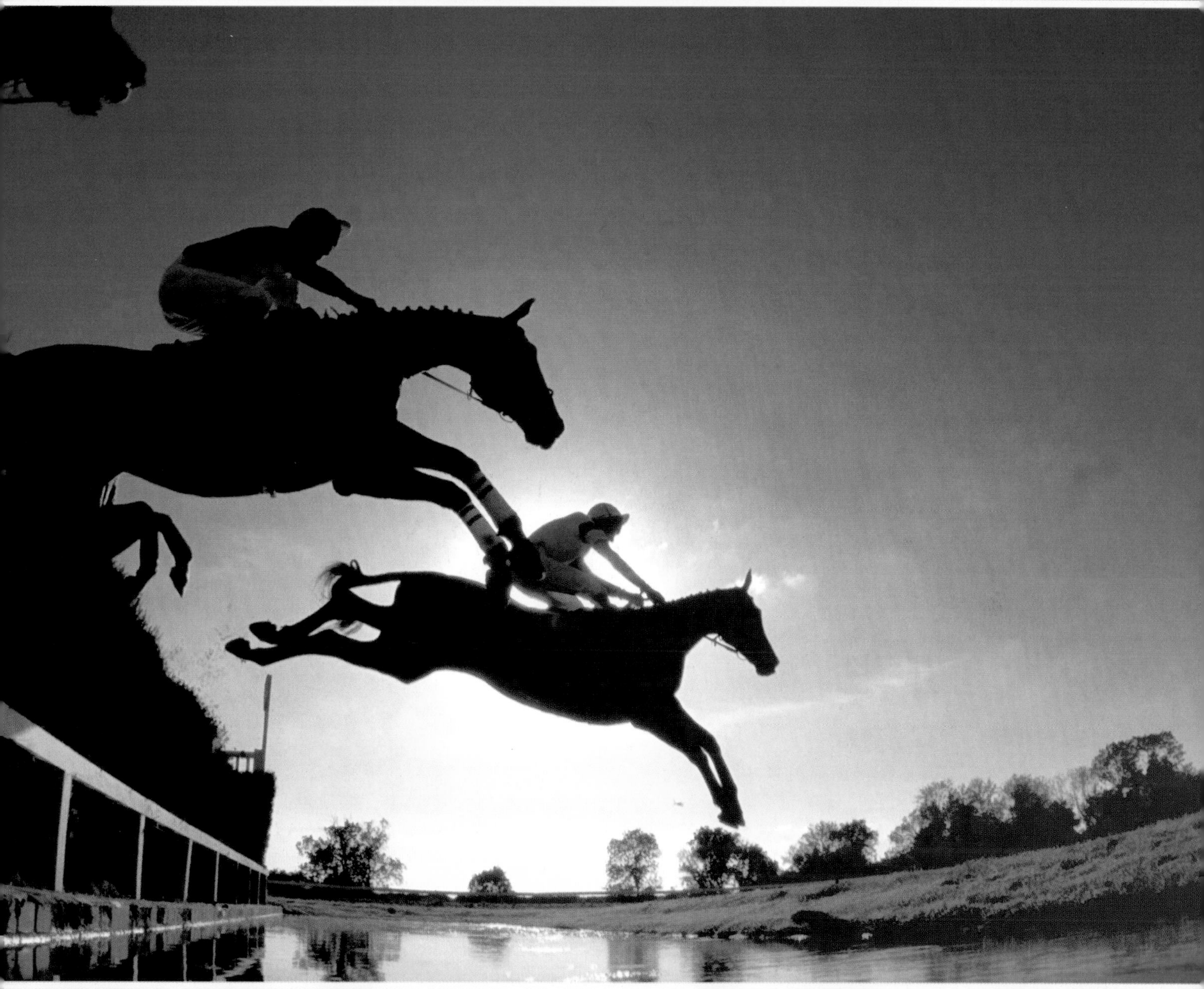

EQUINE ELITE

Red Marauder and Richard Guest win the Grand National

JUNE 9
EPSOM
DERBY

GALILEO THE GREAT

THE WORLD of racing has a new wonder horse. Irish colt Galileo destroyed the rest of the field in the Vodafone Derby with a burst of speed that drew gasps of breath from the packed Epsom crowd.

With two furlongs to go jockey Mick Kinane made his move down the famous straight and his mount pulled away from the rest of the field with every stride.

Galileo finished three and a half lengths clear of second placed Golan, the two were joint favourites at 11-4 at the start.

"It was just unbelievable that the horse could burst away like that from such a class field," said Galileo's delighted trainer, the brilliant Aidan O'Brien.

"I have never had a horse show me that kind of speed before but we knew he had the potential.

"When we first saw him run we knew he had the ability. He's just a natural."

And Epsom great Walter Swinburn, who had three Derby winners as a jockey including the legendary Shergar, had no doubts about Galileo's standing.

"We have seen a very special horse. He sprinted away from a class field and only the very best could do that," he said.

APRIL 7
AINTREE
GRAND NATIONAL

MUDDY MARVEL

RED MARAUDER won the most sensational and controversial Grand National race in years.

Forty horses set out at the start of the Aintree classic in quagmire conditions and only two came home without remounting, with four in total finishing.

Red Marauder, ridden by Richard Guest, finished well clear of second placed Smarty with Blowing Wind third and Papillon fourth, the last two being remounted after falling in the atrocious conditions.

After three days of rain, the race was in doubt right up until a late course inspection.

"I was debating whether we should have gone out there because it was that bad," said Guest after guiding home the 33-1 winner.

"I have never ridden on worse ground and no National will be ridden on tougher going again.

"All I could do was showjump around the course because I knew that any horse left standing at the end would go close to winning.

"Red Marauder is not the best of jumpers, in fact he is probably the worst to win the National, but he's got loads of guts.

"I had a few lucky escapes and there were times when I could not believe that we didn't go down but he kept going and I knew he would because he loves the soft ground."

Despite the lack of finishers, no horses or jockeys were hurt and the riders agreed that it was the right decision to race.

The Foot and Mouth epidemic had put a question mark over the race for a while but fans got a spectacle that few at Aintree are likely to forget in a hurry.

"The advantage with soft going is that there is less chance of the horses getting injured because there is give in the ground," added Guest.

"It was testing conditions and I did have reservations but everyone returned home safely and you can't ask for more than that."

KING IS QUEEN

MARY KING stole the show at the Burghley Horse Trials coming out of hospital to help Britain win the team title.

The 40-year-old from Devon suffered a badly gashed thigh when her mount Star Appeal trod on her as she fell during the cross-country stage of the three-day event.

She received stitches but amazed everyone by returning to the action to finish fourth overall on her other horse, King Soloman III, on the following day.

King finished as Britain's top placed rider with 54.6 points after King Soloman III hit a couple of poles in the showjumping stage.

"My leg was a bit sore when I was walking around but I never felt any pain at all when I was riding," she said after receiving a great ovation at the end of her showjumping round with Britain taking the team title under the new Olympic format.

It was remarkable that King was riding at Burghley in the first place.

Earlier in the year she suffered a broken neck in a training accident and at one stage it was feared that she might not ride at the very top level again.

New Zealand riders dominated Burghley, filling the first three individual places with Blyth Tait taking the first prize of £20,000 on Ready Teddy with 41.4 points.

Fellow Kiwi Andrew Nicholson was second on Mr Smiffy with 46 points and just behind in third was Daniel Jocelyn on Silence with 52.4 points.

CHARLES THE FIRST

PETER CHARLES on the 12-year-old Holstein mare Corrada triumphed in the most famous class in the showjumping calendar – the Hickstead Derby.

A packed crowd at the Sussex arena watched Corrada jump a superb clear round to set a formidable target.

He received two time faults, not helped by starting outside the 45 seconds allowed, but took the top prize with fellow Irishman Billy Twomey on Give Me Remus second alongside 21-year-old Nicky Boulter on Magna Carta, both finishing on four faults.

Boulter and Magna Carta were members of the gold medal winning Young Riders team at the European Championships and are tipped for a bright future.

Heavy rain made negotiating the daunting Derby bank even more tricky than usual and there were 12 retirements and eliminations in the class, including legendary German rider Franke Sloothaak, who retired after Landdame slipped to his knees at the bottom of the 10ft 6in bank.

A first ever Elite Award was presented to Virtual Village Welham and Hiscox Askari in a retirement ceremony before the Derby started.

STABLE TALK

Red Marauder's winning time of 11 minutes in the Grand National was the slowest since 1883.

The race also provided the smallest number of finishers since 1928 when Tipperary Tim beat Billy Barton, the only two runners to finish.

At 35, Red Marauder's jockey, Richard Guest, was the oldest rider in the 2001 Grand National.

Three years before his Aintree triumph, Guest had been banned by the Jockey Club after stewards found him guilty of not trying hard enough in a race. He went to America for six months vowing not to race again such was his disgust at the decision but returned after a change of mind.

Red Marauder's victory was well received in China. Red is deemed a lucky colour in the country and many punters took advantage of the internet to place bets on the horse.

Three-day eventer Mary King broke her neck while schooling a young horse in May and had an operation to have a vertebrae removed, reshaped and put back.

Last to go at the Hickstead Derby, Irishman Kevin Babington on his mount, Carling King, were eliminated after starting their round before the bell.

Mary King at the Sydney Olympics - a year and one broken neck later she was riding high at Burghley

STAR OF 2001

GALILEO

Mick Kinane and Galileo after their Derby triumph

THERE comes along occasionally a sporting star so bright they light up their field of speciality – Muhammad Ali, Ian Botham, Diego Maradona and Pete Sampras are four such outstanding talents. Similarly, one name dominated the world of horse racing in 2001, a four-legged flyer that will be talked about in the equine world for many a year – Galileo.

Even those not particularly taken with the sport of kings may have heard the name because the Irish colt is something special, so special that he is the most valuable horse in the world.

He won the Derby in the second fastest time in the 222 year history of the race, two minutes 33.27 seconds, in front of the biggest attendance at the event for 25 years.

They had all come to see Galileo and he didn't disappoint them. Jockey Mick Kinane just pointed him in the right direction as the runners came down the straight at Epsom and he won by a whopping three and a half lengths. It was the most impressive performance since Shergar galloped home in the same race 20 years ago.

"Only something with wings could catch him when we let him go," said a delighted Kinane as he celebrated his Derby success.

That performance was awesome but Galileo's display in the King George VI and Queen Elizabeth Diamond Stakes in July was even more breathtaking and left the crowd at Ascot stunned at its brilliance.

Fantastic Light provided the biggest challenge the three-year-old had faced in his career and with 200 yards to go they were neck and neck in a storming race, then Galileo stepped up into turbo-charged mode to leave the thousands of fans watching in no doubt that this was a horse of supreme class.

"Great horses come along very rarely and I have no doubt that Galileo falls into that category," said delighted jockey Kinane, who had to get an interim court injunction overruling a decision by the Irish Turf stewards, who had banned him for two days over an alleged careless riding incident at Leopardstown, which would have put him out of the race.

"When I was pulling him up at the end of the race it was as though he had just been out for a gentle canter and nothing more. I have never

seen him tired after a race and that is what makes him so special."

Frankie Dettori, on board Fantastic Light, agreed that he had been beaten by a wonder horse. "It was a great race and we gave the people what they wanted to see," said the livewire Italian.

"We were just ahead at one stage but Galileo just went in to another gear and we can have no complaints about finishing second to a horse of that class."

With the Irish Derby already bagged to complete a hat-trick of wins for the master, the talk in the ring after Galileo's Ascot success was the Breeders' Cup Classic in America and the prospect of the 'winged one' going away to stand at stud carrying the status of the first £50 million horse in history.

That was before Fantastic Light, another superb horse, gained revenge for his Ascot defeat to beat a slightly below par Galileo at Leopardstown in September. A defeat that is likely to confirm that move to stud in 2002.

ONE TO WATCH
VERE PHILLIPPS

I T took the tragic death of his wife two years ago to put Vere Phillipps on the road to a successful career in the world of eventing.

Polly Phillipps died under her horse, Coral Cove, at the Thirlestone Castle Horse Trials in August 1999, an accident that prompted a change in direction for the horse dealer.

Phillipps, an experienced horseman, whose expertise lay in show jumping and hunting, made the decision to switch to eventing – riding the horses his wife had competed on.

He admitted that the move helped him come to terms with his grief, saying: "It did keep me going at times, riding Polly's horses but I also really enjoyed it as well.

"If I sold Coral Cove and then someone had an accident on him I would not have been able to live with that.

"I knew him better than anyone, the way he thinks and how he had been trained in the past. Although I had not evented before, I had jumped loads of different fences on lots of different horses and was probably as experienced over jumps as anyone.

"I felt I could sort out the problems that had affected Coral Cove and caused the accident and decided to give it a go."

And Phillipps did more than give it a go. He has made a major impact in the sport and surprised many with his results.

A ninth place finish on Coral Cove at Bramham in his first year of competition in 2000 was followed by third place at Eglinton, top spot at Auchinleck, fourth in the British Open at Gatcombe and fourth at Burghley, one of the toughest eventing competitions.

The Foot and Mouth epidemic that swept the country in 2001 played chaos with the equine world and just like many horse race meetings, the eventing calendar also suffered.

So convinced that Burghley would join the Badminton Horse Trials in being cancelled, Phillipps worked his horses less than he would normally have done over the year.

But the Trials were given the green light and Phillipps' mount, Coral Cove, arrived at Burghley short of 100 per cent fitness.

The Leicestershire-based rider still achieved a respectable 12th in the individual and also helped the British riders to top spot in the team event, alongside Graham Law, William Fox-Pitt, Pippa Funnell and Mary King.

Further signs that a very successful career is within his grasp.

FACTFILE

NAME: Vere Phillipps
AGE: 39
HOME: Rempstone, Leicestershire
EVENT HORSES: Coral Cove and Biras Creek

• Received the prestigious Equestrian Personality of the Year award in 2000 after readers in the horse world's bible, Horse and Hound magazine, voted him their number one.

• His weakest discipline of the three in eventing (dressage, cross-country and show jumping) is dressage and he now has lessons from Olwen Davies, who also trained his wife, Polly.

• Had never had a riding lesson in his life until he started eventing in 2000.

• Two years after the tragic death of his wife, he married Clea Hoeg-Mudd, who was a close friend of his first wife's.

• As a child he used to sneak in to farmers' fields to ride his pony.

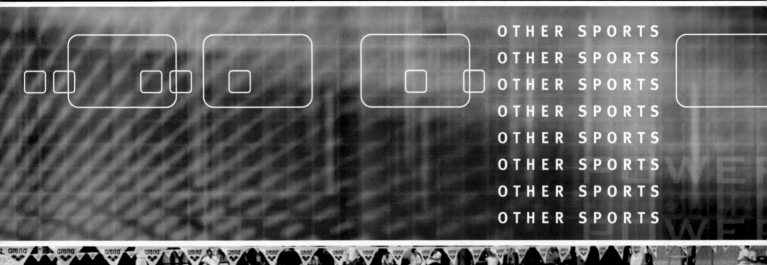

OTHER SPORTS
OTHER SPORTS
OTHER SPORTS
OTHER SPORTS
OTHER SPORTS
OTHER SPORTS
OTHER SPORTS
OTHER SPORTS

OTHER SPORTS
OTHER SPORTS
OTHER SPORTS
OTHER SPORTS

OTHER SPORTS

FLYING FOSTER MAKES HIS MARK

JANUARY 17 Mark Foster became the quickest butterfly swimmer in history over 50 metres at the FINA World Cup in Sheffield.

The British sprint specialist reached the turn in an amazing 10.33 seconds and finished in 22.87 seconds, 0.32 seconds inside Lars Frolander's previous world record.

"I was confident I could go under 23 seconds and really wanted to smash the record, not just beat it," said a delighted Foster after the race.

"This was the race that I have been looking at for a while as a world record chance and I'm really pleased all the hard work has paid off.

"I got off to a great start and knew the record was on after just a couple of strokes. The turn went well for me and it was a great feeling when I saw the time.

"I've been saying for a while that I could take the record away from Lars and I still feel that I might be able to go even quicker."

GOLDEN GIRLS MADE TO WAIT FOR GLORY

JULY 25 The women's 200m freestyle relay team of Karen Pickering, Nicola Jackson, Karen Legg and Janine Belton gave Britain their first World Swimming Championship gold medal in 26 years amid a storm of controversy.

The fab four originally finished third in the pool behind Australia and the United States but the Aussies were disqualified immediately after the race because one of their team, Petria Thomas, jumped into the pool to celebrate before the other competitors had finished.

The Americans were also disqualified after their second swimmer, Christina Teuscher, dived in fractionally before the first one had touched the wall.

So Britain were moved up from bronze to gold, their finishing time of seven minutes, 58.69 seconds, a British record. Then the fun really started.

The Americans were then reinstated as gold medal winners because FINA, the sport's governing body, decided that the touch-pads on the wall were faulty.

Britain appealed against that decision, backed by a number of other countries, and a decision was held over for 24 hours.

Finally the Americans were told they had been disqualified from the event and Britain had their first world champions since David Wilkie's triumph in 1975 and their first ever at a relay event.

For the Ipswich-based Pickering, who also won silver in the 100m freestyle relay, it was a deserved triumph. She has swum for Britain for 11 years and in that time picked up 24 European and Commonwealth medals for her efforts.

"To win gold is amazing and is the result of a lot of hard work," she said after the triumph in Japan.

"We obviously would have liked to have finished first but we have smashed the British record, the gold is ours and no one can take that away from us."

The scoreboard confirms the time - Mark Foster is a world record holder

ARMSTRONG JOINS THE LEGENDS

JULY 29 Lance Armstrong booked his place in the list of all-time cycling greats with his third successive victory in the greatest two-wheel race of them all – the Tour de France.

The US Postal team rider, who overcame cancer earlier in his career, joined an elite band of cyclists to have won the race three times on the trot - a who's who of the legends in the sport – Miguel Indurain, Eddy Merckx, Jacques Anquetil and Louision Bobet.

Armstrong's victory over the 2,100 mile course, that includes some of the toughest terrain in the racing calendar, provided the winner with his best moment in his hat-trick of successes in France.

"I have enjoyed all of my victories in this race because it is the hardest in the world but this one is the best of the lot," said the 29-year-old as he collected his final yellow jersey, awarded to the race leader, before taking in a victory lap of the Champ-Elysees.

"This is the biggest, most beautiful race in the world and now I want to come back in 2002 and win my fourth one."

Few would argue against the king of the mountains achieving just that next July.

ALAIN HITS THE PEAKS

MARCH 11 Alain Baxter produced the best performance by a British skier in 19 years when he finished fourth in the last World Cup slalom of the season.

The Scotsman was only fractionally outside a third place finish and that would have equalled Conrad Bartleski's British record placing at Val Gardena in 1982.

Baxter's fourth spot meant that he finished the World Cup season in 11th place, after starting the year ranked outside the top 60.

"I'm thrilled at the improvements I have made this year and hopefully it can carry on for the Winter Olympics in 2002," said Baxter.

"It's been a great year and to finish fourth in my last race was brilliant. I was third after the first run but was frightened I might blow it on the second one. Fortunately I held it together and the result has given me real confidence for next year."

Baxter, from Aviemore, comes from a skiing family. His parents both represented Scotland in the sport, so have three or four other members of his family and younger brother Noel is a member of the British junior squad.

SILVER LINING FOR ALEX

FEBRUARY 12 Britain's best hope of a gold medal in the Winter Olympics in 2002, Alex Coomber, had to make do with silver at the women's World Skeleton Bobsleigh Championships in Calgary, Canada.

The RAF flight lieutenant led the field for the first three rounds but she was eventually beaten in to second place by Switzerland's Maya Pedersen.

The sport returns to the Olympics for the first time since 1948 at Salt Lake City in 2002 with Coomber amongst the favourites for gold.

Victory would make her the first Briton to take top spot since Christopher Dean and Jayne Torvill's Bolero ice dance routine blew away the rest of the opposition at the 1984 Olympics.

IN THE SWIM

BRITAIN ENJOYED THEIR BEST WORLD SWIMMING CHAMPIONSHIPS IN 26 YEARS WITH THEIR RECORD HAUL IN FUKUOKA, JAPAN IN JULY 2001.

THE FULL ROLL OF HONOUR READ:-

GOLD: Karen Pickering, Nicola Jackson, Karen Legg and Janine Belton in the women's 4 x 200m freestyle relay.

SILVER: Graeme Smith in the men's 1500m freestyle; Karen Pickering, Alison Sheppard, Melanie Marshall and Rosalind Brett in the women's 4 x 100m freestyle relay.

BRONZE: Graeme Smith in the men's 800m freestyle; Mark Foster in the men's 50m butterfly; Joanna Fargus in the women's 200m backstroke; Zoe Baker in the 50m breaststroke.

Graeme Smith smashed the British record in the 1500m freestyle to take silver in a time of 14 minutes 58.94 seconds, the first time a Briton had swum under 15 minutes and only the 12th swimmer in history to achieve that feat.

Unlucky Alison Sheppard finished fourth in the women's 50m freestyle, missing out on a medal by 0.04 seconds, but she did break her own Commonwealth record.

OTHER SPORTS

Cambridge won a controversial
Boat Race after the first restart
in the history of the event

REGIS' DOUBLE DREAM TURNS SOUR

JANUARY 26 Former European 200m sprint champion John Regis quit his new career as bobsleigh brakeman after only three months in the job.

He dreamed of becoming the first man to win medals in the summer and winter Olympics but was forced to abandon the idea after getting frustrated with the political in-fighting amongst the British bobsleigh squad.

Regis finished a disappointing 24th on his World Cup debut as brakeman to Sean Olsson but then decided to switch crews and ride with Mark Tout, who had been reinstated after a drugs ban. His move didn't go down well with the authorities and he was left out of the British Championships.

"I enjoyed the actual racing but if Britain wants to be serious about the sport, they should concentrate on it fully and not on fighting amongst themselves," said Regis.

OXFORD FURY IN BOAT RACE CHAOS

MARCH 24 One of the most controversial university Boat Races in history ended with angry Oxford complaining they had been 'cheated' out of victory.

Only a minute in to the race both crews clashed for at least the third time since the start and Cambridge bowman Colin Swainson lost his oar.

Umpire Rupert Obholzer, a former Dark Blue, stopped the race just as Oxford were forging ahead and ordered the first restart in Boat Race history. The crews set off on equal terms and Cambridge eventually cruised home by two and a half lengths to record their 77th win in 147 races.

"When the crews started clashing I warned them," said Obholzer. "But they carried on and I noticed that Oxford were going off course. The Cambridge man lost his oar and I decided to stop the race.

"Oxford were ahead but I had been warning them when the incident happened so Cambridge could have appealed if I did not start the race again.

"They may think I was unfair on them to order a re-start on level terms when they were ahead but I could have disqualified them after only a minute of the race and that would not have done anyone any favours."

Oxford clearly did not agree and their coach, Sean Bowden, was adamant they had been hard done by.

"Clashing between crews is part of the race and it has happened many times in the past," he said.

"On those occasions the umpire has not stepped in to protect either boat. You just accept it as part of the race.

"Cambridge rowed straight in to us at the start and although I don't blame them for that, they created the problem with their tactics.

"They are a fine crew but we never had the chance to really show our best, that is what has annoyed us more than anything else."

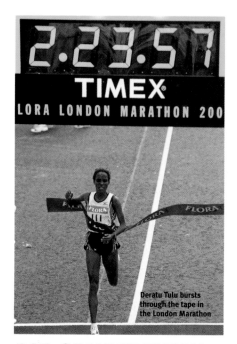

Deratu Tulu bursts
through the tape in
the London Marathon

OAR-SOME TRIUMPH

AUGUST 25 Matthew Pinsent and James Cracknell stunned the rowing world by winning two gold medals at the World Championships in the space of two hours.

The British duo just held off the strong challenge from the Italian crew to win the coxed pairs title and then returned to the water in Lake Lucerne two hours later to beat the Yugoslavs and take gold in the coxless pairs.

There was only three-tenths of a second between the Brits and the Italians in the first race and it looked as though that battle had taken too much out of Pinsent and Cracknell midway through the coxless pairs.

They were lying fourth at the halfway stage with a two second gap between them and the powerful Yugoslav pair of Nikola Stojic and Djordje Visacki in front.

But a magnificent burst took them ahead of the Yugoslavs and despite hitting a buoy with an oar they held on to win in a photo finish.

ROAD RUNNERS

APRIL 22 Abdelkader El Mouaziz won the men's race in the London Marathon for the second time in three years.

The Moroccan stepped up the pace after just over 90 minutes of the race to drop Kenya's Paul Tergat and favourite Antonio Pinto of Portugal to cross the line a comfortable winner in two hours, seven minutes and 11 seconds.

Tergat finished runner-up a minute behind with Mark Steinle coming home in sixth place with a time of two hours, 10 minutes and 46 seconds, the highest placed British runner.

The women's race was a much more dramatic affair from start to finish.

World record holder Tegla Loroupe stopped twice in the first three miles suffering from tightening muscles in her legs and was forced to do stretching exercises.

The Kenyan left herself with a lot of running to do to catch the leading bunch and finally made contact in the closing stages but had nothing left when the pace was upped again and finished well back in eighth.

Ethiopia's Deratu Tulu and Russian Svetlana Zakharova opened up a gap on the chasing pack and Tulu burst clear to win in two hours, 23 minutes and 57 seconds.

But if it wasn't for the smart footwork of race director, David Bedford, she may not have crossed the line at all. The former 10,000m world record holder grabbed hold of a man who raced towards Tulu as she approached the finish, forcing the runner to swerve dramatically.

"I moved sideways quickly when I saw him because I knew if he tripped me I would go down," said the startled Ethiopian after winning her first marathon.

MARATHON EVENT

HOW THEY FINISHED IN THE LONDON MARATHON

MEN

RUNNER	COUNTRY	TIME
A. El Mouaziz	Morocco	2:07:11
Paul Tergat	Kenya	2:08:15
Antonio Pinto	Portugal	2:09:36
Tesfaye Jifar	Ethiopia	2:09:45
Japhet Kosgei	Kenya	2:10:45
Mark Steinle	Britain	2:10:46
Takayuki Inubushi	Japan	2:11:42
Abel Anton	Spain	2:11:57
H. Ramaala	S. Africa	2:12:02
Gert Thys	S. Africa	2:12:11

WOMEN

Deratu Tulu	Ethiopia	2:23:57
Svetlana Zakharova	Russia	2:24:04
Joyce Chepchumba	Kenya	2:24:12
Lidia Simon	Romania	2:24:15
Elfenesh Alemu	Ethiopia	2:24:29
Nuta Olaru	Romania	2:25:18
Alina Ivanova	Russia	2:25:34
Tegla Loroupe	Kenya	2:26:10
A. Fernandez	Mexico	2:26:22
M. Biktagirova	Russia	2:27:14

MEN'S WHEELCHAIR

D.Lemeunier	France	1:42:37
K.Papworth	Britain	1:44:54
D.Weir	Britain	1:50:55

WOMEN'S WHEELCHAIR

T.Grey Thompson	Britain	2:13:55
D.Brennan	Britain	2:36:50
M.Rice	Ireland	3:14:37

Matthew Pinsent - two
gold medals in two hours at
the World Championships

OTHER SPORTS

Sheffield steel the limelight

STEPHANIE'S GOLDEN GOODBYE

JULY 21 Stephanie Cook bowed out of the world of modern pentathlon at the very top with her third major title in under a year.

She was already European champion and Sydney Olympic gold medallist when she started out as favourite for the World Championship title at Millfield School.

And Stephanie didn't disappoint her home fans. A perfect round in the horse riding section left her well in contention for gold in the final discipline, the 3000m.

And she strolled past leader Claudia Cerutti in the early stages of the race to complete her hat-trick of titles in style, taking the gold in the first World Modern Pentathlon Championships to be held in Britain in 20 years.

Cook had always let it be known that she was retiring after the event to return to medicine and take up a doctor's post at a hospital in the West Country.

Cook also added the team gold in the event alongside Kate Allenby and Sian Lewis, with another Brit, Georgina Harland finishing third in the individual.

SPECS APPEAL

JANUARY 14 John Walton became the first player wearing glasses to win the Embassy World Darts Championship when he beat holder Ted Hankey 6-2 in the Final.

Walton, from Sheffield, 50-1 to take the title before a dart had been thrown in the competition, became only the third player, after Eric Bristow and Richie Burnett, to follow up his World Masters success in December with the Embassy world title.

"Beating Ted to win the world title means so much to me because my name is now down in history alongside Eric and Richie," said a delighted Walton, nicknamed John Boy after the character in the TV programme the Waltons.

"It was important for me that I got off to a good start and taking the first-leg when Ted was first to throw was a great boost.

"The only other time I have entered this competition I was knocked out in the first round so it's a bit of a turnaround."

Walton lost only four sets on his way to the Final and his consistency in his head to head battle with Hankey always gave him the edge, with the Sheffield man recording eight

maximum 180 scores in the eight sets as he took the title and the £46,000 prize money that went with it.

Earlier in the month, Phil Taylor won the other version of the world title, the Skol World Championship with a 9-0 win over Canadian, John Part. It was his ninth successive title and the biggest winning margin ever in the Final.

SHEFFIELD STEEL THE LOT

APRIL 1 Sheffield Steelers completed the grand slam of ice hockey trophies with victory over London Knights in the Play-Offs.

They had already bagged the Sekonda Super League title, the Benson and Hedges Cup and the Challenge Cup before overcoming the Knights 2-1, with the winning goal coming in the final period.

Steelers' success at the National Ice Centre in Nottingham repeated the grand slam achievements of the Ayr Scottish Eagles in the 1997-98 season and finished off a campaign that had been dogged by the threat of a strike by their players over late payment of wages.

John 'Boy' Walton celebrates his World Darts Championship triumph

HOWEY'S ABOUT THAT

JULY 27 Kate Howey put five months of injury hell behind her to take silver in the Judo World Championships.

The 28-year-old, who won silver in the 2000 Olympic Games in Sydney, had been out of action since February with a serious shoulder injury that was at one stage threatening her career.

But she returned to the mat in style in the World Championships held in Munich, Germany, and showed no signs of her injury worries as she fought her way through to a showdown with Japan's Masae Ueno, before having to settle for second place.

ELLEN IS QUEEN OF THE SEA

FEBRUARY 11 Ellen MacArthur sailed in to the French resort of Les Sables d'Olonne to complete one of the most amazing feats of bravery, skill and endeavour the world of sport has ever seen.

The 24-year-old yachtswoman finished second to Frenchman Michael Desjoyeaux in one of the hardest ocean races ever, 26,000 miles around Antarctica and back to Les Sables non-stop, circumnavigating the world – on her own.

MacArthur not only completed the course, which was a major feat in itself, but amazingly came in only a day behind the winner in a race started four months previously, and with it became the fastest woman and youngest person ever to sail around the world single-handed.

Her exploits had been followed not only in Britain but right across the globe and there were 50,000 people waiting on the quayside to see her yacht, Kingfisher, limp across the line.

On numerous occasions she was in life-threatening situations on her journey. Only 30 days in to the race she woke to find Kingfisher only 20 metres from an iceberg and certain disaster.

The yacht was blown over while she was up the 90 feet mask making emergency repairs to the sails and she put her own life at risk to go off-course and help another competitor whose yacht had been badly damaged.

Even approaching the final leg of the race, Kingfisher suffered a broken rudder and damaged rigging, and barely made it across the line.

Ellen may have finished second but in many people's eyes – she was the biggest winner of all in 2001.

Ellen MacArthur - perhaps the outstanding sporting star of 2001

MacARTHUR'S MISSION

HERE ARE THE KEY MOMENTS AND STATISTICS AS ELLEN MacARTHUR SAILED IN TO THE RECORD BOOKS AFTER STARTING HER 26,000 MILE JOURNEY, ALONG WITH 23 FELLOW COMPETITORS, AT LES SABLES IN EARLY NOVEMBER.

NOVEMBER 8: Injured a finger and was forced to operate on herself using burning hot wire.

DECEMBER 14: Climbed a mast to repair a ripped sail with 35 feet waves pounding the yacht and forcing it over.

DECEMBER 23: Spent four hours up a mast repairing sails that weighed twice as much as she did.

JANUARY 30: Sailed in to an unseen container and damaged the underside of her boat with 2500 miles still to navigate.

FEBRUARY 9: Problems with the rigging as she sailed towards the finish threatened her stay at sea.

* Her longest spell asleep was only two hours and 50 minutes and most of the time she just grabbed 30 minutes here and there.

* On average she came across 10 icebergs in her path a day, some as big as 200ft long. On waking up to find one only 50ft away, she said: "I have never seen anything so beautiful and so deadly at the same time."

INDEX

A

Aberdeen, 38, 54, 57
AC Milan, 18, 59, 64
Adams, Lee, 136
Afridi, Shahid, 77, 86, 87
Agassi, Andre, 150, 151, 152, 153
Akinbiyi, Ade, 57
Akram, Wasim, 89
Al Fayed, Mohamed, 46
Alaves, 56, 60
Alboreto, Michele, 132
Aldridge, John, 47
Ali, Muhammad, 90
Allardyce, Sam, 50
Allenby, Kate, 186
Alonso, Ivan, 56
Ambrose, Curtly, 76, 89
Anderlecht, 59
Angel, Juan Pablo, 29
Anquetil, Lance, 183
Armstrong, Chris, 27
Armstrong, Lance, 183
Arsenal, 16, 17, 19, 22, 23, 25, 28, 30, 31, 35, 37, 43, 44, 45, 59, 60
Ashes, 76, 78, 79, 84, 85
Aston Villa, 17, 18, 20, 36, 41
Atapattu, Marvan, 80
Atherton, Michael, 76, 78, 79, 81, 88, 89, 90, 91
Atkinson, Ron, 39
Austin, Bunny, 151
Ayr Scottish Eagles, 186

B

Babbel, Marcus, 56
Back, Neil, 114, 117
Bailey, John, 147
Ball, Michael, 63, 65
Ballesteros, Seve, 13
Barcelona (basketball), 127
Barcelona (football), 59, 60
Barmby, Nick, 66
Barnes, John, 52
Barnet, 49
Barnsley, 17
Barrera, Marco Antonio, 140
Barrichello, Rubens, 133
Bartleski, Conrad, 183
Bates, Ken, 21
Bath, 116
Baulch, Jamie, 170
Baxter, Alain, 183
Bayern Munich, 41, 58, 59
Bayliss, Troy, 136
Beckham, David, 63, 65, 66
Bedford, David, 185
Begay, Notah, 103
Belton, Janine, 182
Benfica, 64
Bennett, Wayne, 156
Berkovic, Eyal, 72
Bernoldi, Enrique, 132, 133
Berrigan, Shaun, 156
Besiktas, 59
Bevan, Michael, 77, 82
Birkenshaw, Jack, 87
Birmingham City, 42, 43
Blackburn Rovers, 16, 28, 41, 47
Blackpool, 51
Blalock, Ralph, 126
Boa Morte, Luis, 46
Bobet, Louision, 183
Boateng, George, 32
Bolton, 50, 51
Bordeaux, 57
Botham, Ian, 94
Boulter, Nicky, 177
Bowden, Sean, 184
Bowe, Riddick, 144
Bowyer, Lee, 16, 35
Boyd, Tom, 68

C

Bracewell, Paul, 46
Bradford Bulls, 157, 158, 159, 160, 165
Bradford City, 17, 18, 23, 25, 29
Bradman, Don, 93
Briers, Lee, 163
Brighton, 49
Brisbane Broncos, 156
Brive, 117
Brooking, Trevor, 72, 73
Brooks, Mark, 98
Brown, Craig, 68
Brown, Karl, 126
Brown, Terry, 37
Bruce, Steve, 71
Bruno, Frank, 11, 12, 145
Buchler, David, 33
Burghley Horse Trials, 177
Burke, Matt, 115
Burke, Paul, 115, 116, 117
Burley, George, 17
Burnett, Richie, 186
Burnley, 24
Burti, Luciano, 133
Busby, Sir Matt, 39, 41
Butcher, Mark, 76, 78, 79, 84
Butler, Lionel, 145
Butler, Martin, 51
Byas, David, 77, 87
Byfield, Darren, 51
Byrne, Miles, 98, 99

Caddick, Andy, 78, 81, 83
Caines, Daniel, 170
Calzaghe, Joe, 141
Cameron, Pero, 126
Campbell, Milton, 170
Canberra Raiders, 158
Cantona, Eric, 40, 41, 71
Capriati, Jennifer, 150
Caratti, Cristiano, 152
Carbone, Benito, 18
Cardiff City, 49
Carew, John, 59
Carragher, Jamie, 42
Castaignede, Thomas, 118
Castleford, 159
Celtic, 24, 52, 53, 54, 55, 57
Cerutti, Claudia, 186
Chadwick, Luke, 27
Chamberlain, Helen, 49
Chambers, Dwain, 168
Charles, Peter, 177
Charlton, 17, 28
Charlton, Jack, 69
Chelsea, 16, 18, 21, 25, 28, 57
Chester Jets, 126, 129
Chester, 49
Chesterfield, 49
Cink, Stewart, 98
Clarke, Allan, 24
Clement, Arnaud, 150
Clijsters, Kim, 150
Cole, Andy, 29, 41
Cole, Joe, 72, 73
Coleman, Chris, 46
Collins, John, 46
Collymore, Stan, 21, 23
Cook, Stephanie, 186
Coomber, Alex, 183
Cork, Dominic, 82
Corley, DeMarcus, 147
Correa, Pepe, 145
Corretja, Alex, 150
Coulthard, David, 132, 133, 135
Cove, Coral, 179
Coventry City, 17, 18, 19, 36, 50, 60
Cowdrey, Colin, 91
Cox, Jamie, 86, 95
Cracknell, James, 185
Cram, Steve, 169
Crozier, Adam, 31, 45, 63

D

Crump, Jason, 136
Cruyff, Johan, 39, 61
Cruyff, Jordi, 56
Crystal Palace, 40, 47
Cunningham, Keiron, 157
Curbishley, Alan, 28
Cureton, Jamie, 48, 51

Dalglish, Kenny, 52
Danilevicius, Tomas, 31
Davis, Steve, 108
Dawson, Matt, 114
De Silva, Aravinda, 80
Dean, Christopher, 183
Degerfors, 64
Deportivo La Coruna, 59
Derby County, 17, 20
Derby Storm, 129
Desjoyeaux, Michael, 187
Dettori, Frankie, 178
Dev, Kapil, 94
Di Canio, Paolo, 27, 45
Di Matteo, Roberto, 57
Doherty, Ken, 108
Dominguez, Diego, 117
Donald, Allan, 89, 91
Donewald, Bob, 127, 128
Donington, 136
Dooley, Wade, 118, 119
Dott, Graeme, 108
Douglas, Mike, 102
Dundee Utd, 52, 53, 54
Dunn, Steve, 44
Duval, David, 98, 99, 104, 105
Dynamo Kiev, 24

E

East Stirling, 38,
Ebdon, Peter, 108, 109
Edinburgh Rocks, 129
Edwards, Colin, 136
Edwards, Jonathan, 168, 172
Effenberg, Steffen, 58
Ehiogu, Ugo, 25
El Mouaziz, Abdelkader, 185
Elleray, David, 43
Elliott, Malcolm, 158
Elliott, Matt, 68
Ellis, Doug, 17, 29
Els, Ernie, 105
Endacott, Frank, 158
ENIC, 33
Eriksson, Sven Goran, 63, 64, 65, 66
Essandoh, Roy, 45
Evert, Chris, 150
Everton, 17, 27, 32, 41, 50, 60

F

Fangio, Juan Manuel, 134
Fantastic Light, 178
Farrell, Andy, 162
Farrelly, Gareth, 50
Ferdinand, Rio, 16, 25, 37
Ferguson, Sir Alex, 16, 19, 22, 29, 31, 33, 39, 40, 41, 46
FIFA, 33
FINA, 182
Fiorentina, 64
Flitcroft, Garry, 47
Flo, Tore Andre, 53
Foreman, George, 90
Foster, Mark, 182
Fowler, Robbie, 42, 43, 56
Fox-Pitt, William, 179
Francais Stade, 117
Francis, Trevor, 43
Freedman, Dougie, 47
Frolander, Lars, 182
Fulham, 46
Funnell, Pippa, 179

G

Galileo, 176, 178
Garcia, Sergio, 103, 105
Gardner, Ricardo, 50
Garvey, Adrian, 116
Gascoigne, Paul, 32
Gattuso, Gennaro, 63
Geli, Delfi, 56, 60
Gerrard, Paul, 27
Gerrard, Steven, 56, 66
Gibson, Mike, 122
Gibson, Steve, 26
Giddins, Ed, 86
Giggs, Ryan, 71
Gilchrist, Adam, 76, 78, 79, 82, 83, 84, 85, 92
Giles, Ashley, 80
Gillespie, Jason, 78, 82
Gillespie, Keith, 70
Glamorgan, 87
Gloucestershire, 77, 86
Gollob, Tomasz, 136
Gooch, Graham, 89, 91
Goodman, Don, 51
Goosen, Retief, 98, 104
Goram, Andy, 33
Gough, Darren, 78, 80, 81, 87
Gower, David, 77, 81
Graf, Steffi, 150
Graham, George, 17, 33, 34
Gray, Andy, 10, 12, 13
Gray, Michael, 29
Graydon, Ray, 51
Greene, Maurice, 168
Gregory, John, 17, 29
Griggs, Max, 49
Grip, Tord, 65
Guest, Richard, 176

H

Hakkinen, Mika, 135,
Halifax, 158
Hamann, Dietmar, 19, 62
Hamburg, 32
Hankey, Ted, 186
Harbin, John, 158
Hargreaves, Owen, 58
Harland, Georgina, 186
Harlequins, 116, 117
Harmon, Butch, 103, 105
Harris, Neil, 48
Harrison, Audley, 141
Harrison, Lee, 49
Harrison, Steve, 20
Hartson, John, 17
Hasselbaink, Jimmy Floyd, 69
Hatton, Ricky, 147
Head, Patrick, 135
Healey, Austin, 116, 117
Healy, Ian, 84,
Hearn, Barry, 51
Hearts, 53, 57
Henchoz, Stephane, 44
Henderson, Rob, 114, 115, 122
Hendry, Stephen, 108
Henin, Justine, 150
Henman, Tim, 151
Henry, Drew, 108
Henry, Graham, 114, 115, 122
Henry, Thierry, 22, 30, 31, 44
Herbert, Daniel, 115
Heskey, Emile, 66
Hewitt, Lleyton, 151
Hibernian, 53
Higgins, Alex, 110
Higgins, John, 108, 109, 110, 111
Hillsborough Disaster, 32
Hingis, Martina, 150
Hiscox Askari, 177
Hoddle, Glenn, 17, 30, 34
Holliaoke, Adam, 86
Holliaoke, Ben, 77, 86
Holmes, Keith, 146

Holt, Gary, 54
Holyfield, Evander, 145
Hopkins, Bernard, 146
Hornets, Charlotte, 127
Houghton, Ray, 69
Houllier, Gerard, 27, 42, 56, 57, 60
Howard, Pat, 116, 119
Howarth, Shane, 116
Howey, Kate, 32, 187
Huddersfield, 16
Hughes, Bryan, 42
Hughes, Mark, 40, 71
Hull, 159, 165
Hunter, Paul, 108, 111
Hussain, Nasser, 13, 76, 78, 80, 81
Hutchings, Chris, 17
Hutchison, Colin, 19
Hutchison, Don, 68
Hylton, Mark, 170

I

Illingworth, Ray, 87
Impey, Andy, 57
Ince, Paul, 25
Indurain, Miguel, 183
Inzamam, 82
Ipswich Town, 17, 20, 34, 43
Irvine, Eddie, 133
Ivanisevic, Goran, 151, 152, 153

J

Jackson, Nicola, 182
James, Daffyd, 114
Jancker, Carsten, 66
Jansen, Matt, 47
Jayaprakash, A.V, 80
Jefferies, Jim, 17, 29, 53
Johansson, Jonatan, 28
Johansson, Thomas, 153
Johnson, Andrew, 42, 43
Johnson, Donnie, 126
Johnson, Martin, 114, 115, 116, 118, 119, 120, 121
Johnson, Michael, 171
Johnson, Paul, 158
Johnson, Seth, 63
Johnson, Tommy, 52
Jones, Eddie, 115
Jones, Marion, 168, 169
Jones, Max, 173
Jones, Steve, 87
Jones, Vinnie, 19
Joppy, William, 146

K

Kahn, Oliver, 58, 64, 66
Kaiserslautern, 57
Kallis, Jacques, 94
Karlson, Michael, 136
Katayama, Shingo, 99
Keane, Robbie, 27
Keane, Roy, 24, 31, 37, 59, 71
Keegan, Kevin, 13, 17, 62, 63, 64
Kelly, Gary, 69
Kenderis, Kostas, 171
Kent, 87
Kenyon, Peter, 30
Keown, Martin, 59
Khan, Younis, 94
Kiely, Dean, 28
Kilmarnock, 53, 54
Kinane, Mick, 176, 178
King Soloman, 111
King, Don, 146
King, Ledley, 26
King, Mary, 177, 179
King, Paul, 159
Kluivert, Patrick, 69
Knight, Nick, 82, 83
Knight, Roger, 82
Kuerten, Gustavo, 150

L

Lam, Adrian, 158
Lambert, Paul, 68
Lancashire, 91, 95
Lance, Dean, 158
Lane, Mills, 145
Langer, Justin, 79
Langer, Justin, 84
Lara, Brian, 12
Larsson, Henrik, 52, 53, 54, 55
Law, Graham, 179
Laxman, Venkatsai, 94
Lazaridis, Stan, 42
Lazio, 59, 64, 65
Le Mans, 132
Le Tissier, Matt, 37
Leboeuf, Frank, 19, 57
Leeds Utd, 16, 17, 19, 23, 24, 25, 27, 37, 40, 56, 59
Legg, Karen, 182
Leicester City, 16, 21, 45, 52, 57
Leicester Riders, 126, 128, 129
Leicester, 116, 117, 118, 119, 120, 121
Leicestershire, 77, 86, 87, 95
Leighton, Jim, 40
Lenihan, Donal, 122
Lennon, Neil, 54, 70
Lewis, Carl, 168
Lewis, Lennox, 140, 142, 143, 144
Lewis, Sian, 186
Lewis-Francis, Mark, 171
Leyton Orient, 51
Lillee, Dennis, 76, 85
Linnane, Steve, 158
Lions (British & Irish), 12, 13, 115, 118, 119, 121, 122, 123
Liverpool, 12, 16, 19, 20, 24, 27, 35, 40, 41, 42, 43, 44, 48, 56, 57, 60, 61
Lloyd, Clive, 93
Lloyd, Leon, 117
Logan, Scott, 159
Lomu, Jonah, 123
London Knights, 159, 186
London Leopards, 126, 127, 128
London Towers, 126, 127
Long, Sean, 156, 157, 160
Loram, Mark, 136, 137
Loroupe, Tegla, 185
Lough, Gary, 170
Lowe, Rupert, 30
Lynagh, Michael, 123

M

MacArthur, Ellen, 187
Macey, Dean, 168, 172, 173
Macqueen, Rod, 115
Maddy, Darren, 86
Magilton, Jim, 70
Malcolm, Al, 144
Malcolm, Christian, 168
Maloney, Frank, 144
Manchester City, 17, 18
Manchester Utd, 13, 16, 17, 19, 22, 24, 27, 29, 30, 31, 33, 35, 37, 39, 40, 41, 43, 45, 46, 59
Manuel, Peter, 80
Martin, Casey, 103
Martin, Lee, 40
Martyn, Damien, 76, 78, 92
Martyn, Tommy, 157, 160, 161
May, Peter, 89
McAllister, Gary, 19, 42, 56, 60, 61
McAteer, Jason, 69
McAuley, Kid, 147
McCall, Oliver, 145
McCann, Gavin, 65
McCann, Neil, 68
McCarthy, Mick, 69
McCord, John, 129
McFarlane, Danny, 170
McGrath, Glenn, 76, 79, 84, 92, 93, 95

McIlroy, Sammy, 70
McLeish, Alex, 53
McManus, Alan, 108
McMillan, Craig, 94
McNamara, Jackie, 55
McRae, Shaun, 159
Mendieta, Gaizka, 58
Mercer, Gary, 158
Merckx, Eddy, 183
Meyer, Loren, 126, 129
Mickelson, Phil, 98, 99, 104, 105
Middlesbrough, 17, 20, 25, 26, 27, 35
Middleton, Michael, 141,
Millwall, 48
Millward, Ian, 156, 157, 160
Mims, Billy, 126, 128
Montoya, Juan Pablo, 137
Moody, Paul, 48
Moreno, Javi, 56
Morley, Adrian, 165
Motherwell, 33
Munster, 122
Muralitharan, Muttiah, 80
Murphy, Danny, 27,
Mushtaq, Saqlain, 94

N

Narbonne, 117
New York Yankees, 30
Newcastle Eagles, 126
Newcastle Utd, 31, 32, 41,
Newcastle (rugby), 116
Newport, 116
Nicklaus, Jack, 103, 105
Nicol, Andy, 115
Niedzwiecki, Eddie, 25
Nilis, Luc, 20
Noble, Brian, 158
Nottingham Forest, 40, 52
Nottinghamshire, 87

O

O'Brien, Fergal, 108, 111
O'Driscoll, Brian, 114, 122
O'Leary, David, 16, 27, 59
O'Neill, Martin, 52, 54, 55
O'Sullivan, Ronnie, 109, 110
Obholzer, Rupert, 184
Ogunjimi, Steve, 126
Oldham, 48
Olsen, Morten, 70
Olsson, Christian, 168, 172
Olsson, Sean, 184
Ormond, Jimmy, 95
Owen, Michael, 20, 44, 56, 66

P

Paatelainen, Mixu, 53
Paisley, Bob, 57
Panathinaikos, 59
Pardew, Alan, 51
Parsons, Keith, 86
Part, John, 186
Patel, Sandeep, 94
Paul, Henry, 157, 159, 162, 164
Paul, Robbie, 157, 159
Pedersen, Maya, 183
Peers, Robbie, 129
Pep, Tony, 147
Petit, Emmanuel, 17
Phillipps, Vere, 179
Pickering, Karen, 182
Pinsent, Matthew, 185
Pinto, Antonio, 185
Pintus, Antonio, 25
Pintusevich-Block, Zhanna, 168, 169
Poll, Graham, 19, 29
Ponting, Ricky, 82, 83, 92, 95
Portsmouth, 47

Powell, Chris, 65
Powell, Darryl, 158
Preston NE, 50
Prince Naseem Hamed, 140
Prost, Alain, 132, 133
PSV Eindhoven, 19, 59
Purse, Darren, 42

Q

Quinnell, Scott, 114

R

Radcliffe, Paula, 169, 170
Radford, Lee, 165
Radlinski, Kris, 164
Rae, Alex, 29
Rafter, Patrick, 151, 152
Rahman, Hasim, 140, 143
Ramprakash, Mark, 79
Rangers, 52, 53, 57
Ranieri, Claudio, 16
Raper, Stuart, 158, 164
Reading, 51
Real Madrid, 39, 59
Red Marauder, 176
Redknapp, Harry, 17, 27, 37, 73
Regis, John, 184
Reid, David, 146
Reid, Steve, 48
Ricard, Hamilton, 35
Richards, Dean, 116, 117
Richards, Viv, 93
Richardson, Bryan, 36
Richmond, Geoffrey, 18
Rickardsson, Tony, 136
Ricketts, Michael, 50
Ridsdale, Peter, 25
River Plate, 29
Rix, Graham, 25
Roberts, Andy, 94
Robins, Mark, 40
Robinson, Jason, 114, 115, 123
Robinson, Paul, 63
Robson, Bobby, 17, 22
Robson, Bryan, 20, 25, 26, 71
Roddick, Andy, 153
Roff, Joe, 114
Roma, 18, 64
Rooney, Jamie, 162
Rotherham, 48
Rougier, Tony, 51
Rowland, Jason, 147
Rowntree, Graham, 117
Royle, Joe, 17
Ruddock, Donovan, 144
Rushden and Diamonds, 49
Russell, Jack, 86

S

Saha, Louis, 46
Sale Sharks, 123
Salford, 159
Sampdoria, 64
Sampras, Pete, 151, 152, 153
San Marino, 68
Sanchez, Lawrie, 45
Sangakkara, Kumar, 80
Saunders, Ron, 17
Scantlebury, Peter, 126
Scholes, Paul, 59
Schumacher, Michael, 132, 133, 134
Schumacher, Ralf, 132, 135
Scudamore, Richard, 23, 36
Sculthorpe, Paul, 156, 160, 161, 162, 163
Sealey, Les, 40
Seaman, David, 31, 66
Sergio, Paulo, 58
Shearer, Alan, 22, 62
Sheffield Sharks, 126, 128
Sheffield Steelers, 186

Sheffield Wednesday, 46
Shergar, 178
Sheringham, Teddy, 12, 29, 31, 37, 41
Shrewsbury, 49
Silas, Paul, 127
Singh, Harbhajan, 94
Smith, Chris, 159
Smith, Gary, 55
Smith, Ian, 94
Smith, Jason, 159
Smith, Tony, 159
Smith, Walter, 17
Solano, Nolberto, 31
Solskjaer, Ole Gunnar, 31, 41, 43
Somerset, 77, 86, 87, 95
Souness, Graeme, 47
Southampton, 17, 30, 34, 37
Spasovkhodski, Igor, 168, 172
Speed, Gary, 71
St. Gallen, 57
St. Helens, 156, 157, 160, 161
St. Mirren, 38, 53
Stamp, Phil, 20
Stein, Jock, 55
Steinle, Mark, 185
Stewart, Alec, 78, 82, 83, 91
Stewart, Marcus, 34
Stock, Alec, 46
Stockport County, 47
Stojic, Nikola, 185
Strachan, Gordon, 17, 36, 60, 61
Strupar, Branko, 20,
Sturridge, Dean, 20
Stuttgart, 57
Sulaiman, Jose, 145
Sullivan Ryan, 136
Sunderland, 17, 19, 23, 29, 30
Surrey, 77, 86
Sutton, Chris, 26, 53, 54
Swail, Joe, 109
Swainson, Colin, 184
Swansea, 72
Swinburn, Walter, 176
Sydney Roosters, 165
Szabo, Gabriele, 169

T

Tait, Blyth, 177
Talbot, Brian, 49
Taylor, Graham, 47
Taylor, Mark, 78
Taylor, Paul, 30, 23
Taylor, Peter, 17, 21, 63
Taylor, Phil, 186
Teichmann, Gary, 116
Tendulkar, Sachin, 94
Tergat, Paul, 185
Teuscher, Christina, 182
Thames Valley Tigers, 129
Thiam, Mamadou, 146
Thomas, Hilroy, 129
Thomas, Petria, 182
Thompson, Daley 173
Thorpe, Graham, 80, 81
Tigana, Jean, 46
Todd, Colin, 17
Toia, Anton, 115
Toms, David, 99, 104
Torquay, 49
Torvill, Jayne, 183
Tottenham Hotspur, 26, 33, 34
Trescothick, Marcus, 78, 80, 81, 86, 91
Trinidad, Felix, 146
Tudor, Alex, 78, 95
Twomey, Billy, 177
Tyrrell, Ken 132
Tyson, Mike, 12, 143, 145

U

UEFA, 33
University Boat Race, 184

V

Valencia, 58, 59
Van De Wiele, Daniel, 140
Van der Gouw, Rai, 33
Van Nistelrooy, Ruud, 19, 35, 69
Vargas, Fernando, 146
Vaughan, Michael, 81, 82, 87
Veit, Mario, 141
Venables, Terry, 17, 26
Veno, Masae, 187
Vialli, Gianluca, 16, 19, 21, 25, 47, 57
Viduka, Mark, 24
Vieira, Patrick, 19, 23
Visacki, Djordje, 185
Vivas, Nelson, 28
Voller, Rudi, 66

W

Waite, David, 158, 165
Wakefield Trinity, 158
Walder, Dave, 116
Walker, Jack, 47
Walsall, 51
Walsh, Courtney, 89, 93, 94
Walsh, Gary, 29
Walton, John, 186
Wami, Gete, 170
Ward, Trevor, 86
Wark, John, 34
Warne, Shane, 76, 78, 79, 82, 84, 92, 93, 95
Warren, Frank, 141, 147
Warrington, 159
Warwickshire, 87
Watford, 47, 50
Watson, Lilian, 151
Watson, Maud, 151
Waugh, Mark, 76, 78, 79, 82, 92, 93
Waugh, Steve, 76, 77, 78, 79, 82, 84, 91, 92, 93, 94
Weah, George, 18
Wells, Vince, 86
Wenger, Arsene, 17, 19, 23, 30, 43, 44, 45
West Ham, 17, 25, 27, 37, 45, 72
Westerveld, Sander, 42
White, Craig, 80
White, Jimmy, 108, 109, 110
Wigan Warriors, 158, 159, 164
Wigan, 157
Wilkie, David, 182
Wilkins, Ray, 25
Wilkinson, Howard, 62
Wilkinson, Jonny, 114, 115
Williams, Darren, 23, 30
Williams, Mark, 108,
Williams, Serena, 151
Williams, Venus, 151
Windless, Tony, 126
Winters, Mark, 147
Wise, Dennis, 28
Wood, Keith, 114, 115
Woodgate, Jonathan, 16, 35
Woods, Tiger, 98, 99, 102, 103, 104
Woodward, Clive, 123
Woosnam, Ian, 98, 99
Wright, Richard, 20
Wycombe, 45

Y

Yegorova, Olga, 169
Yorke, Dwight, 26, 31, 41, 43
Yorkshire, 77, 87,
Younis, Waqar, 83

Z

Zakharova, Svetlana, 185
Zalgiris, Kaunas, 127
Zamora, Bobby, 49
Zanardi, Alex, 132
Zola, Gianfranco, 28